THE BIBLE
FOR UNBELIEVERS
The Beginning: Genesis

THE BIBLE
FOR UNBELIEVERS
The Beginning: Genesis

GUUS KUIJER
Translated by Laura Watkinson

SEVEN STORIES PRESS
New York • Oakland

Seven Stories Press
140 Watts Street
New York, NY 10013
www.sevenstories.com

College professors may order examination copies of Seven Stories Press titles
for free. To order, visit http://www.sevenstories.com/textbook or send a fax
on school letterhead to (212) 226-1411.

Book design by Jon Gilbert

Library of Congress Cataloging-in-Publication Data

Names: Kuijer, Guus, 1942- author. | Watkinson, Laura, tranlator.
Title: The Bible for unbelievers : the beginning : Genesis / by Guus Kuijer ;
    translated by Laura Watkinson.
Other titles: Bijel voor ongelovigen. English
Description: Regular Edition. | New York : Seven Stories Press, 2016.
Identifiers: LCCN 2015046819 | ISBN 9781609806767 (hardcover)
Subjects: LCSH: Bible. Genesis--Paraphrases, English
Classification: LCC BS1235.7 .K85 2016 | DDC 222/.1109505--dc23
LC record available at http://lccn.loc.gov/2015046819

Printed in the United States

9 8 7 6 5 4 3 2 1

Contents

The Story of Adam

It began with a word. It was a word that came into my head and didn't belong anywhere. And the word was:

GOD

It was an insubstantial little word, but it appealed to me. It radiated power, but meant nothing and had nothing to do. I thought: This is how everything began. When there was nothing, there was a word that was very powerful, meant nothing, and had nothing to do.

So I gave the word eyes, ears, hands, and feet.

Then, when God could look around, he thought: I can't see anything. What's the point of looking when there's nothing here?

God was all alone in the void.

"That's just the way it is," he said with a sigh. "There's nothing here. I'll just have to make something out of it."

No sooner had the words left his mouth than something happened, and God stared in amazement at his left hand.

"Hey!" he said. "There's something here."

In his hand was a small ball. God stared hard because he had something to look at now. Have I created something out of nothing? he wondered. How is that possible?

7

God pondered for a hundred years, and then said, "It doesn't matter how it's possible. But what can I do with it? That's a better question. What would happen if I threw this ball?"

He looked at the ball and said, "I am . . . *curious!*"

God's heart tingled with excitement. I'm going to do whatever occurs to me, he thought, because that'll be fun.

He counted to three and, *whee!*, the ball flew into the void and burst apart with an earsplitting bang. "BANG!!"

God was startled. "Good heavens!" he exclaimed. "What a big bang!"

There was such awesome power packed into the little ball that bits and pieces went flying in every direction. God hadn't expected that.

This is going to be really big, he thought. Any moment now something's going to happen that'll swallow me right up.

The bits and pieces flew farther and farther apart, creating space.

God had never lived anywhere before, but he was living somewhere now. And it was such a mess. Everything blew apart, crashed and smashed. The sparks flew. It was chaos.

That's what you get for being curious, thought God. But fine, what's done is done.

God thought *he* had made the little ball explode, but perhaps it would have happened without him—who can say?

One thing's for certain, though: God wasn't bored anymore, because everything was so out of hand now. I think this chaos needs some order, he thought. It's tiring me out.

God hoped there was some kind of plan for getting everything in order, but it was such a huge mess that it seemed impossible.

Please let the beginning begin, he thought. He waited patiently for a million years, but still the beginning had not begun.

It's not going to begin by itself, he thought. So maybe I need to *do* something about it. But what? God racked his brains and felt horribly powerless. What could just one god do about so much clutter? Why was he all alone?

Everything I can see came out of that ball, he mused. But where did I come from?

He didn't know. And where were the other gods?

So many questions.

When God realized worrying wasn't helping, he started to think. When exactly had the ball in his hand come into existence? Wasn't it after he'd *said* something?

"The word!" God cried in delight. "The power is in the word!"

It was as if he suddenly understood everything. He even understood what he was. I am a word. An almighty word, a word like an explosion!

It's good to know what you are! Now God was sure he existed.

In the beginning was a word, he thought. And that word was me. So the beginning began long ago.

He realized he could have come to that conclusion earlier and was astounded by his slowness.

One word leads to another. Which word shall I utter now?

He looked around. He'd already noticed a million years ago that the light and the darkness were horribly mixed up together. It wasn't light and it wasn't dark. Everything was wrapped in a kind of haze.

I made it all too gray, thought God. This is going to ruin my eyesight. So what am I going to do about it?

For a few thousand years he searched for the right words, then said, "Let there be light." And there was light.

God saw that it was good, because now he could see everything so much better. He saw an incredible number of stars that were in fact moons. "Planets," mumbled God, then the moons began to circle little orbs. So those were the planets.

"Not bad. Not bad at all," said God. "This is a pretty fine creation."

Did *I* make this or is it all just nature? He thought about it for a few million years and came to a bold decision. "You know what?" he said. "I'm just going to say that *I* made it. And if anyone knows better, they can say so."

A million years are as one day for God, and he found that two days had gone by.

The third day began.

God looked at all those moons spinning around the planets and thought: The stars are too hot, but I should take a closer look at these planets. Maybe I'll find a place where I feel at home.

He took his time, so the day lasted a million years.

Most of the planets were as dry as dust and as cold as the moon, but he discovered a planet that was blue with water.

That looks like a nice spot, thought God, because where there's water, there's . . .

He didn't get any further because he had no idea what he wanted to say. I don't have any words for this yet, he thought, but I can feel deep down that water is good for something.

When he came closer, he saw the water was full of mud. That was a bit disappointing, because there was nowhere to stand. Fortunately he knew the word "spirit," so he could hover like a spirit over the mud.

The water needs to be separated from the mud, he thought, then there'll be land on one side and sea on the other. It'll be possible to walk on the land and swim in the sea. When that's done, I'll call this planet "earth," because it's a good place to take root.

Volcanoes started exploding everywhere. High mountains formed, and deep valleys. The water flowed into the deepest valleys and the land dried out.

"This is a start," said God, "but it still looks a bit dull."

The sea moved in endless undulations and the land swirled around, but nothing else happened.

This place really needs something else, thought God. But he didn't know what. He thought about it until he came up with a new word. That word was: "plant."

And something appeared. It began with little green things in the sea. Then those little things climbed up onto the land and started growing like wild.

"Ah, that's more like it," said God contentedly. "Here are the plants."

He watched as the plants grew stronger and taller. Some of the stalks became so thick that he saw they were trees.

"If I made all of this, I must be a pretty good creator, even if I do say so myself," said God. But there was no one on earth to agree with him and that was too bad.

That was the third day. Then the fourth day began.

There were days and nights, but day was gray and night was too.

"There needs to be a clear difference between day and night," said God. "So that I have plenty of light for creating during the daytime and can sleep soundly at night."

He thought for a few hundred years, then said, "Day must be light and bright, and night must be dark as pitch."

No sooner had the words left his mouth than the light and darkness were driven apart.

"Wait just one moment!" cried God. "I'm not finished yet. Between day and night, there needs to be twilight. That'll be nice and cozy."

It was the first time the word "cozy" had ever been uttered in the universe. God wanted to feel cozy because he was all alone. And that's why we have twilight as night falls.

Maybe it was the coziness of twilight that triggered God's longing—a deep longing that made his heart hurt.

I am longing, he thought. I'm full of longing for something, but I don't know what.

He longed all day, then evening came. That was the end of the fourth day.

It turned darker than ever before. The next morning, the light was so bright that God lay there blinking for half an hour before getting up, but he'd never had such a good night's sleep. He felt fit and ready to create some very special things.

The fifth day began.

God got up and decided to take a walk along the beach. The sun was shining and the sea was nice and warm. He walked barefoot into the water and thought: This is all very beautiful and magnificent, but it'd be good, just for once, to meet someone.

In the sea there was only water and the sky above was empty too. It's no fun being me, God thought. If no one knows me, my existence has no meaning.

God needed someone who knew about him. So he looked out over the sea and waited. He'd surely have stood there for a million years if something hadn't suddenly come by.

It was a tiny little thing, not much of a thing at all. So when God first saw it, he didn't think much about it.

There was a current in the sea. The water tugged at God's legs. From left to right. And then God saw that the little thing, which didn't seem like much of a thing at all, was actually very special indeed—the water was moving from left to right, but the little thing was going from right to left. *Against the current!*

God was so amazed he couldn't speak. The little thing floated farther and farther away. He ran after it so he wouldn't lose sight of it.

It's not a plant, he thought. It's something else. But what can it be? God was speechless.

It's a willful little thing. It does whatever it wants to, he thought.

And suddenly he realized: *That little thing has a will of its own. It's like me!*

God stood still for a moment because his head was spinning. His heart was flooded with an emotion he'd never felt before. He instantly found just the right word for it: this was "happiness."

And he did a little dance in the sea.

"I obviously must have made you up," he said to the little thing, "but I didn't know I had it in me."

He looked around. Where was it? The thing had disappeared.

"Fish," he thought. It's called a fish.

God was disappointed because the fish had swum away.

It's nice that something has a will of its own, he thought. But what good is it to me if it doesn't pay me any attention?

He walked up the beach, but he didn't notice all the sudden splashing in the sea. Thousands of fish, big and small, were leaping out of the water to escape a shark. God didn't see, because he was sunk in important thoughts.

He looked at the empty sky and a word popped out of his mouth: "Birds."

He said the word and the air filled with the sound of beating wings. Birds, large and small, glided effortlessly around. They played with the wind and chirped songs about love and jealousy.

God marveled at all that beauty and saw that it was good.

He hoped a little bird would come to perch on his shoulder, but the birds didn't seem to know he existed.

But I'm less alone than I was yesterday, thought God, and he felt satisfied as he walked home.

It was dark, and then it was light again. The sixth day began.

God got up after another good night's sleep and boldly ventured inland. The plants were blooming and growing, the birds were nesting in the trees, but otherwise the land was empty. There should be creatures that live on the ground, too, thought God—creatures that crawl and jump and walk and run, because I think that would be a fine sight to see. He knew what he had in mind, but couldn't come up with the right word. This is going to be another day that lasts a few million years, he thought, but that doesn't matter. I have all the time in the world.

Up on the mountains, down in the valleys—God was everywhere! But there was no one else around.

Creatures, he thought. I want creatures. He looked around. He heard the trees rustling in anticipation, but nothing happened. The right word had not yet been spoken.

Every million years, one letter came to him. So, after six million years, there were six letters hovering around God's head, but he couldn't make a word out of them: an *A*, another *A*, an *I*, an *L*, an *M*, and an *N*.

It was quite a puzzle, but suddenly he got it: "ANIMAL! Yes, wild animals! Beasts! Livestock! Everything that moves upon the ground!"

He said it and felt a mighty tickling on his ghostly toes. Toes . . . Well, of course, God doesn't have actual toes, but he definitely felt something tickling. A column of ants was busily climbing up his bare legs. Oh, God wasn't wearing any clothes yet, by the way.

Worms wriggled up out of the ground. Grasshoppers jumped all around and mosquitos buzzed about his head. Every kind of creature you can imagine was there, including a beast with long ears happily skipping over the green grass. God looked at it and said, "Rabbit."

A flock of sheep came past, bleating. Cows with fat udders stood mooing in the meadow. And God thought: They really need milking. A snake strutted over a slippery rock, because snakes still had legs back then. All the animals you can think of simply came into being without God lifting a finger. They came out of their holes, had a good stretch, and began to live as if it were the most natural thing in the world.

God couldn't believe the abundance. There was so much to see that it seemed like creation was finished. The animals and plants that populated the world were a delight to his eye. God was having such a wonderful time that the sixth day lasted a few million years. And yet, he still felt a great sense of longing.

Something's missing, he thought. There's an empty space inside me.

The animals were busy living their own lives and not paying attention to God. He had no one to talk to, because the vocabulary of the animals was so limited. They just said "moo," "squeak," or "oink," and had no sense of higher things.

What I'm longing for is a good conversation, thought God. What I really need is an animal who is aware of my existence and who can talk.

What should such a creature look like, though? More or less like me, thought God, but unfortunately I have no appearance.

He happened to be standing with his ghostly feet in the clay, which gave him an idea. He dug into the clay with his hands and started kneading away. What would I want to look like if I *did* have an appearance? he wondered.

He began to mold the clay and, after a couple of hours, he considered the result. It's not at all bad, he thought, but I think there's something similar already in existence.

He pondered this. Which animal did his work of art remind him of? It wasn't the rabbit, and it wasn't the cow, or the bat, and no, it wasn't the elephant either. It looked more like an animal he'd seen swinging through the trees. What was its name again?

"The ape!" God cried enthusiastically. Yes, that was it! His clay statue looked like an ape! He was very pleased at the thought, since the ape was a smart and agile creature with clever hands and feet. An apelike animal was definitely a good starting point.

Its appearance isn't a problem, thought God, because that's just perfect. The insides are going to need some tweaking, though. This creature needs more brains, and I'll have to do something about those vocal cords.

It was no sooner said than done.

Then life had to enter the clay.

God had noticed that the animals sucked air in and blew it back out. They seemed to need it to live. So God took his clay doll and blew air into its nostrils. The doll started to move, blinked, looked around, and asked, "Who am I, where am I, why am I?"

It was a miracle! This animal could speak! And how! It started asking important questions right from the start. For a moment, God was speechless.

Then he said, "You are Adam. That means 'man.' You are on earth because someone has to keep an eye on things. And when you have a free moment, you have to sing my praises."

"Oh," I said, because this Adam was, of course, me. "And why can't I see you?"

"Because I'm a word!"

And then I remembered. When I'd awoken, that was the first word I'd thought of: "god."

I looked around. At first, I had no idea what I was looking at, because I didn't have a word for anything apart from God.

"Go ahead," said God. "Don't be afraid. Go forth and discover the world. It's very beautiful. I made it all myself."

"Did you really?" I replied. But I could hear from the resounding silence that God didn't like my question.

"Listen, my friend," he said. "I didn't make you so you could pester me with questions. I made you so there would be someone to see how mighty I am."

God didn't seem to realize I'd made him up myself.

"So what happens now?" I asked.

"I'll take you to Paradise," said God, walking invisibly ahead of me.

It wasn't far, because in the beginning Paradise was everywhere, but especially between the rivers.

When God stopped, I knew I was there. "This is a garden," he said. "You'll need to do a bit of work in it, but then you'll have everything you need. Do you like gardening?"

"Er . . . yes," I said. I had no idea what gardening was, but it sounded like fun.

Then God vanished into thin air and for a time he was nowhere, because he wanted to rest.

That was the end of the sixth day.

I'd been given the job of looking after the garden, but there wasn't much to do. I picked the occasional apple, pear, or plum, pulled a few vegetables out of the ground, and that was pretty much it. For the rest of the day, I sat there watching all the animals around me. They were so much busier than I was! The young animals played together, while the older animals searched earnestly for food and fought each other. They also did something that for the sake of convenience I'll call "screwing." I didn't understand the purpose of this activity, but it certainly looked amusing. Over time, I came to understand that you needed two to play that funny game, and that's when I realized I was alone.

"I don't like this one bit," I said out loud. "I want someone too."

"You have me, don't you?" said a voice behind me. I didn't need to turn around to know who it was. It wasn't an elephant or giraffe. It was, of course, God.

I didn't answer him immediately, because I needed time to think. Did I "have" God? Could I search earnestly for food with him, have fights and . . . um . . . play funny games with him?

"That's true," I said politely, "but I don't have anyone else besides you. I'm all alone."

"So what?" said God. "I'm alone too, aren't I? Why don't you get a dog?"

I didn't know what a dog was, but I didn't argue. I was sure I didn't want a dog. I wanted someone who looked more or less like me, but . . . different.

"Are you really alone?" I asked. "Are there no other gods but you?"

"I find that question rather inappropriate," said God. "Didn't I just say I'm alone?"

I suspected God might be fibbing a little, so I held my tongue, but in my mind I easily dreamed up a dozen more gods. Our silence held until I said, "I'm only human and it's not good for a human to be alone."

"All right, then," said God. "I will make a woman for you, but it's going to cost you an arm and a leg. No, on second thought, make that a rib."

"No problem," I said. "I have ribs to spare."

"And one more thing," said God, "when another human being comes along, you'll have what's known as a 'difference of opinion.'"

"Oh," I said.

"That's when you say, for example: 'This is a lion.' And she says: 'No, it's a goat.' Do you understand? You'll have constant contradiction."

"Then I'll just say, 'It is so a lion!'"

"Wrong!" cried God. "That's exactly what turns a difference of opinion into an argument. She'll say, 'Tisn't!' You'll say, 'Tis!' And I don't want any fighting in Paradise. What you have to say is, 'You're right. This is a goat in the form of a lion that doesn't bleat, but roars.'"

"Fine," I said. "That's what I'll do." Because I was prepared to do whatever it took.

"Now for the really dangerous bit," said God. "One day she'll say, 'You know that god of yours? You just made him up yourself, didn't you?' And what will you say then?"

"Then I'll say, 'Yes, you're right. I made him up myself in the form of a human being that doesn't bleat, but roars.'"

"Wrong!" God exclaimed. "That answer is so insufficient it will only create unbelievers. You'll have to tell her this: 'But it was God Himself (with capital letters!) who whispered the idea in my ear.'"

I didn't answer him because I needed to think. How did this work? If I'd made something up myself, it couldn't have been made up by someone else. Or could it?

"Think about the word 'inspiration,'" said God helpfully. "An inspiration is a notion breathed into someone. Into you. By me, of course. But that doesn't mean the thought isn't yours."

I have to confess that at that moment my eagerness got the better of my powers of reasoning. I didn't want to be alone anymore. It really didn't seem to matter if God was a product of imagination or inspiration.

"Whatever the case," I said. "I want a woman." It was my first time uttering the word "woman"—a word like a breeze rustling the leaves on the trees.

"Fine," said God. "Go lie down, because I need to put you to sleep for this operation."

I lay on the soft moss of Paradise.

"Relax, let go. Think about nothing. Make yourself completely empty. Listen to the sound of the universe," said God, and so on, and so on. Eventually I became so bored that I fell fast asleep.

When I awoke, God was nowhere to be seen. I looked around and saw I was still alone. A deep sense of sadness overwhelmed me and I cursed the figment of my imagination that I'd named God.

"Empty promises from a no-good god," I grumbled. "If he carries on like this, I'm going to choose a different god to worship."

Dispirited, I walked to the banks of the Tigris. I thought a cool dip in the water would do me some good. When I heard the sound of the river and saw a couple of sweet cocodriles, or cocodiles, or crocodiles (I always have a problem with that word), bobbing about in the water, I cheered up a little.

Then it happened. Right in the middle, where the river was

deepest, a head rose out of the water. Two big, dark eyes stared at me, the mouth opened wide, and white teeth flashed between the lips. Then the head shook its long hair, which whipped around in a shower of droplets.

This animal has no name yet, I thought in surprise. This is a creature I don't know.

I was drawn irresistibly to those eyes, those lips, that swishing hair. So I walked into the river to take a closer look at the new creature. Before the water was up to my knees, the head started to scream. It gave me a huge fright and I ran back to the riverbank. I didn't stop running until the shrieking turned into a kind of cackling bird sound. Then I spun around.

The animal had come closer. Its shoulders were now out of the water. They were beautiful shoulders that gleamed in the sunlight. An arm rose up and a finger pointed at me. The cackling rattled away, higher and higher. I have no idea how it happened, but a sound welled up in my throat and, before I knew it, I was cackling back. The animal and I cackled at each other and I felt a happiness I'd never known.

Later I realized this was "laughter," but I didn't know that at the time.

The animal waded cackling toward me, and little by little its body rose out of the water. I stopped laughing. "My Lord and my God," I sighed. "Now that's what I call a creature." At the same moment, it occurred to me that perhaps this was not a creature, but a god. A cackling god. And when I saw its two round breasts, the same kind of breasts that mother animals feed their young with, I assumed God must have made a woman for himself. That thought cut through my soul. I wanted to cast God into the outer darkness to make him invisible for all eternity, so this goddess would know nothing of him.

She stepped onto the riverbank. Her body glistened in the sun and I saw how heartrendingly naked she was. She beckoned me over. Nervously, I went to her, scared I might do something wrong and lose her.

She pointed at my manhood and said, "If I'm not mistaken, you're a man."

I'd noticed the same thing myself, and it would have been foolish to deny it.

So I said, "That's right." Then I realized she wasn't a goddess, but a human being. I'm not sure why, but the blood rushed to my head and turned my face as red as the setting sun.

"I don't know where I came from," she said, "but I know I was looking for you."

"You're one of my ribs," I said.

She looked at me as if I were a slug. Fortunately, that didn't last for long, because once more she burst out laughing.

"Say that again," she said, still hiccupping with laughter.

"God made you from one of my ribs," I said, a little uncomfortably.

"Oh," she said. "So which rib was it? Why don't you show me?"

I felt my ribcage and had to admit that I didn't know. None of my ribs seemed to be missing.

"I'd like you to think before opening your mouth, honey," she told me. Then she took hold of my head and pressed her lips to mine. I'm not going to tell you what happened next, but it was very nice and snug indeed.

In the beginning we were beside ourselves with joy, and that was followed by years of contentment until finally, like a lazy cat, boredom crept in. Life was too easy and everything was allowed. We heard nothing from God all that time, but as soon as I thought to myself that something really ought to be forbidden . . . he was there like a shot.

"You haven't thought about me for a long time," he said. "Too busy with that wife of yours?"

"Oh, you know," I said. But God was right. Our love had caused me to neglect him shamefully.

"Well, anyway, there's something I forgot to tell you," he said. "I actually meant to forbid you to do something, but in all the commotion it slipped my mind."

"I thought as much," I answered. "Something should be

forbidden, because when something's forbidden it leads to temptation. And temptation creates excitement. And excitement means there's no boredom."

God was silent for so long that I worried my line of reasoning had confounded him. I had come to realize that thinking for yourself leaves God speechless.

"Do please tell me," I said. "Whatever it is that you forbid, I shall obey with thanks because I know it's for my own good."

I heard him sigh with relief. I was once again Man as he had imagined me.

"Listen carefully," he said. "In the middle of the garden there's a tree that bears what appears to be wonderful fruit, but in truth it is not good to eat; it would turn you sour. Then you would know the difference between Good and Evil. So you are not permitted to eat from that tree."

I was disappointed because it wasn't much of a commandment. There were hundreds of trees in Paradise and they all had delicious fruit, so why would I be bothered by that one tree and its wicked harvest?

"Is there a problem?" asked God.

"A problem? No," I said.

"You won't forget to tell Eve, will you?"

"Your Will be done," I muttered grouchily.

God vanished in resounding silence.

"God?" asked Eve. "The god who cut the rib out of your body?"

"The same," I said.

"And that god has suddenly told us we're not allowed to do something?"

"That's right."

Eve pulled a carrot out of the ground, washed it in the river, and started munching.

"Are you sure you didn't just invent this god so you can boss me around?" she asked, snapping the carrot between her teeth.

Her question took me by surprise. I wanted to give her an answer, but I was gasping for breath. It felt like I'd been thumped in the stomach.

"He is the god who made heaven and earth," I finally spluttered. "And he made you too. He was here before I thought him up."

Eve offered me a bit of her carrot but I wasn't hungry.

"That doesn't make much sense," she said. She stood up. "I'm going to take a look at this tree. Which one is it? Show me the way."

I realized that I didn't know exactly which tree God meant. How could I find the middle of the garden when it wasn't clear what shape Paradise took or where it ended?

Eve walked briskly ahead, her hair blowing brightly in the wind.

"It doesn't matter exactly which tree it is," I shouted at her back. "What matters is that you know not everything is permitted."

Eve stopped and turned around. I nearly bumped into her.

"Are you chickening out?" she asked.

My God, I thought, she's so beautiful! I wrapped my arms around her and tried to kiss her, but she pushed me away.

"First I want to see the tree," she said. "Then we can kiss and cuddle again."

I had a strange sensation. Eve had never imposed any conditions on our love before. I didn't like her doing so now, and yet I felt that life had become more exciting since God had revealed his commandment. We were about to have a difference of opinion, and I suddenly understood what "disunity" meant: we were no longer one, together, but two, apart.

"Fine," I said. "Then let me lead the way."

As I walked ahead, I felt strangely alone. How was I to know which tree God meant? When I see the tree, I'll know, I thought. I need to have faith.

Paradise had always been my home. This was the first time I'd ever felt I was in unfamiliar territory. I began to realize there were things to know that I didn't know about. I felt a painful hunger for knowledge, and I knew God's commandment had awakened that hunger within me.

We walked along paths that animals had made, into places we'd never set foot in. I saw strange birds that had no name yet and crawling, creeping things that looked like creatures from a bad dream. But the weird and wonderful are all part of life, I thought. I want to know everything. Life had never been so exciting as it was on our search for the forbidden tree.

"I love going somewhere I've never been before!" cried Eve.

So she felt the same way: she wanted knowledge. Something wild, even reckless, flowed into my body, as if I were about to become a god with knowledge of everything.

After we'd been walking for hours, I began to study the trees one by one, but each tree looked as innocent as the next. If I wanted to convince Eve, I would have to find an awe-inspiring tree, a tree with a prickly demeanor and a suspicious appearance.

"Show me the way," I whispered.

I heard God mutter something, but I couldn't hear what he said.

We went so deep into Paradise that there was no path, and we had to sweat and toil to carve our way through. When I was close to exhaustion, it finally dawned on me that any tree could be the forbidden tree. It wasn't about the tree but the commandment. Right at that moment we came to a clearing with a single giant tree in the middle that overshadowed everything. Breathless, we stopped and stared. We didn't say anything, but we both knew what the other was thinking: This is it.

This was a tree so old that it had seen everything, a tree that had absorbed all the wisdom in the world. Time had battered its trunk. It was covered in scratches, bumps, and lumps. Its twisted limbs grew out at strange angles, desperately searching for the light it was blocking from itself. And from those same weary branches hung heavy fruits that glowed red in the light of the sun.

No doubt about it. This was the Tree of Knowledge.

"That tree looks cranky, but its fruits are so tempting," said Eve. "It feels like they were made just for me."

"If they weren't tempting, there'd be no need for the

commandment," I said. "They look delicious so that we can feel what it means to be obedient."

Eve's silence was audible, so I knew she was thinking.

When the silence went on for too long, I said, "Well?"

"You do realize this god of yours might be a strange thought that popped into your head when you weren't quite awake, don't you?" she said.

"Even strange thoughts can be true," I told her. I had to think very quickly because I knew this was important. "When I look at the moon, I sometimes think it's not flat, but round like an apple."

"Ridiculous!" cried Eve. "You can see it's flat, can't you?"

"Sure," I said. "But maybe I'm looking at it wrong. A thought is a figment of the imagination that might be true, but I don't know for sure. And about God—when you look around, don't you wonder who made all this? And when you hear a voice saying, 'ME! It was ME who made this, I am the Creator,' that could be true, couldn't it?"

"Could be," said Eve, her voice full of resentment.

I could feel her resistance spinning around me like a whirlwind and was overcome by a fierce love for her.

"What about now?" I asked eagerly. "Will you kiss and cuddle with me now?"

"No," she snapped. "You can do it with that god of yours."

We spent the night under the Tree of Knowledge, without touching each other. I slept badly, and every time I woke up, I wondered why God was standing between us like a wall. I called out to him because I wanted an answer to my question, but he didn't appear.

"When I need you, you're not there," I whispered. I felt this was a bitter truth, a law that would last into eternity, and one I would have to try to live with.

Another question was troubling me: Why had I found Eve's resistance so exciting? Did I need her defiance to relieve my boredom? What *was* love?

I looked at Eve and saw that she was sound asleep. How was it possible that anxiety had taken hold of me but she was sleeping with a smile on her face? As I looked at the forbidden fruits above my head, my body flooded with a longing for the unknown. What did the world outside Paradise look like? Were we the only people or were there others? If there were others, would they be just as desirable as Eve? What was good, and what was evil? The longing for knowledge is like a sharp knife cutting deep into the flesh. It carves away at the soul, but the peculiar thing was that I felt the pain of longing as desire. God had forbidden it, so I did not eat from the tree, but, at the same time, it seemed strangely as if he wanted me to disobey him. Would I find my purpose only through disobedience? That seemed like a possibility, but I was afraid to find out. I didn't fall asleep until day was dawning.

When I awoke, the sun was already high in the sky. Eve was sitting up straight with her back to me. I reached out my arm and stroked her with my fingertips. I could feel that she was eating and my stomach started to rumble.

"I'm hungry," I said.

Without turning around, Eve said, "Here, eat." She held out her arm so I could see the red fruit in her hand. She had taken a couple of bites and I saw the fruit was white inside. I sat up to take it from her but couldn't raise my arms. They hung limply at my sides. It was only then that the shock hit me. The fruit Eve had eaten—the fruit she was offering—was a fruit from the Tree of Knowledge.

"Eve!" I heard my voice in a high-pitched shriek asking her: "What are you doing?"

"I'm eating," she said.

"Yes, but what? What are you eating?"

She casually shrugged her shoulders.

"A fruit from this lovely tree."

I was beside myself with fear. I saw God before me as a raging bull, bellowing and charging, and about to run us through with his horns. Where could we hide?

"But why?" I screamed.

"I'll tell you when you stop making such a fuss."

She brought the forbidden fruit to her mouth and bit into it. As she looked around, I saw the juice trickling down her face. I found her repulsive yet irresistible. I could barely look at her but wanted to lick the juice from her chin.

Snorting, the bull came to a halt. I watched as he puffed two columns of steam out of his nostrils and tore at the ground with one of his front hooves. As I realized he was giving me time to listen to Eve's story, I grew a little calmer.

"Tell me about it," I said.

Eve turned around, took a long look at my face, and sighed contentedly.

"All right," she said. "This morning a snake came scampering along."

"Scampering?" I said. "Snakes don't have legs."

"This one did," said Eve. "All snakes had legs once upon a time, didn't they?"

"Well, they used to," I said. "But if a snake has legs now, it's an iguana."

"Well, this was the old kind of snake, the kind with legs," said Eve.

"It was a snake in the form of an iguana," I suggested.

Eve sighed. "It was a snake with legs, and the snake said . . ."

"Hang on just one minute!" I cried. "Snakes can't talk. They hiss."

"It was a snake with legs and it could talk, smart-ass!"

I could see she was getting angry, so I said, "It was a snake in the form of an iguana that didn't hiss, but talked."

"Yes, that's right," said Eve. "Can you just keep quiet for a second and listen?"

"I'm all ears," I said.

"Good. So this snake came scampering up this morning and spoke to me. It said, 'Good morning, Eve,' and I realized it wasn't just any old snake, but a god in the form of a snake."

I was about to protest, but she gave me a threatening look and I managed to keep my mouth shut.

"The snake climbed into the tree, crossed its front legs, and said, 'Adam's god is an excellent god, but there's something he's not telling you.' Well, I was naturally curious, so I asked, 'And what might that be, my dear snake?' 'I'm not really supposed to say,' it said. 'But maybe I will, because it's you.' Then it started hissing and I couldn't understand what it was saying. 'Go on, snake, tell me please!' I begged. 'If you eat from the Tree of Knowledge, you will no longer need a god,' it lisped. 'You'll become God's equal because you'll know everything, just like him.' 'What kinds of things would I know?' I asked. 'That you'll die,' said the snake. 'And because you know you'll die, you will not only do good, but also evil. Only then will you truly become human. Right now you're no more than talking animals.' 'But what does it mean to die?' I asked. 'You won't find out until you eat from this glorious tree. So you can choose. Do you want to remain a talking animal or become a human with knowledge of things, like Adam's god?' I didn't have to think for long. 'I want to know, my dear snake,' I said. 'I want to know everything.' The snake stretched out, picked an apple, and held it up to my mouth. 'Then eat of this fruit,' it said. 'And be born again, this time human.' I didn't hesitate. I took the fruit and bit into it. At that moment, the snake lost its legs and slid down the tree. Before I could take a second bite, it had already slithered out of sight. Then you woke up and saw me and were startled, but there's no need to be afraid. The fruit tastes good and it'll clear your head. Here, take a bite."

I looked around helplessly. Where was God? He was nowhere. The bull had disappeared and I suspected I'd dreamed it. Eve and I were alone.

If I ate the fruit, I would *know*, but there would be disunity between me and God. We would no longer be as one, but as two. Maybe that was what I was longing for so much. I wanted to break free, so I could say: This is me and that is you. An act of disobedience was needed in order to make God someone different from myself.

"You don't have to, you know," said Eve. "If you don't feel like it, I'll eat it by myself."

How could I enter into a dialogue with God if I never spoke out against him?

Oh no, it wasn't Eve tempting me, but my own thoughts. And even to this day I don't know for certain that my thoughts were not also his. Did he want to make us into humans, the only creatures in his creation capable of contradicting him? Could it have been God hiding inside Eve's snake-with-legs?

"Give me that damned fruit," I spat out. "I want some too." I took a bite.

Nothing happened, nothing at all. Eve had mentioned a clear head, but when I looked into her eyes, I could see she was far away, dreaming in broad daylight. I waited. Maybe the fruit needed time to take effect. I don't know how long it took, but I noticed the world around me was slowly changing.

As I looked at the trees around the clearing, I grew afraid. They were no longer trees but long stakes penning us in as prisoners. I stood up and said, "I want to leave this place."

I looked around for Eve but she wasn't there. "Eve!" I cried.

"Hang on. I'll be there in a moment," Eve called from a nearby clump of bushes.

I broke out in a sweat. "Come on. Hurry up!" Paradise had placed one wooden hand around my throat and was squeezing. I was struggling to breathe.

When Eve emerged from the bushes, I couldn't believe my eyes.

It looked as if she'd partly transformed into a bush herself. When she came closer, I saw that she'd ingeniously covered her breasts and hips with leaves by knotting supple twigs together. Her breasts and hips! The very parts I was so fond of! I searched for them under the leaves and in my mind the curves of her hips became excessively round, and my eyes lifted up to her breasts until they swelled above the leaves and I grew dizzy with excitement. It was as if all my blood had left my face and raced to my manhood, which I quickly hid with both hands. Dang it! I was getting a stiff dick! I was ashamed because I was naked and Eve could see my excitement. She chuckled and seemed to find me amusing. And so I realized once and for all that we didn't have the same sense of humor.

I took her by the hand and dragged her away. Once we were among the trees, I broke off a leafy branch and used it as a temporary cover for my hilarious manhood.

"Why the hurry?" Eve cried breathlessly.

"Because God is on our heels," I called back to her.

She pulled away from me and stood there, panting.

"Don't be so silly," she hissed. "There is no god. And I invented that talking snake just for you."

She laid one hand on my chest and caressed me, her hand slipping down to my leafy branch.

"Come on," she said. "Let's find a good spot where we can get nice and cozy."

I really wanted her, but just as I was about to give in to her sweet temptation, I heard God's deafening voice.

"Adam, where are you?"

"Nowhere, Lord God," I said anxiously. "I am nowhere at all."

"Come on, lover," whispered Eve. "Do you want to kiss my breasts? Here they are." She untied her twigs and her breasts came tumbling forth.

"What have you done, Adam, that you must hide from me?" God asked in a thunderous voice.

"Nothing, Lord God," I said. "Really, nothing at all."

"Who are you talking to?" asked Eve. "I'm here. Why don't you talk to me?"

"Have you eaten from the Tree of Knowledge?" asked God. His voice boomed all the way down to my innards and I was terribly afraid.

"Only the tiniest morsel, Lord God," I said spinelessly. "And it was *her* fault."

"Her fault? You mean Eve led you astray?" asked God.

"Yes, Lord God."

"You are my man," Eve whispered in my ear. "And I want to have you."

But my arousal had flagged and was drooping sadly.

"This is what happens when I am not enough for you," thundered God. "You are the one who insisted on having a woman, are you not? Did you not know I am a jealous god?"

"No, Lord God," I said.

"Well, you know now," said God. "Things will never be right again between me and that woman, and I shall sow disunity between you and her. Now listen to the rest of your punishment."

God began to list a litany of miseries.

Eve tied her leafy twigs around her breasts again.

"Are you a real man?" she shouted angrily, interrupting God. "Or should I go look for another one?"

Luckily for me, there were no other men.

I took some animal skins and fashioned a garment that would later be known as pants. I knew why I did it: I didn't want to show what I was made of. Eve knitted a dress out of sheep's wool to protect her from the mosquitos. At least, that's what she said, but I knew better. She wanted to hide herself from me to kindle my desire. And it worked. Her body became an obsession to me, which made me ashamed. The Tree of Knowledge had complicated everything that had always been so simple and natural. Love had become so complex.

I whittled a stick to a sharp point to protect us from the wild animals and said, "Come on, we need to leave Paradise."

"I couldn't agree more," said Eve. "This place is going to bore us to death."

"That's not what I meant," I said. "We're being thrown out because we're bad."

"We're running away," said Eve, "because we're curious about the world."

This was the disunity God had sown between us. Sometimes we did the same things, but for very different reasons. In fact, we were always at odds.

"In pain you will bring forth children," I said.

"Yes, of course," she said. "Do you think the animals have an easy time of it?"

"By the sweat of our brows we will earn our bread."

"What do you mean? Why did you say that? There's always sweat streaming down our foreheads anyway, isn't there?"

"We are going to die."

"Well, yes. What did you think? That you'd have eternal life? Then you should have eaten from the Tree of Life."

I stopped and looked at Eve's face. Did she mean what she was saying or was she making fun of me? Where had that Tree of Life business suddenly come from?

"Didn't you know God kept the Tree of Life hidden from us?" she asked. "Because he was scared we'd live forever, like him."

I could see that she meant what she was saying.

"Stop talking nonsense, you silly woman."

I shrugged and started walking again. It was better not to respond to everything she said. Eve's god was not my god, or she had less sense than I had.

We walked and walked. When we'd reached the dry and dusty desert plain, I turned around. The gate to Paradise lay behind us.

"Do you see that angel with his flaming sword?" I asked. "We can never go back."

Eve put up her hand to shield her eyes from the sun.

"The air's shimmering," she said. "I don't see anything else."

I sighed and fell silent. I realized that a woman has barely any spiritual life to speak of.

"An angel," she said. "Is that a god too?"

"No," I snapped. "There's only one god and that is God." It just slipped out. How could I know if there was only one god, not a thousand?

"Oh," she said. "I was just asking."

We roamed around the world and life was hard. I learned to hunt, and I tamed a few sheep and goats, while Eve concentrated on digging up edible roots and tubers. God didn't get in touch, so sometimes I wondered if he still existed. We suffered hunger and shivered with cold, and our skin burned beneath the scorching sun, but we no longer had any time to be bored. We never knew what was in store for us: one day we'd be making our way over high mountains; the next we'd be following a river that wound its way through a deep ravine. One day we'd be living in abundance; the next day, we'd nearly die of exhaustion and thirst.

We had children. The first son we called Cain, the second Abel. It was a struggle to keep them alive, but our efforts were rewarded: they grew up to be strong boys who helped out when Eve and I were shorthanded. When Cain was ten years old and Abel nine, we began to have some spare time. We would sit together in the evening, gazing at the moon and the stars. I don't know how it happened, but I started to tell my story. About how the world was made, how Eve and I came into it, and why we were driven out of Paradise.

It's strange how the same story can have such a different effect on two different people. Cain was happy with everything: he thought we were right to eat from the Tree of Knowledge; he didn't care that God was nowhere to be seen; he enjoyed life, no matter how hard it was. Abel, though, became furious.

When he was young, I saw his anger only on his face, but as he grew older, he put it into words. Unpleasant discussions arose, which went something like this: "The two of you are bad," Abel said. "God wants nothing to do with you, and that's why he's silent. Why don't you try to make it up with him?"

I had no answer to that, but Cain said, "Why? With or without god, the sun will come up again tomorrow and we will have to go to work."

Eve giggled.

"Mother!" exclaimed Abel. "What kind of person talks to a snake?! Do you not understand what you've done?"

Cain raised his hand threateningly.

"Don't talk to your mother like that!"

This scene was repeated dozens of times.

I was glad my story had made an impression on Abel, but I was worried about the ferocity with which he condemned us.

When Cain became angry, Abel remained silent, because Cain was stronger, but Abel's fury remained. He wanted to hear my story over and over again. I patiently told him everything he wanted to hear, and he listened, but Cain no longer paid any heed.

Eve warned me more than once.

"A god who sets people against one another is a bad god," she said.

When two brothers started to hate each other, that was bad. But where did that Evil come from, if not from God? Was there another god at work? I was confused.

Abel was not. Abel was certain about everything, and so I clung to him as if he were the father and I the son. I followed him into the field where he tended the sheep, and I listened to him.

"God is great! God is great!" he called all day long.

"Abel," I said carefully. "I don't know if he can hear you. God is a notion."

"But you've seen him yourself, haven't you?"

"I have seen him in my mind's eye," I said. "When I close my eyes, I can see all kinds of things: a mountain, a sheep, my big toe."

"God is great! God is great!" cried Abel, with spit coming off his lips. "He revealed himself unto you."

I thought long and hard about that word, but I could make no sense of it.

"What does 'revealed' mean, Abel?" I asked.

"You had a revelation, through which the existence of God was disclosed."

"You could put it that way," I said, "that I brought God into existence."

Abel's face turned pale. He sighed and shook his head, so I realized I'd said something wrong.

"God is great!" he screamed.

Startled, I pressed my hands to my ears.

"We must serve him humbly and make sacrifices," he bellowed right through my hands, "or a great misfortune will befall us."

Then I realized that Abel was *scared*. He feared God. I remembered my own fear, which I now thought was so ridiculous that I couldn't help laughing.

"My dear Abel," I brayed. "God sometimes grumbles away inside my head, but in reality he is nowhere without us. I swear it to you. There is no need to be afraid."

I shall never forget the look he gave me, the deep frown, the furrowed brow, the furiously clenched fists. I had offended him and I didn't understand how. My laughter died so quickly that it made my stomach ache.

"Come on, Father," said Abel. "Let us choose an animal to sacrifice. We must make amends, for you have offended him with your disrespectful words."

I trotted after Abel like a sheep because I had no idea what he was planning to do.

We walked straight through his flock, his sheep parting for us. Suddenly Abel dove on top of one of the animals, threw it onto its back, and trussed its legs together. He drew his stone knife from his belt and raised it high in the air.

I grasped his arm. "A-Abel," I stuttered, "my dear son, what are you doing? This is a fine, healthy ewe, why not take a lame one or a useless ram? That'll taste just as good, won't it?"

"We're not going to eat it, Father," growled Abel. "We're going to burn it for God."

Then I knew for sure that my poor son had lost his mind and I cried out in my despair: "But, son! It'll stink! Do you think God likes bad smells?"

Sadly he was stronger than I was. He pulled himself free and stabbed the knife straight into the throat of the poor sheep, which, still full of the desire to live, had to give up the ghost. I fell onto my knees and thought: Innocence dies—and it dies for nothing.

Abel built a table of stones and laid brushwood upon it. He took the bleeding sheep's body in his arms and placed it on the wood. Then he made a fire.

As the fleece began to singe, it gave off a nauseating stench. I pinched my nose shut and shouted, "I don't know which god you're doing this for, but he can't have any sense of smell." I stood up and ran home.

I hoped God would make it clear to Abel that he took no pleasure in people burning animals, but I was disappointed. When Abel returned home, he was beaming.

"Father," he said with delight. "God has accepted my sacrifice!"

Eve and Cain sat in silence by the fire and appeared not to have heard what Abel had said.

"Mother?" said Abel. "Did you hear?"

Eve poked the fire. I knew her; she looked calm, but I could tell she was furious.

"I heard that you burned a sheep," she said icily.

"For God, Mother, only for God."

"Precious food," said Eve. "Burned."

"But, Mother," said Abel. "God has to eat too."

Cain laughed gruffly.

I could see my family falling apart and I smelled the danger. Abel would always be our son, no matter how strangely he acted, but I could hear a sharp hostility in Cain's laughter.

"First he was a word," snapped Cain. "Then an inspired notion. Is he supposed to be a belly now? And if he's a belly, does he have to poop too?"

Don't offend him, I thought. Please, don't offend him.

How is it that belief in God makes a person so easily offended?

"You are cursed," said Abel. "God has cast you out."

Cain looked at me and grinned. "Is that true, Father?" he asked mockingly. "Has god-with-the-belly cast me out?"

I couldn't answer because Eve was holding the glowing poker under my nose.

"Tell Abel I'll bash his head in with this poker if he ever says anything that horrible again."

Terrified, I backed away.

"Did you hear me, Abel?" she said.

"Yes, Mother."

Nothing else happened that day, but a deep hatred grew between the two brothers. Eve and I watched helplessly.

I remember one day Cain saying to us, "Of course, you should have eaten first from the Tree of Life, and then from the Tree of Knowledge, because now death awaits us and that doesn't sound like fun."

Again we were helpless.

"We didn't know the Tree of Life existed," said Eve.

"Because we had no knowledge," I said.

That was true, and still we knew that we should have thought about it more carefully before taking action. Our rash behavior had put us in debt to our sons.

Cain had learned to plant seeds and grow food. He had discovered a type of grass with edible seeds that could be used to make bread. He worked the land. His shoulders grew broad, bulky cords of muscles rippled across his arms, and his legs seemed to grow out of the ground like trees. I went with him into the field to help him, but I was not accustomed to hard work and by the end of the day all my muscles ached. But still I preferred to spend time with Cain than with Abel, the son from whom I was becoming estranged. He sometimes drove his sheep straight through Cain's fields, shouting, "Death to the godless ones!"

Then Cain would pick up his hoe and run after Abel.

"Come here," he screamed, "and I'll give your pious head a good whack!"

Abel scooted off like a hare. The sheep, suddenly without a shepherd, panicked and ran in all directions, but regrouped when Abel had reached safety and whistled for them.

One time, when Cain returned breathless to me after such a fit of rage, he said, "We need to talk."

He indicated that I should sit down. Then he sat opposite me and stared into my eyes. I was surprised, because Cain was not a man of words.

"Father," he said. "There is no god."

I felt a stab in my heart, because Cain had touched upon my own doubts.

"How do you know that?" I asked. But I didn't really want to hear his reply.

"He told me so himself," said Cain.

I burst out laughing, but Cain didn't laugh along with me. "It was an inspired notion," he said. "I have revealed God's absence."

I shivered, because the world seemed empty and abandoned. "God" was the first word that had come into my mind and I had become attached to it.

"I tried to make a sacrifice, just like Abel. I took a sheaf of my best wheat and burned it for God. I waited until the last of the smoke was gone, but God remained so silent that it hurt my ears. Then I became angry and cursed him. 'Why will you accept Abel's sacrifice but not mine?!' I screamed. 'That's not fair!' Then I heard a voice that said, 'Because I do not exist. I exist only for those who believe in me.' 'But that's awful!' I cried. 'If you exist, you must exist for everyone.' 'No,' the voice said. 'You can manage fine without me. If you do good, then you can look anyone straight in the eyes, can't you? If you do evil, then sin lies in wait, eager to sink its claws into you. So you must be strong.' Then it was silent and I knew that man is alone in the universe."

I looked into his eyes and saw that he was longing for a word from me: consent, approval, love. I could give him the last of the three.

I said, "My son, whatever you believe or do not believe, you are my child." I placed my hand on his head and said, "Even if God is not with you, I am."

We looked into each other's eyes for a long time without saying anything. I felt his loneliness and I knew no love in the world could calm my son. He would search, all his life, without knowing what for.

But I had no inkling of the horror that would cross his path.

I did not understand why Abel took pleasure in provoking his brother. It was as if he wanted to make Cain look small so that he would seem bigger himself. Usually Cain just shrugged his shoulders or muttered under his breath. But one day Abel said, "I know why God accepts my sacrifices and not yours."

Cain scowled.

"Do you want to know?"

"No," said Cain. "I don't care, because there is no god."

"I'm going to tell you anyway," whispered Abel. "It's because I'm a better man than you. God protects me. Nothing can happen to me, because I'm good."

Eve jumped to her feet.

"Out of this tent!" she yelled. "Clear off to your sheep. I don't want to see you for a few days." I could see she was incandescent with rage and I admired her for it. I sometimes became angry, too, but fury paralyzed me, making me helpless.

Eve was the only one who commanded an almost timid respect in Abel. He slunk off without another word.

Neither Eve nor I could find words to console Cain, so we said nothing. As the silence resounded inside our heads, Cain suddenly said, "I want a woman."

I knew those words would come one day and I'd been dreading the moment for years. There was no woman.

Eve giggled and told me, "This is going to cost you another rib, honey." She was in the habit of using sweet words when she was making fun of me.

"So I'm off to look for one," said Cain.

Eve and I looked at each other. We both knew we shouldn't dash his hopes, so I said, "That's a good idea. It's time to leave your mother and father." I felt lousy because I believed we were alone in the world, but I was afraid to tell him so.

"Wait until the harvest's over," said Eve. She was excellent at avoiding trouble for as long as possible. We had no way of knowing that delay would have fatal consequences this time, because God had not warned us.

Maybe he didn't know, any more than we did. Perhaps I shouldn't overestimate his capabilities.

Then the day came when our world collapsed and I understood what it meant to live outside Paradise. For the first time, we experienced the death of a person. We lost two sons: one to death, the other to life. The love between Eve and me was destroyed. Grimly, we lived on, without any joy. Life didn't matter to us; we longed only for death.

That was the day Cain ran wailing into the tent and threw himself to the ground at our feet. His forehead was bleeding.

We looked down at him in silence. His body shuddered and shook like an animal being slaughtered.

"Father! Mother!" he groaned, and then, like a little child: "Daddy! Mommy!"

I knew what had happened. I had seen Cain's fury whenever Abel humiliated him. I knew it, but I didn't want to accept it. My mind went blank.

"An accident," he mumbled. "It was an accident. I didn't mean to do it, I really didn't."

God, my God, I thought, why have you forsaken him? He is a good man. There is no fault in him.

"Pull yourself together," said Eve sternly. "Get up. Dry your tears and tell us what happened."

I could see Cain was shocked to hear his mother's voice, as if he hadn't expected her ever to speak again. He leapt to his feet, bleeding and sweating, but he wasn't crying any longer. Stuttering and stumbling over his words, he told his story. It came down to this: Cain met Abel out in the fields. Abel seemed to be in a good mood and they got to talking. They chatted about this and that, but then Abel brought up The Sacrifice again.

"Let's do over," he said. "Let's make a sacrifice together. I'll sacrifice a sheep and you can sacrifice a sheaf of wheat."

They each made a table of stones, which Abel called "altars," and placed their offerings on them. They lit fires. As the smoke began to rise to the heavens, Abel asked, "So? Do you hear anything?"

"Nothing," said Cain.

"Close your eyes," said Abel. "Kneel down. Concentrate, think about nothing, relax, let go."

Cain kneeled down, closed his eyes, concentrated, thought about nothing, and let go.

"You still can't hear anything, can you?" jeered Abel. "I can.

God is speaking to me. He is calling me his son. But he wants nothing to do with you."

Furious, Cain jumped up and raised his hand to Abel.

"Go on, brother. Hit me," cried Abel. "God is with me. Nothing can happen to me."

"Oh, no? Really?" roared Cain. He snatched a smoldering sheep's bone from Abel's altar and hit him. He heard Abel's skull crack and the blood came gushing out of his head like a fountain. His body fell to the ground with a thud.

"That's put a stop to your bullshit, eh?" screamed Cain. "Where's god now? I thought nothing could happen to you? Well? Speak up. Where's god?"

But Abel did not reply.

Cain kneeled down beside him and shook his shoulder, but there was no life left in him. Cain wailed in misery because he was the first man to see proof that humans are mortal. Stunned, he sat beside his brother's body with no idea what to do.

After sitting there for hours, life slowly returning to him, he had a strange idea. He didn't know why, but he wanted to hide the death from sight. He had to conceal the corpse so that no one would see it.

He dug a pit and placed Abel's body in it. Then he covered it with the stones from Abel's altar.

When nothing could be seen of Abel, he heard a voice that said, "Where is Abel, your brother?"

Cain clenched his fists and shouted, "So now you come! Now that I no longer believe in you, you speak to me. Too late!"

"But, to get back to my question," said God, because that's who it was, "where is Abel, your brother?"

"How should I know?" grumbled Cain. "Am I his nursemaid? He said that was you."

"What have you done, Cain?" asked God. "Don't you hear your brother's blood crying out from the earth?"

"My ears are open wide," said Cain, "but all I hear is the bleating of the sheep."

"You have killed him," said God.

"You called him your son, but you did not protect him," said Cain.

Then God got really angry.

"You are cursed!" he thundered. "Leave this place where the earth has opened its mouth wide to receive your brother's blood, the blood you spilled. If you remain here, I shall ensure your land yields no crops, for I am against arable farming. That is why I did not accept your foolish sheaf of wheat. Man should wander the earth with sheep and goats, never settling anywhere. As fugitives and vagabonds, you will roam."

Cain was silent for a long time because he needed to think. Then he said, "I made a sacrifice, but you said nothing. My brother humiliated me in your name. I struck him, but I did not know that a man can die from a single blow. You were nowhere when I hit him. So I think your punishment is too harsh. If I must wander the earth and there are others besides my parents, they will say, 'That man has no god. We will kill him.'"

Then God was silent for a long time because he too needed to think.

"You have a point," he said finally. "Of course I am guilty of nothing, because I am God, but your sacrifice was well meant and I really should have said something nice about it. So I will protect you. If anyone kills you, they will suffer vengeance seven times over."

"That sounds good," said Cain, "but even if I am avenged seven-fold, I'll still be dead."

God was growing impatient. He wanted to be finished with this, so he said, "To make it up to you, I shall place a mark on your forehead so that no one will strike you dead."

Then, all by itself, Cain's right hand took ahold of a sharp stone and carved a sign into the skin that covered his forehead. Later, after Eve had stopped the bleeding, she thought the sign meant "this way up," but I heard from someone else that it signified: "This unbeliever is my son."

We were completely broken, but now that a hundred years have gone by[1] I can think about Cain's story a little more calmly. It surprises me that you can speak to a god you are certain does not exist. I remember what surprised me most was that God protected Cain from an imaginary danger; after all, there were no other people on earth who could kill Cain, were there? At least, we'd always been under the impression that we were alone, and God never told us any different. And yet, over the course of a hundred years, we began to have our doubts. Was God hiding something from us, just as he had hidden the Tree of Life?

Abel was dead and Cain departed. He settled east of Paradise, in the Land of "Nod," which means "to wander." We tried to ignore our grief and to love one another, but death dwelled within our hearts. We were alive, but the life had gone out of us.

When we were about 130, Eve gave birth to a son, whom we named Seth. He was the consolation of our lives. Our great love for each other never returned, but we now had someone between us who brought peace. Like me, Seth was content with his life, even though he was the only child in the world.

And so we lived peacefully together for another eighty years without Seth ever asking for the company of a woman. The thought didn't seem to occur to him.

One day, when we were pottering about outside the tent, a huge cloud of dust appeared on the horizon. We paid little attention to it, since we were accustomed to seeing wandering herds of camels. As it came closer and we had to wrap cloths around our heads to protect ourselves from the dust, I heard voices and I froze in fear. I fell to the ground because I thought we were being visited by the gods, and I cried out for help but God was silent. The herd stood still and the dust settled. I saw figures on the backs of the camels, but I didn't dare to look, and I bowed so deeply that my nose touched the ground.

Then I heard Eve laugh as she hadn't laughed for years. It

---

1 Adam lived to the age of 930.

sounded like the cackle she'd made that first time, when she rose out of the water and saw me.

"Stand up, you fool!" she cried. "They're people! People!"

I looked up and saw a person, and another one and another, men and women, sitting up high on their camels.

I should have been glad, but I was horrified.

"I want a woman," whispered Seth, but I didn't listen—my world was falling apart before my eyes. We were not the only people on earth! I felt betrayed by my own story of creation. Had I lost two sons to a god who existed only in my mind? Or had God been making a fool of me?

The camels kneeled down and soon the strangers were standing.

I stood up, my knees shaking. A man asked, "Are you Adam?" And I thought: Is this God? He knows my name!

But the man said, "I am Enoch, your grandson."

It was the first time the word "grandson" had been spoken in my universe and I couldn't immediately place it.

"The son of your son Cain," said the man.

Eve gave a squeal, leapt at this stranger and hugged him.

"Grandson! Grandson!" she cried with delight. "How's my boy? My Cain?"

"He's well," said Enoch.

"We're not alone in the world, Adam," cried Eve with her arms still around the stranger. "Rejoice."

But I did not rejoice. I would have preferred my view of the world to have been correct. I was outraged.

"How can you be my grandson?" I asked. "Does Cain have a wife?"

"Of course he has a wife, you dummy!" screamed Eve. "What a question!" And turning to Enoch, she said, "How's your mother, grandson?"

"She's fine," said Enoch. "She sends her best wishes."

"Father," Seth whispered in my ear again. "I want a wife."

Enoch must have heard him.

"Uncle," he said. "I have brought three young women for you, all three in the prime of life, no older than eighty, glowing with health, and the proud owners of all their own teeth."

He beckoned the women closer. They were dressed in colorful robes, they wore glittering rings in their ears, and their lips were unnaturally red. They disgusted me. Seth gaped at them with his mouth open wide and his eyes bulging.

"Where have all these people come from?" I said to no one in particular.

"From Cain's city," said Enoch. "The city he named after me, Enoch, in the Land of Nod."

I had no idea what a city was, but I was silent because I didn't want to appear stupid.

"A city? What's that?" asked Eve, and my toes curled with shame.

"It's a place where many tents all stand together," Enoch told her. "Tents made of stone. Houses. Hundreds of people live there."

"Oh, that sounds wonderful!" exclaimed Eve. "I want to go to the city!"

I felt forsaken by God. I had never been so alone. The very word "city" annoyed me. Firstly, those people shouldn't have even been there. Secondly, why did they all have to live clustered together? How did they make their living? The three women wiggling their hips before Seth's eager eyes didn't look as if they'd ever had to bend their backs over a stubborn piece of land. Their hands gleamed like flowers in the sunshine.

"If Seth wants a wife, she's staying here," I grumbled. "We're not going to the city."

"No, no," said Enoch, "that's not the idea. If Seth chooses a wife, she belongs with you."

I didn't know how to respond. I had no need for a stranger in my family, but I realized I couldn't forbid Seth to take a wife.

"Let him choose," I said glumly.

Seth looked like a rabbit staring, helpless, into the eyes of a snake. He looked, but his tongue lay limp in his mouth. Not a word came out.

"First let's have a nice bite to eat and a drink," said Eve.

So we had a nice bite to eat and a drink.

Where had Cain found his wife? That question will remain unanswered, since Enoch did not know.

"She was there and he found her," he said simply. "There were lots of other people. And the sons of God saw how beautiful the daughters of men were, and they chose the women they desired."

Sons of God! I wanted to put my hands over my ears so I didn't have to listen to Enoch's blasphemy, but they lay in my lap as if paralyzed.

"So the descendants of God dwell among us," Enoch said, "people with a divine spirit within them. There are a number of them in the city. When they speak, others cannot help but listen. They have the gift of the word."

Silence usually reigned in our tent, but this man from the city could not be silent; he talked and talked. The women blathered right through it, and a thick broth of words sloshed from one of my ears to the other. I love strong, simple words, on a bed of silence. Great, thick torrents of words make my head as heavy as lead.

They stayed for seventy-seven days, because Seth could not choose. On the seventy-seventh day, when I thought I was going insane, I screamed, "You can't choose? Then take all three!"

So he took all three.

Enoch departed with his entourage, peace returned, and Seth lay groaning in his tent with his wives for months. That proved contagious, and Eve and I added a few more sons and daughters to the family.

God remains as silent as Abel's grave unto this very day.

The Story of Ham

All my life I have tried to find favor with my father, but I have not succeeded. He has cursed me for saying the wrong things.

I am Ham, son of Noah, father of Canaan.

When Noah was approaching six hundred, he started to behave strangely. He went half-naked through our village, declaring that people were wicked and that God was angry with them. I loved my father, so I was concerned.

"What are they doing?" I asked. "What's so bad about them?" I was almost one hundred years old myself. I thought I had the right to ask such questions.

"They are doing wrong," Noah growled. "I'll say no more than that. Why are you interfering? Is it not enough that your father says they are wicked?"

"Of course, Father," I said. "But be careful. It's not what people like to hear."

"They cannot harm me," he said. "God is with me."

His words annoyed me. What can be done when a man takes refuge behind God's broad back?

One day, when he returned from the village, beaten black and blue, Shem and Japheth tended him lovingly, but I sneered, "God must have been taking a nap."

Of course I shouldn't have said that, but I was worried, because I loved my father. My brothers were more obedient than I was, but I doubt they cared as much. My love for him burned within me. I longed for his love in return, but I did not receive it.

Noah didn't need any people; he had God. The god of Adam, our forefather. His story has been passed from father to son, along this line:

Adam's son Seth begat Enosh, Enosh begat Kenan, Kenan begat Mahalalel, Mahalalel begat Jared, Jared begat Enoch (of whom it is said that he walked with God, and he did not pass through the realm of the dead but flew straight into God's arms), Enoch begat Methuselah, Methuselah begat Lamech, and Lamech begat Noah, my father, whose name promises that he will bring comfort.

I would appreciate if it you could learn to recite these names by heart—in reverse order too.

Adam's story was passed down through all those forefathers by word of mouth until it finally ended up with Noah, who in turn told it to Shem, Japheth, and me. He praised the faith of Abel, but my father was a crop farmer like Cain, the man he loathed from the bottom of his heart. Noah grew crops, even though he knew God did not love such farmers. My grandfather Lamech had told him clearly that God cursed arable land. God loved nomadic herdsmen.

So what happens to a devout man when he realizes his daily work offends his god? He becomes afraid and develops an aversion to life. Some people are able to choose another profession when they become unhappy, while others turn to drink.

Noah turned to drink.

Whenever he was drunk, he was moved by the spirit. He staggered through the streets and his insults kept people from sleeping.

"Robbers and murderers! God will wipe you out like rats!" Shem and Japheth gently tried to bring him back inside, which sometimes worked but usually did not. I, on the other hand, tore

into him and called him a dumb drunk. I wanted to shake him out
of his delirium.

My father was not entirely wrong. Owning land led to blood
and mayhem, since there were always border disputes. There was
thievery, there was murder. There was rape and abduction, but
these didn't seem to me like good reasons for a man to go out of his
mind. I don't know if it was the alcohol, but my father's eyesight
grew worse and worse, until finally he went blind. His blind eyes
saw things that weren't there and he talked nonsense, so everyone
laughed at him.

Our village was in a region that was ravaged by lengthy droughts.
We had to spray the thirsty land with water from deep wells. People
would bash each other's brains in for the sake of water; it was more
precious than gold.

Noah became obsessed with water. On the rare occasions it
rained, he would run outside and skip around in the downpour
until it stopped. Then he'd stomp in the muddy puddles for a
while, like a little boy. He was drunk then, too, but not on wine.

One day, when he collapsed in his tent, soaked through, he said,
"There will come a day when the rain doesn't stop and the water
will engulf everything. The earth will be washed clean of iniquity,
for God has seen that all people are wicked, except for me."

My mother and my brothers nodded meekly, but once again I
was stupid enough to speak up.

"Yes," I said, "the whole village is full of praise for your incredible goodness."

He knew the whole village hated him, so my mockery did not go
unnoticed.

"Who are you with?" he asked bitterly. "Me or them?"

"You *and* them," I said.

A worrying silence fell. My father's sightless eyes seemed to be
peering at me as if I were a mangy animal. I loved him, but the wine
had destroyed his mind, and he had grown impossible to reach. He
lay down on his couch and closed his eyes.

Then suddenly, unexpectedly, an idea came to me that was so

crazy I started laughing even before I'd said it. I said, "You'll have to build a boat."

It was a joke, nothing more. I'd hoped to make him laugh, but he didn't laugh, because he'd fallen asleep.

The next day he called us together, my mother, my brothers and their wives, and my wives and me.

"Listen," he said, "God has told me I must build a boat."

I wanted to shout out, "That was me! Not God. And it was just a joke." But this time I wisely kept my mouth shut.

"A boat?" asked Shem. "But, Father, where do you want to go sailing with this boat?"

"Here," said Noah, "because God will wash away the people from the face of the earth with a huge wave, and—along with the people—the animals, insects, and birds, since he is sorry he ever made them."

"Ah, that's too bad for God," I said. "All that hard work for nothing."

Noah fell silent. His eyes seemed to see and to pierce me through.

"Which of my sons was that?" he asked.

"Ham," I said.

Noah nodded.

"Why do I always hear mockery in your voice? Why do you have no respect for your father?"

I said nothing, because he wouldn't understand that it was not respect I wished to give him, but love.

"God regrets his creation," he said. "He wants to make a new start, because no trouble is too much for him. He is going to wipe out all the people and all the animals."

"Except for the fish," I said. "And the waterfowl."

I don't know why, but I just couldn't help making fun of him. Almost everything my father said tickled my funny bone, yet my laughter was not an expression of joy, more of despair. I wanted him to see me, but he was blind to everyone and everything. Was I the only man who longed to be seen by his father? I didn't know. My brothers showed no such sign. They listened to Noah breathlessly and with reverent adoration, as if he were a god.

What does that really mean: respect? It seems to me like a kind of heartlessness, shown by those who stand at a safe distance and watch in silence as a person or a god comes to grief. Respect is the undoing of both people and gods, as everyone—person or god—needs to be lovingly mocked if they are to survive in our hearts. If my father had known about love, he would not have cared about respect, I'm sure of that—but he did not know. He knew only his honor and his drink.

"Ham," said Noah. "Do you want to come on board with me?"

"Yes, Father," I said. "If our wives and children can come too."

"Your wives can, but not your children."

"All right, Father, we'll let your grandchildren drown."

Neither my brothers nor my mother dared to laugh, even at that. Shem and Japheth stared at me in horror, but it was their father, not I, who had coldly condemned their children and mine to death.

"It is God's will," he said.

"Oh," I replied. "Well, that's fine, then."

I was almost certain my brothers would think he'd gone too far now. They would leap up, they would fly at my father's throat. They would scream at him to get lost and take his god with him, and to keep his pious paws off their children.

But nothing happened. They listened, pale and full of respect, to the man who was planning to destroy their lives.

"I have to make a boat of cypress wood," said Noah. "Which of you is going to help me?"

A bewildered silence followed, because who wants to contribute to the downfall of his own family? My brothers were as silent as the grave and I too intended to keep my mouth shut. Then I thought: Do I believe in the fantasies of an old drunkard whose mind has been ravaged by alcohol? Do I believe God wants to destroy his own creation? Why not build a boat for my father if it gives him pleasure? A boat in the middle of the bone-dry land, a boat that will never see water.

So I said: "Me. Father, I will help you."

"Ham? You?" I saw the amazement on his face.

"Yes, Father, me. But on one condition."

"Aha!" cried Noah. "Of course! A condition. Just for once, my son Ham won't be a smart-ass!"

"Yes, Father," I said. "On one condition. This smart-ass will only help you if you do not drink a single drop of wine while we're building the ship and you don't take any wine on board when the flood comes."

Again that searching, sightless look. I asked myself why I loved him. Was it really love or was it a desire for recognition? What was loveable about this man? Why didn't I break away from him and leave with my family for some other country?

"A son who criticizes his father?" asked Noah.

"Criticism? Fine. Go on drinking your wine—and ask someone else."

He waited in sullen silence. I could see Shem and Japheth were becoming agitated. They knew what Noah was waiting for but they didn't make a sound.

All their lives, my brothers surrounded themselves with silence, never sharing a thought with anyone. They were submissive to my father and afraid of their own emotions. They were suspicious of each other, but less so of me because my father hated me. Now a new situation had arisen: I had offered him my help and they had not. They believed in our father's prophetic gifts, while I didn't. That was the difference. His prediction of a coming flood paralyzed them with fear. I admit that I took pleasure in their confusion. Just imagine: Japheth's ten-year-old son led his blind grandfather by the hand, day in, day out, and took him wherever he wanted to go, but the boy would not be allowed on board!

Really let that sink in. Do not let it pass you by. That was the commandment of Noah's god.

I could see a terrible future ahead for my people: not because of their faith in God, but because of their faith in a prophet like my father.

"We're going to need people to work the fields," Japheth finally managed to say. "While the ship is being built, we still need to eat, don't we?"

"The sheep have to be fed and the cows milked," said Shem.

"The housekeeping done," said my mother.

"The children fed and dressed," said my sisters-in-law.

No one wanted to work on the idiotic boat except me, though I felt my favorite wife's support when she laid her hand on my back. Perhaps she thought I had a plan, but I did not. It had been an impulse, nothing more.

"Fine," said Noah. "My son Ham will build the boat. It must be made of cypress wood. Build different rooms within the hull and coat it with pitch, inside and out. Make it three hundred cubits long, fifty cubits wide, and thirty cubits high. You must leave an opening one cubit high all around the top so the light can come in. The door must be built in the side. The boat must have a ground floor with two more floors above."

"That's not just a boat," I said. "That's an ark."

"That's right," said Noah. He stood up. "Come, let us begin."

The problem was that no cypress trees grew for miles around and we had never seen a boat in our dry land. We had only heard rumors of the existence of floating wooden houses and people who moved in them across the water.

We stood outside. It had not rained for a long time; the land was as dry as dust. All the way to the horizon, there was not a tree to be seen.

Noah walked about two hundred yards to the east, then he stopped.

"This is the place," he said. "This is where it should be."

"Father," I said. "There is no wood."

"Then make sure we get some," he said simply.

"But, Father," I said. "It's going to take a while."

"That doesn't matter," he told me. "I'll wait for you." He sat down in the prickly, dry grass.

I looked at him and saw he was serious. How could he assume I'd just dash over the horizon, chop down a few hundred trees, and still be back before sunset?

"Couldn't we make the boat a bit smaller?" I asked. "About

the size of a washtub?" For the millionth time I tried, against my own better judgment, to get through to my father by making a joke.

"No," he said, "because we're taking animals too."

"Animals? What kind of animals?"

"Two of every kind that exists, a male and a female."

I dropped down onto the sand beside him and tried to get my thoughts in order. We were going to build a boat on dry land and we were going to house all the animals in it, two by two.

When I'd managed to form some kind of idea of what he meant, I said, "Including the elephants?"

"Yes," said Noah. "Including the elephants."

"But not your grandchildren?"

"God has to draw a line somewhere."

"Not even instead of a couple of warthogs?"

Noah didn't answer. I could see tears in his eyes and I realized he was a prisoner of his own insanity.

"God is not very kind," I said.

"A father must be strict," said Noah. "Friendly fathers are no good to anyone. Go fetch the wood."

I tried to hate him, but instead I was filled with compassion, and I hated myself for it. Why could I not be a strict son? Why did I not despise him for the god that dwelled within him? Why was I trying to save a man who was past saving? Devoting oneself to a hopeless love is supreme folly and evidence of a weak character.

I leapt to my feet.

"Go home," I said. "This is going to take months."

But Noah didn't move from the spot.

"If I catch you drinking a single drop of wine, I'll burn everything I've built."

Noah gestured toward the distant horizon, where I had to go.

Unlike my beloved father, I had many friends in the village, and that was handy, because I wasn't going to get anywhere without some help. The first one I visited was Jered, the carpenter. I told him the whole story and he roared with laughter.

"I don't know why I'm doing this," I said when he'd finally stopped laughing. "I must be an idiot."

"I think it's an interesting idea, though," said Jered, "building a boat in the desert. Perhaps it might draw down some rain from the clouds."

I told him the dimensions of the boat that my father had specified, but it didn't help much. Neither of us knew what a boat looked like.

"We'll just build a big wooden box that we assume will float," said Jered, "because it's not as if it'll ever actually have to float, is it?"

When Jered said that, a plan began to take shape in my mind. I thought: Oh yes, this boat is going to float. I didn't know exactly why I thought that. I just thought: Father is blind. It doesn't matter what the boat looks like, but it does have to rock and sway.

"Just as well you and your family are filthy rich," said Jered, "because this is going to be an expensive job."

"It's in everyone's interest for my father to stop yelling at them," I said.

Jered just grunted and I realized I couldn't count on the solidarity of the local community. I was risking everything I owned to help Noah quit the drink and to get my father back. Was it love or greed? And can you really *have* a father if he's decided long ago that he doesn't like you? Those were the questions I asked myself, but I didn't come up with any answers, because I didn't want to know. In a way, I was just as obsessed by the idea as my father was—and therefore blind to reality.

When Jered and I had made an estimate of the price of the timber and transportation, he called his people together and we got down to work.

Noah constantly sat at the edge of the construction site and had all his meals brought to him. At night he allowed my mother to cover him up, but he did not sleep with her. He drank only water, but still his madness did not diminish. He even managed to inform the workers on the boat of their impending doom on a daily basis.

They shrugged. I continued to hope he would fall silent one day and realize that his terrible thoughts were the result of his excessive drinking.

How was I to know that Noah's god was incapable of handling his own rage? It's hardly surprising that a man wants to see the gods as more thoughtful and wise than himself, isn't it? How can anyone live with a god who wants to destroy his own creation, thereby proving himself a failure? If I had known such gods existed, I would have told everyone to build their own ark, right under Noah's nose. But the thought never occurred to me. It fills me with disgust. If the gods are even crueler than humans, I want nothing to do with them. But I do hope that one day a human will rise up and teach them justice.

I didn't believe a flood would ever come; my only aim was to put an end to my father's folly. I wanted to shake him awake, once and for all, by appearing to go along with his plan, and then triumphantly revealing my deception. So, together with my friends, I constructed a huge stage upon which I could present a deception as realistic as possible. We dug a large hole and lined it with clay, which, like the cypress wood, had to be transported from far away. Under the hot rays of the sun, the clay turned as hard as stone, and we filled in any cracks that appeared. Then we built the boat at the bottom of the pit. We crafted and waterproofed hundreds of wooden tubs. The whole village had lots of fun and, for years, our construction was the main force that united our community. It was as if we were erecting a monument to laughter, to a priceless joke, or—let's not beat about the bush—to humor as an antidote to my father's deadly seriousness.

To our surprise, our absurd creation actually ended up looking magnificent. By the light of the setting sun, our joke transformed into a work of almost unseemly beauty. It defiantly radiated uselessness, amply compensating us for the drops of sweat we had poured into its construction. We had devised a form of enjoyment that exceeded the pleasures of dice games and made intoxication redundant. Those of us who were less receptive to beauty became drunk on the strong resinous scent of the cypress wood. Noah listened all day to the sound of our hammers and saws. In the evening, when silence fell, I took him by the hand because he wanted to touch our work. And, every time, I saw surprise in his shaking hands. This son, the one he loved least, was carrying out his instructions with a precision that demonstrated supreme devotion.

He tried not to let his satisfaction show, but instead made remarks that sounded like stern reprimands. That was the only way he knew how to talk to people.

"The elephants need to go at the bottom."

"Of course, Father."

"You have to work faster."

"Yes, Father."

I did not obey but slowed the pace of the work whenever I could, in the hope that Noah would see sense as time went by. I ran out of funds but still there was no stopping me. I sold some of my land to my brothers and every day I slaughtered a sheep for the carpenters. My wives began to complain, since they had to work what land of ours remained, and my children had to roam farther and farther from home to tend the sheep.

My brothers did their best to make my father distrust me, jealous of the time I was spending with him because of my work on the ark.

"Father, Ham's boat is becoming a monster."

"It's going to sink like a stone."

But Noah saw through them.

"Ham may have a big mouth and treat his father like a dog, but he's the only one of my sons who was prepared to carry out God's command."

I couldn't call it love, but I saw this scant recognition as some kind of precursor to love. I know, I'm a lost cause. I realize now that a man of god like my father will never give himself entirely to a human being, not to my obedient brothers, not to my caring mother, let alone to me.

The first year, the rain did not come and the sun burned our skin. We barely needed to heat the pitch that we used to seal the inside of the ark. The vapor that rose from it in the bone-dry wind stank to high heaven. It was no fun anymore but still everyone pressed on. Strangers came from near and far to gaze in amazement at our work of art. We sold hundreds of miniature arks, which Jered manufactured in his workshop. Our village became famous. More and more villagers opened up little stores selling all kinds of trinkets. Business was booming. My father did not drink a drop of wine, but the more successful everyone was, the more fiercely he cursed them.

He too became a tourist attraction. His fame galloped before him. When the strangers grew tired of gaping at the ark, they began to challenge Noah.

"Come on, old man, we want to hear you rant and rave."

"Do you have one of your fine fire-and-brimstone sermons for us?"

Noah put up with the jeering for a short while, but then he furiously rose to his feet, leaning on his stick and pointing up at the heavens with his other hand.

"Your laughter will die on your lips when you watch your children drown before your very eyes." That's what his sermon boiled down to. I could have hit him—what kind of person threatens others with the death of their children? At such times, I could draw no other conclusion than that the man was wicked through and through, but everyone else just laughed at him. As time went by, I began to follow their example.

Back then, I still believed it was possible for laughter to ward off Evil. Maybe I even thought mockery could cleanse a tainted heart.

"Venerable prophet!" one of the outsiders cried. "Your boat will be filled to the brim with animal poop and piss. You'll suffocate in the stench!" Or "The lions will think you're a tasty snack."

Jokes like that.

I have to confess that my attention gradually shifted. I'd started my ridiculous task in order to save him, but as our prosperity increased and I began to understand that we owed our renown to my deranged father, I realized that it was essential for him to stay deranged. It seemed there were two ways to make a living: slogging away in a field or coming up with some crazy scheme that made you famous. Our village became a tourist destination. The visitors sometimes stayed for weeks, looking for some variety in their monotonous existence, for money, for women, for an exciting life. My brothers both opened inns, which made them lots of money, and my mother sold colorful fabrics and jewelry.

The ark was in danger of losing its position as the center of attention and so Jered and I came up with something new: we started to manufacture animals. We made elephants, lions, wolves, turtles, and lizards—any animal you'd care to name. All our animals could move: we hid people inside the large animals, and the smaller ones were for pulling along. Every week we organized a long procession of animals going to the ark, two by two.

We presented the story of the ark and the coming flood, the prophet Noah, and his angry god, so vividly that it took people's breath away. Some of them even started to believe in Noah's prophecy, throwing themselves to the ground and begging for forgiveness. At first I couldn't contain my laughter, but I soon realized these idiots were what made our spectacle so appealing, and I learned to watch them with a straight face. Our fame grew and the strangers who visited our village came from farther and farther away and some spoke dialects that were almost incomprehensible. Most came only to have fun and to mock Noah; the converts were in the minority.

When Noah had finished yet again strewing his curses over the throngs, I would ask him my new question: "Father, some people have repented of their sins and asked God for forgiveness. What about them?"

"Too late!" Noah would cry. "There's nothing God can do about it now. They will drown along with the rest."

I became aware that it was the terrifying aspect of this god that made him so attractive to many people. Shivers even ran down the spine of those who believed in nothing. They expressed their fear by ridiculing Noah and his devout converts, but I could sense they didn't feel entirely comfortable. I discovered that people have a need for anxiety and I realized that a shiver down the spine is a form of sensual pleasure that can be turned into financial gain.

Within three years I had recouped my losses and began to make a profit, but that same year I started to grow anxious myself. A man from the east arrived, said he had traveled for four weeks, and spoke a dialect I had difficulty understanding. He caught my attention as he studied our construction with interest, listened calmly to Noah's ill tidings, and watched our procession of imitation animals with a smile. Not a word passed his lips at first, but one day one of his servants asked if I would agree to meet him, because he had something to say to me. I granted his request because he had aroused my curiosity.

After we had exchanged pleasantries, he came to the point.

"You know, it's quite possible that your father is not insane," he said.

I did not react, because of course my business was based on the idea that my father might not be crazy, even though I knew better.

"You have no need to conceal your feelings from me," said the wise man from the east. "I know what you're thinking. If my father behaved like yours, I would think the same. But I shall tell you a story that has been told in my family for as long as anyone can remember . . . When you dug the pit where you built your boat, did you find any shells?"

I nodded.

"Well, those shells come from sea creatures. The question is: How did those creatures ever reach this dry land? Now for the tale that's told in my family—according to this story, all the lands you see from here to the horizon, and also the land I come from, twenty-eight days from here, were once sea: the result of a huge flood. The sea came falling from the sky in the form of rain and swept across the land like a roaring wave that engulfed everything—all except one family who had built a boat because the father, just like yours, had predicted the flood. But there's an important difference between my ancestor and your father. Your father puts the flood down to an angry god, whereas my ancestor reached his conclusion from the shells. He simply thought: If the sea was here once, it could return. And so he built a boat as a precaution.

"I have traveled far and wide and everywhere I went—to the east, the west, the south, the north—people told me a story about a great flood that once destroyed everything and was survived by just a few people. What seems to be land can become the ocean floor, and what appears to be sea can dry up at any moment, since the earth is young and restless. The story told everywhere has now reached your father. And maybe he's right. Perhaps the sea is returning."

I was speechless, because my father's crazy yelling suddenly had a foundation in reality. I felt my anxiety rise up within me like a fog. Was it really true that an old, addled drunkard knew more than his healthy, hardworking fellow men? It couldn't be! It shouldn't be!

To overcome my confusion, I quickly came up with a question.

"If the people of your land believe a flood is possible, why don't they all build boats?"

The wise man nodded.

"That is the great mystery of the human mind—it knows about danger but does little to avert it."

Then one year it began to rain heavily. The pit beneath the ark filled with water and the story of the wise man from the east haunted my mind.

"Is this it?" I asked Noah anxiously.

"Are the animals here?" he asked.

"No," I said, "but you'd better go into the ark anyway."

But Noah didn't want to. He stayed where he was in the pouring rain.

The rainfall was spectacular, the ark rose inside its pit, with its roof high above the houses. Rivers ran through the streets, houses flooded, some collapsed, a child drowned. I had never experienced anything like it before and I thought: If this is possible, then anything is possible.

But Noah was right: just as suddenly as the torrential rains had started, they stopped. The sun dried the village, the houses were repaired or rebuilt, the dead child buried. The ark, though, remained afloat in its basin for a long time. We topped up the water with our wooden tubs whenever the level started to drop and we kept the ark afloat for a year, to the amusement of the visitors, who saw a boat bobbing about in the middle of the desert.

It was only then that I started to wonder why we had not built such basins before to store water. Why do humans make themselves dependent on the favor of the gods? Why do they not act themselves? I had sold all my farming land to my brothers and had eaten my flocks. I did not need any more water. I was rich. Out of kindness, I encouraged people to build water basins, but no one did so. Instead they begged the gods for rain, which did not come, year after year, as the gods make a pastime of not listening to prayers. And when they bring rain, they bring too much or too little. They want to see people suffer because they are jealous of us. It took years before I understood why. Have patience—I will reveal the reason to you when my story is ready for it.

Now that I had seen how dangerous water could be, I secretly built a hidden room in the ark, suitable for hiding my four children as stowaways. Only Jered knew about it, but he laughed at me and cried out that I had lost my mind, just like my father. He was, of course, right. While I was working on it, I could feel that I was not in my right mind, and that an unreasoning fear had taken hold of me.

I know now that my lack of reason was like my father's piety, an attitude I had long resisted, but which still crept in like a thief in the night. It was the uncontrolled fear that invites the gods to heap their disasters upon us. When people are scared of water, they build dykes, canals, and levees to control the water, not boats, because that just makes us playthings of the gods. It is our devout need for complete submission rather than wise intervention that actually brings disaster upon us. The gods seize their chance when we are weak; when we're strong, they lie low.

For another three years it was as dry as a bone, the ark stood firmly on the ground, and our tubs were empty. The only water we saw came from our wells. And then, one day, when the sky was clear blue and the sun turned the earth into a skillet, it finally happened. A harmless little white cloud appeared on the horizon, no bigger than a clenched fist, an insignificant little cloud that gave no cause for celebration, since there was clearly no rain in it. But along with that pitiful little cloud in the sky, an immense cloud of dust appeared on the horizon, higher and wider than we'd ever seen in our lives. There was no wind, so no one could understand how the dust cloud had formed or how it was moving. But it was most definitely moving—and it was coming our way. Everyone made ready for an approaching sandstorm, because that was all we could compare to the strange phenomenon, but there was no storm. Then we heard a rumbling sound and the ground trembled beneath our feet, but there was no thunder.

I was standing near the ark, terror stricken. I had no idea what was happening, and then I heard the roar of my father's voice: "Today's the day," he yelled. "They're coming! Throw the doors of the ark wide open!"

I didn't know what Noah meant, but I instantly obeyed. I lowered the enormous loading ramp on its chains and the ark gaped open like the maw of some mythical monster.

In a few generations no one will believe what happened next. They'll just say: You can't take that kind of story literally. But I saw it with my own eyes. The huge dust cloud was caused by an endless procession of animals, not our imitation animals this time, but real ones. In an orderly fashion, they walked two by two, with two milk-white bears leading the way. They headed straight for the mouth of the ark and filed inside, calmly, deliberately, going straight to their own quarters as if someone had sketched out the inside of the ark for them and they'd memorized the layout. I didn't believe in miracles, but I saw this miracle unfold before my very eyes.

When all the animals were in the ark, Noah walked unaided up the loading ramp and headed inside, but before he disappeared into the darkness, he turned and shouted: "Bring God's chosen ones inside. The water is coming!"

I had no time to decide if I believed him or not. I fetched my own wife and children and guided them into the ark, my children hidden under their mothers' skirts.

On the way, I bumped into Jered, the man without whom I could never have built the ark.

I said to him, "Come with me, I'll find somewhere to hide you."

But he replied, "You're out of your mind."

I said, "That's right, I'm out of my mind, but come with me anyway."

"Do you think I want to drown in dung?" asked Jered.

I looked at him and could see in his eyes that he'd rather die than have to live under the rule of Noah's god, and for a moment I too was seized by doubt. Was it not better to die proudly than to survive with the help of an irrational god? A good question, but I was not brave enough to choose death. I embraced my friend, thanked him, and felt devastating shame as I dragged myself into the ark. At Noah's command, my brothers and I pulled up the loading ramp until it closed almost seamlessly.

So there we sat, inside our wooden coffin that stank of pitch and dung. The women were wailing, and I could hear my stowaways crying, but I could think of no way to comfort them.

"Are there children on board?" Noah screamed above the din of the animals.

"Yes, Father. Mine," I called back.

"Get rid of them. They're not allowed to come."

As I looked at this man, who was foaming at the mouth, my heart sank into my shoes. What was to become of the world if this man counted as good and God had chosen him to survive?

"Father," I yelled. "My children are staying on board. I will kill anyone who lays as much as a finger on them."

"Why yours and not ours?" cried Shem and Japheth.

"Because, damn it all, the two of you obeyed Father and I did not," I roared.

"Father, let us bring our children on board." My brothers were desperate, but they did not dare to save their children without our father's consent. Noah said nothing. Not only his mouth was silent, but his whole face. He looked like a cold, blind statue.

It was too late anyway.

I'd been expecting rain, but the first water came across the land.

The wind rose and quickly developed into a violent storm. The sand lashed the ark, and the air screamed like a woman in childbirth. There was a thunderous din as if an army of a-thousand-times-a-thousand giants was approaching. Then came the blow.

A giant fist thumped the ark on its side, and the ark listed and flew through the air. The trusses groaned as if dying, but did not break. The ark slowly righted itself, yet still seemed to be whizzing through the sky like a shot arrow. I climbed to the top floor and hauled myself up to the hole I'd made in the roof. The stench of dung poured through the narrow hatch like thick smoke, burning my eyes. I stuck my head out and, through my tears, saw what was happening. We were not flying. We were floating! We were floating on a furious, churning torrent of white-crested waves. The roar of the water drowned out everything else. It was only after I'd dried my tears that I saw the pieces of wreckage all around, with people desperately clinging on, their mouths wide open. I knew they were screaming and crying, but I couldn't hear them. I saw many of them drown without a sound. The sky turned black and it began to rain. It was as if heaven had opened its sluicegates; it didn't rain in drops but in shafts as thick as fingers. They beat like drumsticks on the roof of the ark, so hard my ears were ringing. The rain drew a curtain between me and those other people, but I knew they were drowning out there, my friends, my friends' wives and children, my brothers' children, Jered.

I dropped back down because I could no longer bear the sight of the world. I fell to my knees amid the rodents, a broken man. What kind of god was this? I couldn't keep down the contents of my stomach and everything came pouring out. The animals sniffed at my vomit and gobbled down anything useful. Disgusting, but it was behavior I could at least understand. If only we had remained animals! Oh Adam, oh Eve, what did you do? You saddled me with a conscience and a deep disgust for my own vomit.

I dragged myself to my feet and realized I was facing the choice of whether to remain in this dreadful life or not. Jered didn't want to be saved by my father's blind god, so he'd taken the honorable way out. I had not. I had dishonored myself by shutting myself away in a stinking coffin while, outside, people were drowning and being torn apart by flesh-eating fish. I had seen shrieking birds land on the floating corpses and peck out their eyes.

I could have preserved my honor by jumping overboard and joining the people who were being swept away like so much garbage.

But I did not, and I despised myself for it.

Then came the day when the rain stopped and the flood eased. A babbling calmness descended upon the world, interrupted only by the screeching of birds landing on the roof of the ark, fighting for a place to perch. The outer wall of the ark was black with insects, and inside we were plagued by clouds of furious mosquitos.

Noah wanted us to chase the birds from the roof, since they were not supposed to survive, but no one took notice of him. Blind though he was, he killed as many mosquitos as he could, but he could not exterminate them all. He scraped the insects from the wall with a spoon, but every spot he cleared was immediately reoccupied: many more creatures were going to survive than his god had decreed. Thousands of waterfowl bobbed around on the floodwaters, and swallows soared above the floating wreckage and uprooted trees, where hissing snakes lay in wait. High in the sky, vultures drew their circles of death.

It was a paltry triumph, but better than nothing: Noah's divine mission had not gone entirely according to plan. Not enough consideration had been given to the details.

"Father, what are we going to do about all those cackling birds on the water?"

I asked my father such questions with childish glee, because a man like me, who had lost his honor and vomited at his own cowardice, knew only one pleasure: tormenting others.

"Kill them! Kill them all!" Noah screamed with despair in his voice.

I felt like a little boy pulling off a spider's legs one by one.

"Great idea, Pops," I said. "Here's your stick. Good luck!"

He called for my brothers but they pretended not to hear. They had been struck dumb by grief and useless rage.

We floated around for weeks and the boredom was like a poison racing feverishly through my veins. I thought up things to hit Noah harder and deeper. "Look over there, Father," I told him. "There's an island floating toward us, made of lashed driftwood. It must be ten times the size of the ark. And this will come as a surprise, Father. It's inhabited! Oh, what a wonderful sight! So much life all together in one place!"

Noah snarled something.

"What did you say, Father?"

"What?"

"What do you mean, 'what'?"

"What is living on that island?"

"Oh," I said. "Didn't I mention that? It's children, Father. Let me see . . . ten, twenty, thirty. I guess it must be about a hundred children."

"That's impossible!" roared Noah. "They're all dead!"

"Please forgive me, Father," I whispered. "Of course. You're right. They're dead. They are dead children pretending to be alive."

I took pleasure in the terrible confusion he was obviously suffering. What was true—and what was not?

"Maybe God realized too late that children are innocent and so he gave them this semblance of life."

Noah was choked by silence. He may have wanted to speak, but I'd rendered him speechless.

"Your god murdered thousands upon thousands of innocent children because he was too furious to think his plan through properly. To console himself he has put a hundred dead children on an island to imitate their existence, so that he can still somehow maintain the feeling that he is good."

Noah tore himself out of his silence, leapt to his feet, and screamed, "That cannot be true! They are real children. They're alive."

"So what's it to be, Father?" I asked. "Are they alive or are they dead?"

"They're alive," he snarled. Then he dropped to the floor.

I remained silent, since I wanted to leave him dangling from the noose of his own making for as long as possible. I knew that a simple sentence was forming in his mind, a sentence of just five words that would cut his tongue and make it bleed. I hoped he would have the courage to utter that sentence, though, because I wanted him to feel the pain.

I heard him groan.

"Is something wrong, Father?"

He gave a deep, heartbreaking sigh. Then he said it.

"Maybe my grandchildren are there."

I left him hanging until the silence became unbearable even for me.

"What did you say, Father?"

"My grandchildren. Go see if they're there."

I could see he was suffering and I was petty enough to take pleasure in it.

"I'll go take a look," I said, "but if they are there, what then?"

"Then nothing! Go see!" he bellowed like a cow in heat.

"No, Father," I said. "I won't take a look until I know what's supposed to happen to those children."

And then the truth came out. I didn't know beforehand what that truth would be, but I knew it existed, somewhere in that blind, addled head of his.

He hid his face in his hands and I heard him sobbing. It was the first time in my life that I'd seen my father cry, but I didn't care. No, in fact, it filled me with disgust.

"He has allowed them to live," he whispered. And then, with a voice like a volcano erupting, he roared: "GOD IS SORRY, DAMN IT. GOD IS SORRY!"

I was stunned. I gaped at my father first as if he were a raging bull, but that image soon gave way to the image of a man broken down by his god. Behold the man, I thought to myself, collapsing like a donkey under his burden. Behold the man who bears on his shoulders a divinity too heavy.

I laid one hand on his shoulder, determined to free him from his god forever.

"His regret comes too late, Father. I made up that island. All the children are dead."

I was naive and it made me cruel. If a man does not want to be free, no one can free him.

"You are lying," he gasped. "They are alive, because he's sorry." Sweat dripped into his blind eyes.

"They are dead," I said, "because in his rage he did not think of justice. A hothead's remorse is poor compensation. You would do well to cast aside this god and take a new one."

I understand now that no advice helps when a person is possessed by a deity. That person can no more part with his god than an apple can cut out its own core.

We floated around for almost a year until the water had receded and the ark ran aground on a mountain. It turned out that hundreds of people had found refuge on islands like the one I'd imagined, but my brothers' children were not among them. My father wanted nothing to do with these survivors who had no place in his vision of the world. He slumped on the floor like an empty sack and pestered us for wine. But there was no wine.

Finally there came a day when enough land had dried up for us to leave the ark.

The earth was horrifyingly empty; so were our hearts. We set to work in silence, embittered by the sheer weight of our losses.

Noah heard our silence, he felt our ice-cold hearts, and not a word passed my mother's lips. He sat huddled on the ground, usually with one hand in the air, as if hoping his fingers would catch some sign of life.

Sometimes he cried out hoarsely, "He will never do it again. Truly. Never again."

But no one said anything in reply. My obedient brothers completely ignored him. Now and then I briefly laid my hand on his head so he would know someone was there, but that was all I could do.

"He will never do it again. Never again will he curse the earth because of human beings, or because everything made by humans is wicked. He has accepted that now. Never again will he kill everything as he has done."

Endlessly he mumbled away to himself, endlessly he repeated the same thing: God regretted his bloodlust. He would never do it again.

I was unmoved. What good was remorse without penance?

Whenever it rained, Noah grew anxious.

"Is there a rainbow in the clouds?"

No one replied.

"Fine, then. Don't say anything. I know there's a rainbow in the clouds, because God said, 'The rainbow in the clouds will for all coming generations be the sign of the covenant between me and you and all living creatures of the earth.'"

"All right, Dad. Now could you please keep your mouth shut for a while?"

No, he could not.

A year later, life came back to him. He stood up, leaning on his old stick, and called out: "My sons, come here." There was authority in his voice once again. So Shem and Japheth immediately went to him and I too was unable to resist my obedience.

"Listen and obey," said Noah. "God has commanded me to

plant a vineyard. I have no need for a vineyard myself, since I haven't drunk wine for years, but God wants a vineyard. My blindness will not permit me, so you must carry out God's command in my stead—and forthwith."

I was the only one who burst out laughing.

"I assume it's Ham who's laughing?"

"Yes, Father, it's me."

"And why does my son Ham laugh?"

"I imagine God gave you another command: that for the sake of your health you should drink the occasional cup of wine."

He was silent for a long time and seemed to be listening to something.

"No," he said finally. "God has not spoken on that subject."

"I'm sure he will in time," I said.

My sons, Cush, Mizraim, Phut, and Canaan, were sitting beside me and I saw that they were biting their tongues so as not to burst out laughing. But their merriment, like mine, had nothing to do with actual joy. The prospect of their grandfather starting to drink again did not delight them.

"May I take the liberty of refusing this assignment from God?" I asked.

Much to my surprise, Noah said, "You may refuse because you built the ark. But your brothers may not."

So my obedient brothers set to work. God alone knows where they got the vines from, but of course it was years before they could produce their first wine.

And, immediately, it all went wrong.

My father had been like a dead tree all those years, pointing up at the heavens with his bare branches, still exuding threats, and standing gloomier than his own pitch-black shadow. I thought I knew what was on his mind: that sea of corpses. Without realizing, he was driven by an impotent rage against the god he worshiped. His fury took the form of his customary bad temper; he drove away his wife, his children, and his grandchildren; and nothing remained of him but a few bones inside a sack of rock-hard leather.

As soon as he had wine, he began to drink without restraint and staggered around babbling once more. He took his drunken self to the villages of tents that survivors of the flood had set up and began cursing everyone all over again. He disgusted me and I was determined to seize the first opportunity to free myself from him.

One day he became so intoxicated that he went and lay down in his tent with no clothes on. I happened to walk in on him and saw him lying there. Filled with contempt, I backed out of the tent and bumped into Shem and Japheth.

"Your father is as drunk as a lord and he's lying on his bed in his birthday suit," I said. I spat out the words and they tasted bitter as gall.

So Shem and Japheth took a cloak, draped it over their shoulders, walked backward into the tent, and covered their father's naked body with their faces turned away, so as not to see him naked.

I admired their behavior: I would have done the same if I had known beforehand what state my father was in. But I was less appreciative the following day when they told my father all the gory details of what had happened.

"It was terrible, Father. Ham was trumpeting it all around, to anyone who would listen, saying you were lying in your tent not fully clothed, and using the most terrible words, and all the while he was cackling like a hen because he wanted to dishonor you as much as possible."

I stood there, together with my eldest son, Canaan, and said: "Listen carefully, Canaan, and hear your uncles cook up a story to suit their own purposes. These are the same men I saved from death."

Trembling, my father rose to his feet, his eyes full of an alcoholic's tears. He held his free hand in the air and pointed a finger at the sky. "Cursed be Canaan!" he roared. "Canaan shall be his brothers' servant, the lowliest servant of all."

My father turned his anger not on me, but on my innocent son. Not once did he say my name, and so it was like I no longer existed.

"May Canaan be the servant of Shem. May Canaan be the servant of Japheth."

I had disappeared so completely from the face of the earth that my brothers had suddenly become Canaan's brothers.

I allowed my father to vent his rage until he withdrew, exhausted, to his tent. I looked at Shem and Japheth. They did not dare to meet my gaze. Then I turned to Canaan and said: "Come on. We're leaving."

I didn't mean we were off for a stroll. We took down our tents, saddled our mounts, and loaded up our donkeys. I said farewell to my mother, and then we set off on a journey in search of another land and another god. But to my disappointment I realized that all gods in all countries are jealous of people, since people live and gods merely exist.

Canaan would serve no one. We settled on the coast of the Great Sea. Mizraim traveled onward and settled on the banks of the Nile, and then Cush went along that river, farther to the south. Phut, though, went first to the east, then to the south, until he arrived in the land that is known as the Land of Gold.

And so we scattered across the world to be free and no man's slave. I never saw my father again, nor his god. Should anyone read this story in the future, he will find it hard to believe they ever existed.

The Story of Shelah

I am Shelah. My great-grandfather was Noah, the man who built the ark, my grandfather was Shem, my father was Arphaxad. He was conceived when my grandfather was one hundred years old, two years after the flood. He was a child to replace the children who had perished in the flood.

When I was thirty, I left my parents and headed to the east with my pregnant wife, where we settled on the plain near Shinar.

I have to confess that my departure was not entirely of my own free will: I was driven to it by my restless nature. Family life weighed heavily on me. A son had no way to escape the authority of his father, who in turn was expected to remain subservient to his own father. I fiercely longed for freedom and even as a child I believed it lay somewhere beyond the horizon. The words "far away" awakened dreams within me of a limitless space where people were free to move and free to think.

I grew up among crop farmers, but my spirit was too uneasy for me to tie myself to a piece of land. When I was young, I did not understand what was wrong with me, and my misunderstood longings often expressed themselves as moodiness. I looked for arguments with everyone and became very good at finding them. People thought I was unbearable and they were right. I found myself impossible, too.

When I realized that my objectionable behavior was an attempt to silence my longings, I tried to hold my tongue so my desire could speak up. I remained silent for years and that too drove those around me to despair, but in that silence I found the right words, and so I understood myself better and began to consider my future.

To my surprise, I found a woman who truly loved me and who was prepared to follow me wherever I went. Milcah was beautiful and compliant, while I was known for being taciturn and difficult. But she saw through me and awoke within me the man she saw with her clear gaze. My tongue loosened and we talked about all our feelings and desires. It was she who encouraged me to say fare-well to my land and to my family, since I would wither if I stayed.

"Even if you leave, you will never be without your family. You carry with you your memories and all the stories you have been told. People will try to tell you that you cannot live without them, but life is everywhere, no matter where you go."

How did she know these things? She must have thought at length about my longing, and better than I had myself. Or perhaps she too had dreamed of far away since she was a child and had sought a man who, like her, felt drawn to the horizon.

When she became pregnant, we decided to pack our belongings, for we wanted our child to be born in a new world.

How do you tell your family that you're leaving and plan never to return? Every word, every sentence I came up with—I knew it would be met with anger: insults, curses, maybe even violence. Milcah saw me worrying and she laughed at me.

"Leave it to me," she said. "I'll do the talking."

When her pregnancy was starting to show, I called our families together, with a trembling heart. We sat in a circle and, after we'd exchanged pleasantries, my wife stood up.

"I am speaking on behalf of Shelah, my husband," she said, "because he does not have the gift of the word, and I do."

Sheepishly, I grinned around the circle to show that I agreed with my wife's words.

"Shelah does not like to speak, but he is a good listener and so he was not deaf when God's voice spoke the following words to him: 'Shelah, depart from your land, leave your family, and go to the land I will show you.' Thus spake the god of Adam, Abel, and Noah to Shelah, your son. It pains him greatly that he must leave you, but who would not yield to a command from almighty God? Any man who would resist him is a fool, even though that obedience may cause sadness."

She spoke for a long time, but I was too surprised to take in what she said. As I looked around, I saw faces that were serious, yet serene. Our mothers cried silently. The word "God" had worked wonders.

When she reached the end of her speech, no one protested. Our fathers and grandfathers solemnly embraced us, giving us their permission to leave.

Back in the seclusion of our tent, I asked her, "Where did God suddenly come from?"

"From my heart," she replied. "The voice of your longing is God's voice. All the voices inside us come from him—the voices of love and anger, of jealousy and compassion. There is not one voice inside us that does not come from him."

"Oh, I see," I said, but I doubted it was true. I could have listed about five voices within me that most definitely did not come from God.

I did not argue with Milcah, though, because she had made it possible for us to leave. We loaded our belongings onto our beasts of burden and set off for the land that "God"—or rather, I—would reveal to us, but I had no idea what kind of land I was looking for. And what would I do there? How would I earn my living? All I knew about was growing crops. I knew nothing at all about anything else. Although I had freed myself from my family, little had changed inside my head. When I thought about my future, I pictured myself doing the same work I had always done: plugging away at a piece of land. We traveled for weeks and all that time I saw the world through the eyes of a farmer because nothing else occurred to me.

When we reached a lowland plain near Shinar, I saw the ground there was very fertile. The plain was crossed by wide rivers that had deposited rich clay on their banks, year after year. I knew I had arrived in the land for which I had longed.

But Shinar was not only a land, it was also a city. Other people had gotten the idea that they might find their fortune on the plain of Shinar. They had used the river clay to make bricks and build homes. I'd never seen houses made of bricks before, but I knew from stories that such buildings had existed in the time of my forefather Noah. They had fallen victim to the flood, and the technique of baking clay had been lost.

At first, the city filled me with disgust. The thought of living in a home fixed in one place, imprisoned in a brick box with a roof on it, made me anxious. Besides, the houses were so tightly packed together that you could hear your neighbor snoring. I had no idea what compelled people to form groups and to pin themselves down to a measured-out plot of land.

But I have come to see that my restlessness was driven mainly by my curiosity. That's why I understand my ancestor Eve's disobedience so well. She wanted to know. She hungered for knowledge. Maybe the forbidden fruit didn't even taste that good, but that was not the point. There was something in that fruit she did not know and that's why she had to eat it.

I bought a plot of land and industriously set to work on the soil, but the city was buzzing inside my mind like an annoying wasp, giving me a vague kind of headache. I couldn't simply ignore the unknown—it was there, it was making me restless. It wanted to make itself known.

When our son Eber was three months old, he developed such a high fever that both Milcah and I were afraid he would die. Then we remembered that the man who had sold us our piece of land was not only a big landowner but also a doctor. And so, for the second time, we set out for the city, but now with our newborn son. The first time I had barely taken in anything about the city because I was basically in a state of panic. Suddenly so many people all together, thronging along narrow streets, so much shouting, so many smells—I couldn't cope with the unknown and so I closed myself off to it. I realized later that Milcah had seen more. She was delighted by the clothes the women were wearing, while I had not even noticed any women.

Our doctor muttered to himself as he massaged Eber's little tummy to loosen his bowels. Then the doctor gave our son a medicine that cooled his fever within an hour. After he had spoken a few incantations and invoked his gods, the doctor declared that Eber would live, and we took him at his word.

Back on the street, I was so relieved that it felt as if I had been given new eyes. If the city housed such learned men as our good doctor, it could not possibly be a bad place. My eyes took in everything and my ears opened wide.

And then we heard the music . . .

At first it was only a jumble of sounds, and I could see Milcah, too, did not know why our ears were listening so eagerly. But we stopped walking because we felt that it had some meaning, even though we did not understand exactly what. After we had lingered for a while, listening to the sounds, the noises began to mingle, and I heard them skipping around and playing together like lambs.

Milcah and I shared a look and could tell from each other's faces that we'd made the same discovery: we could hear a beauty that was like birdsong and yet it was so human that it absorbed us completely. My feet wanted to hop and jump, but I kept them under control for the sake of my dignity. Milcah gently swayed her head like a reed in the breeze.

We tentatively walked through a gate, looking for the source of this enchanting sound, and came to a courtyard overshadowed by a huge tree at its center. Under the tree sat three men and a woman. The sound was coming from their hands.

Since then we've learned what music is, and we know what

instruments are. When the musicians stopped playing, one of them was so kind as to place his instrument in my hands. I plucked impotently at the strings and found I could not make music: the music came not only from the instrument but, more importantly, from the skilled fingers of the player.

While working on my land, I often thought back to that discovery. Sometimes I turned to look at the silhouette of the city. There were people living there who had so refined the movements of their fingers that music flowed from them. They had practiced for years and years. Where had they found the time?

Then I thought about the ark my grandfather Shem had built together with his brother Japheth, and how they had given up everything they owned in order to protect the family from the coming flood. They had sold all their land and livestock to Ham, their lesser brother, who had mocked and taunted them until it became clear that the ark attracted many curious visitors and there was lots of money to be made.

Like the musicians from Shinar, they had sacrificed their time and possessions to become experts at something that was out of the ordinary and it had made them wealthy. I was beginning to understand how I might calm my restless heart. I had to go in search of skills I did not yet possess. I needed to become acquainted with the world and discover what options I had to improve life for me and my family.

I toiled in my field for seven more years, and then I'd had enough.

"We will become poor and perhaps be hungry," I said. "But I want to go to the city to learn."

"You have heard the voice of God again," said Milcah. "He will provide for us."

I was about to protest, but I held my tongue and thought: The voice of God? Maybe it is. Perhaps there is no difference between my voice and his.

Or maybe it was something else. I was surprised that Milcah immediately agreed, and I wondered if I had perhaps put *her* longing into words and if she might be the god who had whispered my thoughts into my ear. Whatever the case, we sold back our land to our good doctor and moved to the city.

I bought a ruin there with a partly collapsed roof, then spent weeks clearing away the rubble so that the floor was habitable. We stretched our tent cloth between the walls to protect us from the hot midday sun. Since I intended to rebuild the house, I looked for work in the brick factory on the banks of the river. After I got home, my hands worked to exhaustion, I labored for a few more hours by torchlight at a sawmill. And so I learned to work with bricks and wood, but Milcah and Eber only saw me when I tumbled semiconscious into bed. That was the price they and I paid for our new life.

When the house was ready, I had more time to reflect on my future. I had discovered that building with wood and bricks gave me great pleasure, so I decided to offer my services as a designer and constructor of buildings. But no matter how hard I tried, no one wanted to hire me.

I had taken the rubble from my house to a big dump just outside the city, where over the course of the years a thick layer of waste construction materials had built up, through which not even a single blade of grass could grow. I was impressed by its size. Without even meaning to, the people of the city had laid a foundation upon which a twin city could be built if needed. And that gave me another idea.

I wanted to make a name for myself, so that I might be known throughout the entire city and receive commissions. I meant to build something that would amaze the folks in the street because nothing like it had ever been seen anywhere in the world.

"Make a name for myself." I'd borrowed that expression from Milcah, because she'd already made her name in Shinar. Everyone knew she heard the voice of God while others heard only the sighing of the wind or the rustling of the reeds on the riverbank. And if people did hear voices, they heard a host of gods' voices all mixed together, each with its own message: a threat, a warning, or a blessing. Milcah heard the voice of the Most High God, loud and clear, with just one message at a time.

Milcah's ears only opened up, though, if she was first paid generously. Her growing clientele ensured she barely needed me anymore.

"God has spoken to me," I said. "I am going to build something extraordinary."

Milcah stared at me as if she'd seen a ghost and I understood why. Never before had I used God's name to lend approval to my own desires.

"That was not God," said Milcah testily. "It was your own aspirations. You say you are going to build something extraordinary, but you mean that you are going to build a tower, so high that it reaches the clouds. The tower of your ambition."

A tower. Although I had never heard the word before, I immediately knew what Milcah meant. And I also knew that by speaking that word she had transformed my vague longing into a definite idea.

"If that is so, then ask God what he thinks of my plan," I said.

"God is silent," said Milcah. "But I doubt that he likes your aspirations."

"I want to be the best at something," I said. "I want to do my best. Why shouldn't I?"

"You want to make a name for yourself, but I am afraid God will prevent that," said Milcah. "Your tower will perhaps have a famous name, but you will not."

"I would be delighted if Shinar and my tower were to become more famous. It's better to live on as a tower than as some man from the past whose bones are dust and no one knows where they lie."

Milcah said nothing.

I looked at her. The city had turned her into a different person. She was no longer the simple girl I had married, the girl who loved me unquestioningly. Her thoughts darted off in all directions and what she said sometimes took such complicated turns that I couldn't follow her.

I never would have imagined that Milcah's god would speak out against me one day. Why was she allowed to make a name for herself while I was not? Was her god jealous because he was rarely on my mind and yet still I led a happy life? I don't know. Perhaps all gods are jealous of people. Milcah had given me the idea of a tower, but at the same time she'd said her god did not want a tower. What was I to make of that?

Then I remembered the Tree of Knowledge, the tree God himself had planted in Paradise but whose fruits were not to be eaten, even though he knew the fruit called Knowledge is irresistible to humans. What did the god want from Adam and Eve? Did he want them, in spite of their human curiosity, to resist the forbidden fruit, or did he want them to disobey and to emulate him? I'm afraid that, deep down, he wanted obedience.

I was going to build a tower, and that fearsome undertaking would bring me a wealth of knowledge, perhaps more than any other human being. Maybe I would discover secrets that the earth, the sky, and the clouds concealed from us, or secrets about the nature of humankind and the gods, because anyone who undertakes something inevitably acquires knowledge.

Merely by formulating these thoughts I began to feel I was on the verge of a major discovery: that what the gods feared most in humankind was knowledge. I didn't know exactly why, but I saw a vision that the gods fade away in the light of excess human knowledge. I saw that they thrive on ignorance. But at the same time it was as if the gods were intent on bringing about their own demise by tempting humans to gather the very knowledge they feared.

I decided that, given my own lack of knowledge, I could not know what the gods wanted and I doubted that Milcah knew any more than I did. I was going to build a tower that would reach into the clouds and make our city famous all over the world.

First I made a model out of wood. The tower would consist of a long path to the top, a spiral road that would rise very gradually. The second ring would lie on top of the first, then would come the third, and so on until the block stretched up to its highest point, up where the clouds float. The path would be wide enough for donkey carts. Spaces could be built into the vertical walls for accommodations, stables, and storage rooms. The tower would become a city in the air teeming with people, and it would even be possible to plant gardens up there to supply the city with food.

I was proud of my design, as I was certain no one had ever come up with anything like it before and that I therefore had a unique opportunity, but Milcah just laughed at me.

"This is the dream of a fool," she said. "This thing can never be made by human hands."

She was undoubtedly right, but it was the sort of rightness I loathed. I'd rather be a fool spitting on his palms and eagerly embarking on an impossible task than a person who is right.

So that's what I did. I began building my spiral road upward, working on my own for the first seven years. I knocked a pole into the ground and used a rope to mark out a circle so large that a hundred of Noah's arks would easily have fit inside. I went back and forth with my donkey cart to the quarry at the foot of the mountains. I loaded rubble and laid the foundation for my road, which was to be five yards wide. I leveled it with grit from the brick factory. Of course my circle couldn't be absolutely circular, because the road had to curl upward like a snail shell. I didn't know how to calculate for the deviation and so about halfway around the circle, hoping for the best, I began to make the curve a little tighter, until finally the head lay beside the tail, but two yards higher. I worked on that first ring for seven years.

I have to confess I was so obsessed with my tower that I made little contribution to my family's happiness. Milcah drifted so far from me that I struggled to understand her. It was as if we spoke two different languages. I didn't earn a penny, so she was the one supporting the family. I stayed with her, since without her I could not continue to build my tower.

"You are disobeying God," she said every day. "He wants you to do something useful."

I shrugged my shoulders, because she made a living from her

oracles and I didn't see what was so useful about incomprehensible gibberish or predictions that sometimes came true and sometimes didn't.

"I occupy myself with the spirit," she said, "and you with earthly mud."

To my son Eber, though, I was a hero, probably because children think earth is so fascinating that they do not see it as "mud." His mother tried to keep him away from the tower, but when she wasn't paying attention, he would slip out the door and I would see him pushing his wheelbarrow around the building site. I had explained my plan to him and his eyes sparkled when he realized how high the tower was going to be.

"Will I be able to touch the clouds?" he asked.

"When we're standing at the top, I'll lift you onto my shoulders and you'll be able to touch the clouds with your fingertips."

How could Milcah not be at all curious about the clouds? "Spiritual life"—what exactly did that mean? I couldn't make head or tail of it, and so I went on working steadily, every day, until my hands bled.

As I began work on the second ring, I noticed that the number of people mocking me was decreasing and that some were showing genuine interest in my tower, probably because they could now see that I would rise up into the sky, ring by ring, higher than the surrounding hills, higher than any person had ever been.

The first to join me was Zippor the birdman, a madman who had wondered all his life why stones fall down and not up, and upon what manner of substance the birds float and fly. He started by walking up the first ring because, as he explained, he wanted to rise slowly. When he reached the end, he flapped his arms and jumped, but of course he fell two yards like a stone. Luckily he didn't break anything.

"You're not high enough yet," he said.

From then on, he helped me, because he thought the substance upon which humans could glide must be found at a higher level than whatever birds used.

At home, when I enthusiastically told Milcah that I was no longer alone at the building site, she replied: "The sky is for the birds and the spirits of the air, not for human beings."

"Why not? And how do you know?" I asked. Her nagging was really getting on my nerves.

"I know because that's how it is," she said.

"You have to research things first if you want to know about them," I muttered.

"You don't need to research what you already know," said Milcah.

"Ah, wife!" I snapped helplessly.

"Your curiosity is disrespectful," Milcah snapped back. "If a man wants to know something, he must present his question to the gods and politely await their response."

"And what if they remain silent?"

"Then he is not permitted to know the answer."

I stifled a yawn, not wanting to offend Milcah. "Oh," I said, and hoped that would be the end of the discussion.

"Why don't you listen to your wife? Why are you the only one in the city who does not respect me?" she shrieked.

I ran out the door.

The second man who joined me was Jobab, the director of the brick factory. He said, "If you succeed in building a tower that reaches the clouds, Shinar will become famous all over the world. Everyone will want to live here and no one will ever leave."

"What do you think?" I asked. "Will I succeed?"

"No," said Jobab. "Not a chance."

"Why not?" I asked in dismay.

"Because you are alone. Thousands of hands are needed for this task, and several generations."

I wanted to say that my son was helping me, and Zippor the birdman, but I remained silent because I knew Jobab was right. I had embarked upon a hopeless task that also displeased the gods.

"But that's the appeal of your project—it's completely pointless," Jobab continued. "Have you heard the story of Noah's ark?"

I nodded but didn't mention that Noah was my great-grandfather.

"The pointlessness of a boat in the middle of the desert enchanted people. It drew them like flies to a pot of honey."

Jobab looked at Zippor the birdman, who was lumbering past, flapping away in search of air that was dense enough to bear his weight.

"Its purpose must be formulated as absurdly as possible," he said. "The clouds aren't high enough. The tower has to reach higher than the clouds, since its boundless folly is what makes the ambition so appealing."

I have to confess that his words wounded me, because if the construction of the tower was boundless folly then I was a boundless fool. There's a difference between thinking oneself a fool and others calling you one. Yet I continued to listen attentively to Jobab, because he smiled as he spoke his words of insult and was the very image of affability.

"Let's build a tower that reaches to heaven. That will make us famous and then we will not be scattered across the face of the earth."

We! Jobab had said "we." I couldn't believe my ears. *We* were going to build a tower, the two of us! If I was a boundless fool, then he was one too!

"You have laid a good foundation," he continued. "But in fact it's nothing more than a rising spiral path made of rubble and soil. Let's make blocks of clay and bake them in the fire. We can use the blocks of clay as bricks, with pitch as mortar."

My hurt feelings vanished from my foolish mind without a trace. I opened my arms wide and embraced him.

"Jobab, you madman! You believe it's possible, too, and that we can build a tower up to heaven!"

"No, I'm not saying that," said Jobab. "But this isn't about whether it's possible or impossible. It's about giving it a go."

I didn't understand, but perhaps it's not necessary to understand people as long as you're able to work together and achieve something. We said goodbye, but not for long, as Jobab promised to get straight to work in his factory, making bricks.

I called for Eber.

"My son," I said, "return to your mother and stay with her. Do not come to the tower again. It makes her sad, and I have enough help now."

I quickly turned my head away, because I could not bear to look at his face. It was as if I had slapped him.

"Go," I said. "Run. Your mother will be pleased."

I turned on him and felt his bitter silence piercing the back of my neck like the point of an arrow. I'd hurt him. He wanted to build the tower with his father, not sit at home with his mother. He heard my words but did not understand them. The people of Shinar all spoke the same language, but what is language exactly? Sometimes it seems most like a tool for sowing confusion and incomprehension, even though at first one might think it was intended to clarify things.

I did not understand myself either. Only later did I come to realize that I had sacrificed Eber to the world Milcah represented: the world of gods, spirits, prayers, sacrifices, and incantations. I gave Eber back to her because I feared she would turn people against me and my tower, but I regretted having surrendered him to the enemies of curiosity.

I say "enemies" because Milcah had followers. They spent their time singing and dancing around my house to honor the gods, or sacrificing animals and reading their entrails to decipher the wishes of the gods. They were always going into ecstasies and then their screams and shouts would fill the air.

They were all of the opinion that our fate was entirely in the hands of the gods and that we could win their favor only through humble obedience. Almost everything humans devised or did for themselves aroused the anger of the gods, with results such as stillborn children, horrendous diseases, attacks of insanity.

I sacrificed Eber for the sake of domestic harmony, but it did not help. I returned home exhausted one evening to find a wife who'd lost her mind. As soon as she saw me, she started to scream. Maybe words were hidden within her shrieks, but all I could hear were shrill noises.

When she had calmed a little, I managed to figure out a few sylla-bles and the occasional word. I was tired, and my fists were itching, because I didn't know what I had done to deserve this frenzied rage, but of course I held myself in check. I have never hit anyone in my entire life.

Perhaps that was what Milcah resented most about me: that I was not a real man, that I did not put her in her place, by force if necessary. She wanted me to be fully occupied with dealing with her, not with a tower or anything else outside our home.

I'm just guessing, though. I don't know anything for certain.

Maybe she invoked her gods to get even with me for my neglect. I think it's possible that her piety was about nothing more than seeking attention and power. Who dares to contradict the mouth through which the gods issue their oracles? Milcah was a queen who wanted to be made subservient but, since her husband could not subjugate her, she had become a furious goddess who would tolerate no contradiction.

What had angered her this time? Jobab. The name of Jobab, the director of the brick factory, had driven her into a rage, because Jobab was a rich and powerful man respected throughout Shinar. The rumor that he was going to work with me on the tower had rippled around the city and reached Milcah before I could inform her myself.

I managed to make out the following from her screams: I was a seducer who made people's heads spin, a reprobate who would bring about the city's downfall, an ungodly man who brought about divi-sion between God and humankind, a rebel who thought he could take on the gods, a corrupter who would drag others along with him to their doom. People should not want to know things, people should work and pray, praise and worship, nothing else. I should cease the construction of my blasphemous tower immediately and ask Jobab to forgive me for the temptation to which I had exposed him.

But the worst was still to come.

She threatened me with the life of our son Eber, whose name means "he who comes from the other side."

"If you go on like this," she told me, "you'll force me to send Eber back to where he came from—to the other side."

I knew what she meant by "the other side" and the terror almost stopped my heart from beating. I had heard of desperate souls in utter distress who had resorted to sacrificing a child to the gods in order to appease them, but those stories were about people who lived far away. No one in my family had ever suggested such a thing and, as far as I knew, such atrocities had never occurred in Shinar. I refused to believe that the tower was the cause of Milcah's despair and I came to the conclusion that her followers, or perhaps the spirits and the gods, had driven her insane.

My mind was made up: I had to put an end to the situation. Talking no longer helped, as we spoke two different languages.

"Milcah, my queen," I said, "you know how much I love you, but I am leaving you. I have returned our son Eber to you, but you have not accepted my sacrifice. You reproach me for every step I take, every action I perform, every word I speak. You will only be satisfied if I act like a dead man in the realm of the departed, a shadow of myself."

To my surprise, my words silenced Milcah. She looked at me with big, bulging eyes. Compassion flowed through my body, and my knees started to buckle. She was beautiful. I saw the simple carefree girl before me that she once had been and I almost succumbed to that sweet memory.

But I pulled myself together. The city changes some people into wanton libertines, and gives others ideas that would never take root in the lonely countryside but that, within the confined space of a house's four walls, are able to develop in all their toxicity.

"I have to leave you," I said, "because I am driving you to despair and you are extinguishing any spark of life within me."

She seemed to want to say something, and her mouth opened, but I silenced her with a gesture. I saw her surprise; I'd never imposed my will on her before. There was only respect in her eyes. I realized the part I was playing was the man she had been longing for, a man who could handle her, who could make her hold her tongue, the kind of man I did not want to be. Again it was language that had us talking at cross-purposes: the word "man" doesn't mean the same to everyone, any more than "woman" or "god."

I looked around our living room and realized everything I owned was at the tower. I could go. I called Eber. "Son," I said, "say goodbye to your mother."

The scene that followed can hardly be described, but I had to take my son away from his mother. He wasn't safe with her. I did it, but all my life I'll bear the burden of the grief I inflicted on them both. Perhaps none of it would have been necessary if I hadn't started to build the tower, or if I'd stopped in time. That may be true, but I doubt it. The gods always find something to set people against each other. I believe it's better to ignore them, since no matter what we do, they always have their way.

My family was not the only one torn apart by the building of the tower. After Jobab had ordered a dozen of his workers to concentrate solely on baking, transporting, and laying the clay bricks and digging for pitch, some of the locals became caught up in our enthusiasm, while others anxiously awaited the wrath of the gods. The majority watched with folded arms, supposedly giving expert advice but mainly interested in how best to turn our immense efforts to their advantage.

Milcah's devoted followers organized parades around the tower, blowing horns and ringing sheep bells, in the hope that the strength of their protest and the help of their gods would cause the tower to collapse. We workers, we did not mock them, we paid no attention to them, we had no time, we were working. But those watching— the people who had no useful opinion but plenty to say—enjoyed themselves at the expense of both the pious and the workers. They laughed at every setback and misfortune that befell us. They called out whenever Milcah's procession went by, "Blow harder! Ring louder! Your gods are fast asleep!" and thought themselves most amusing.

Those people could not conceive of someone building a tower to elevate humankind above this plain and ordinary life without there being any personal profit in the matter, nor could they imagine that there were people who believed it was necessary to use horns and bells to urge the gods to intervene if they thought humanity had taken a wrong turn. In fact they couldn't imagine anything outside their own field of vision. Money, beautiful clothes, fun, getting drunk, sex— that was as far as their imaginations stretched. When they drank to "life," the word meant something quite different to them than it did to Milcah or Jobab or me. I suspect language will cause plenty of problems for our people in times to come.

Among all three groups—the workers, the pious, and the indifferent—there were some who moved from one camp to another, and that tore families apart.

After another seven years, when the group of workers had grown to around one thousand, we realized that a new city was developing at the base of the tower: a city of tents and shabby huts. For a long time my tent had been the only one at the foot of the tower, but now it was surrounded.

By that point we had reached the eighth ring and were looking down from above at what was more like a stinking garbage dump than a city. All the beggars from miles around seemed to think the tower would offer them protection and sustenance, but what awaited them was contempt and hunger, unless they were persuaded to join the pious or us. Many of them did so, but just as many opted for a life of indolence. They grouched, grumbled, and expressed their indignation about all the injustice in the world but did nothing to improve their situation.

By "life," they didn't mean activity, anticipation, or the slightest ambition, but an unjust and immutable fate.

One day Jobab took me aside. He said, "I must speak to you. Something is brewing among the people."

I looked at him in surprise, because something had been brewing among the people for years. It had destroyed my marriage and those of many others.

"There is a group of the pious who believe they need to give the gods a hand," said Jobab. "One of my workers happened to overhear a conversation in which very dangerous things were said."

I sighed. I was used to having threats and curses hurled at me; they were my daily diet.

"Just ignore it," I said. "And keep on working."

"Listen, Shelah," Jobab said sternly. "Open your ears and try to understand what I'm saying. Hear what these people are saying. They're saying: 'God put man on earth with two feet and not two wings to fly. Man must toil on the ground, serve God, obey him, restrain his curiosity, and be thankful for the task God has given us on earth. If man starts building towers that reach into the sky, perhaps he will discover how God's secrets work, or learn how the birds fly, how God went about his creation, or how to live eternally. If we do nothing about the construction of this tower, it will be only the beginning of a long series of blasphemies.'"

My ears rang because it felt as if I were hearing Milcah's screams. I had heard it all before and was sick to death of such incomprehensible gibberish. I cried out: "Every one of these words is as empty as a rumbling stomach. They mean nothing. The language these people babble is from another world. It's unintelligible to anyone with sense."

Jobab gripped me by the shoulders and gave me a good shake.

"It would do you good to try to understand languages other than your own. Listen. Hold your tongue until I've finished speaking."

I fell silent. His words crunched in my ears like gravel. A numbing tedium filled my mind. I had such loathing for people who want to kill life stone dead that I felt more like vomiting than listening.

"Good," said Jobab. "Now for their conclusion. They said, 'It is right and useful that we beg God for help, but we must do more. We must preserve his honor and mercilessly punish the sinners without anyone being able to point an accusatory finger in our direction. Have you seen those poor wretches at the foot of the tower? They are bitter and angry at everything that moves, because they have no future. What might those people be capable of doing if they were rewarded with the assurance of God's blessing? Why don't we make use of the boundless energy their hatred gives them, but which is now locked away inside their raging hearts?'"

Jobab stopped speaking and looked at me expectantly.

My ears had opened whether I wanted them to or not. I finally heard the danger. The tedium had been forcibly expelled from my mind.

"God. God's honor. God's blessing," I mumbled. "Language is bursting apart at the seams. I no longer know what its words mean. Is 'God' another word for unbridled rage? And if that is so, why do people not say 'Rage' instead of 'God'?"

"Now is not the time for profound thoughts," Jobab said firmly. "You need to understand what's going on. They are organizing a war against the tower and promising those poor wretches happiness and wealth if they start killing for God. They are calling their war a holy war."

"Language! Again!" I screamed. "Language, which is rotten to the core! How can a war be holy? How can they believe it's possible to seize happiness and prosperity by cutting someone's throat?!"

Jobab looked at me helplessly and shrugged.

"Only the animals comprehend each other without any misunderstandings. Since the time of Adam and Eve, we have not wished to be animals, and so we've grown entangled in thought. That's just the way it is, and the confusion of languages will only increase. Those are the facts. Don't waste any words on them. We need to act."

At that moment, we were joined by a gasping Zippor the birdman.

"Listen," he said. "Birds fly because they're made of air. Our eyes deceive us. We think everything is matter, but matter cannot fly. Birds are mirages."

Jobab and I looked at each other and burst out laughing. We must both have realized at the same time that Zippor, too, had entangled himself in language and that no one would be able to understand what he was talking about, even though each individual word he put forth was perfectly clear.

When we'd stopped laughing, I quickly searched for words to get rid of Zippor.

"You have spoken most eloquently, Zippor," I said. "Your erudition increases by the day, but now you must leave. Jobab and I have something to discuss."

I could feel myself blushing, since flattery is perhaps the most nauseating form of deceit, but it had the desired effect: Zippor slunk away. Language can be not only an inextricable tangle, but also a slippery snake that hisses and wriggles and ties itself in knots. Would it not be better to remain silent for the rest of my life?

"Now for the strangest thing," said Jobab, once Zippor was safely out of earshot. "Do you know who they have chosen as their first victim?"

"Me?" I asked. "You?"

"No, neither of us. It's Zippor the birdman, who would not harm a fly and just goes around spouting nonsense."

My mind creaked to a halt. Zippor was the most naive, most harmless, the most foolish man I knew. Anyone who wanted to harm that innocent soul could not be right in the head. I think my face must have been one big question mark, because Jobab attempted to answer the question I couldn't utter.

"I can only guess," said Jobab. "They think the tower has driven Zippor insane and that his insanity is contagious. Zippor is searching, he wants to know, he is hunting for insight. He has the sickness of Adam and Eve whose hunt for knowledge brought about their downfall. They think: If someone had gotten rid of Adam and Eve in time, we'd still be living in Paradise."

"The earth is not supported by anything, the earth floats," I mumbled.

"What did you say?"

"The earth floats," I repeated. "I heard Zippor say that recently. The earth is a ball full of air. I heard his words, but I can make no sense of them."

Jobab shook his head and sighed deeply.

"I am not bothered by his nonsense, but there are others who think he contradicts the gods."

We sat together in silence for a long time, not knowing what to do. The city was falling apart. Words had acquired so many different meanings that we could scarcely be said to share a common language, and if language no longer served as a means to connect people but was more like a battlefield, how could anyone live together?

I heard the creaking of cranes, the squeaking of wheels, the shouting and cursing of laborers, sounds that were so familiar to me that it felt as if they had always been there. But for the first time I felt suspicion eating away at the familiar: How loyal were our own people? Were some among them not working wholeheartedly, but instead forging sinister plans? How easy would it be for one of them to crush me at a single stroke by "accidentally" dropping a heavy stone from a higher ring?

I leapt to my feet, ashamed at having feared for my life.

"We need to warn Zippor," I said. "He has to leave. Does he have family far away from here?"

Jobab stood up and laid his hands on my shoulders.

"You know what Zippor is like. He'll tell everyone whatever you say to him. It's better if our enemies don't know we're aware of their plotting."

I felt despondent, and I despaired at his good sense. I had always done whatever occurred to me and said whatever was on my mind. I didn't know if I could live with my hands tied and my tongue still.

"Listen," said Jobab. "I'm going to arm a number of my men. I will tell them to guard Zippor. I will send others into the city with instructions to keep their eyes and ears open, so we know what's going on there. And in the meantime we will continue with the building. We will not allow ourselves to be intimidated."

I nodded, but I confess that from that day on I began to see the tower as a threat to our society. I wondered if it would not be better to stop the construction work, no matter how sad that might be.

For years I didn't understand why Jobab was so much more self-assured than I could be. That was because I hadn't noticed that he spoke a different language too.

The construction of the tower had transformed Shinar into a vibrant city. Jobab would not think of giving up. The tower was attracting visitors from all corners of the world, and not just poor wretches and fortune seekers, but also wealthy merchants, major landowners, and shepherd princes. I should have known, because I'd heard the story of Noah's ark so often that I could recite it from memory. I'd always overlooked one aspect of the story: the commercial success of the pointless.

Building a boat in the middle of the desert was so foolish and indeed pointless that it made people hopelessly curious. The pointless is apparently irresistible. I imagine that if all the inhabitants of a city agreed to walk around on their hands on Fridays, then the city would be packed with curious onlookers every Friday, not in spite of but *because of* the utter futility of the spectacle.

Jobab spoke the language of money. The influx of people meant that the city needed new houses, stores, even palaces, and Jobab provided them. Brick by brick, he built himself a fortune.

I had nothing against that, but the threat of violence made me start to doubt. Was the tower really worth human lives? It had cost me my marriage and had forced me to take my son Eber into my protection. I could feel the tower overshadowing me, and I grew numb. Would I have to go on building until the first person was killed?

On one such day of doubt and gloom, Milcah suddenly appeared before my tent. She had a couple of heavily armed men with her and for one anxious second I feared for my life, but Milcah simply stepped forward and held out her empty hands to show that she came in peace.

"Listen," she said. "I have a message for you that comes from the gods. They have held a meeting because they are concerned about your tower. They decided to send one of their number down below to see what's going on. And this is what their emissary said when he returned to the meeting. He said: This is one people and they speak one and the same language, and what they are doing now is just the beginning. All they are planning to do lies within their reach. They will learn to fly, they will learn to extend their lives infinitely, they will learn about the substances that make up creation, and ultimately they will make us redundant because they themselves will become gods. Let us go to them and create a confusion of languages so they can no longer understand one another."

Milcah looked into my eyes to see if her words had gotten through to me.

"This is what the Most High God has decided," she said then. "This is going to happen because you wanted too much and left too little to the gods."

I looked up at her and for the first time in ages I understood her and I believed, heart and soul, that she was right. This was what the gods had decided. I could feel it inside me as an undeniable and bitter truth: this was going to happen.

Milcah leaned forward and kissed my forehead. Before I had recovered from my surprise, she fell to her knees, bowed deeply before me, and kissed my feet.

"Come back to me," she whispered. "Come back, abandon the tower to the sun, the wind, and the rain, and it will gradually perish. You will be lord and master in our house once again. I will submit to you as you submit to the Most High God who rules over gods and men and whose secrets are sacred to us."

She stopped speaking, but still lay at my feet like a slave. I couldn't even look at her. I have a loathing for submission and Milcah had never before been submissive to me.

"Rise, my queen," I said.

She stood, but did not look me in the eyes, as if she wanted to show how our relationship would be in future. I assume her god had imposed this servility on her, and I was seized by a violent aversion to anything connected to the supernatural. What do the gods have to gain from our humility? Do they enjoy complacently playing with their living dolls for all eternity? Are they really that childish, or are they just misunderstood?

"Jobab will not sacrifice the tower to the gods," I said. "He will go on building even without me, but I am willing to return home. On one condition: you must make sure nothing happens to Zippor the birdman. There's no fault in him."

Milcah flinched as if I'd hit her.

"But Shelah, my lord, how can I protect a man who is doomed to die? Do you not understand that he has become the symbol of the folly, the arrogance, the blasphemy of the tower?"

No, I did not understand. Language was playing tricks on me once again. I understood the words but not their meaning. The confusion of languages had begun long before the gods had decided upon it. They had "predicted" a process that had been set in motion years ago by humans themselves.

"Zippor is not a symbol. He's a person," I said. "I will remain at the tower for as long as he is threatened."

Now she looked into my eyes and I had to endure her gaze. Are you familiar with the expression of those who proclaim divine truths? Their eyes seem to look, but they do not see. Their gaze passes no farther than their eyelids and is caught upon their lashes. A thick curtain comes down and a gate locks with a sound like thunder.

"Mukkendrok da fobelst erdo napolok," said Milcah, turning her back on me.

I realized the confusion of languages had entered a new phase. She walked slowly away from me like someone who expected to be called back, but I did not call her.

I loved her, but could not bear her; she loved me, but rejected everything within me. If love is anything more than a persistent misunderstanding, which language can express it perfectly? I know of none.

I watched as my wife disappeared among the tents, together with her armed entourage. Milcah could no longer walk around the city without bodyguards. She was constantly bothered by overenthusiastic followers who thought they would live happily ever after if only they could touch her robe. It was alarming that so much folly had taken hold of the city in such a short time, and how great the confusion had grown in people's hearts.

I stood up and called my son to me.

"Eber," I said. "Where is Zippor?"

"I do not know," he said. "Am I Zippor's keeper?"

I heard an unfamiliar surliness in his voice. Now what? Did my son not understand me?

"We are all Zippor's keeper," I said sternly. "Anyone who does not defend innocence cannot be called human."

Eber sighed.

"I don't know why, Father," he said, "but it seems like your generation speaks a different language from mine. Isn't every man responsible for his own safety?"

"Absolutely," I said. "Except for people like Zippor, who have been given such little weight they are like birds at which the lion playfully swipes its paw."

Eber shrugged his shoulders. I could tell he thought I was an idiot and that irritated me.

"So do you have a god who thinks you should not protect those weaker than you, you blockhead? Go find Zippor and bring him to me," I barked.

To my relief, his cockiness came clattering down like a badly built house. I didn't care if he understood me just as long as he behaved like a son submitting to his father's authority. Without a word, he turned and ran to find Zippor.

Then I heard a great clamor in the poor people's tent camp— shouts, the clash of weapons —and I saw black smoke rising, and women and children ran screaming toward me. I resisted the urge to flee and instead, drawing myself to my full height to show I was not afraid, I raised my hands in the air to bring the crowd to a halt. It worked, and they stopped before me dripping in sweat and with panic in their eyes.

"What is going on?" I asked. Then they started shouting, all at the same time, so I couldn't understand a word. I waved my arms to silence them and then pointed at the woman closest to me. "You," I said. "Talk."

She started to talk, very quickly, and the sounds she made rolled from her mouth, loud and clear, and yet I could not understand her. I froze in fear. Had it already happened?

"Woman!" I roared. "Why do you not speak the language of Shinar? Why do you bombard me with a language no one knows?"

My words scared her, but that wasn't the strangest thing—the women were also scaring one another! As soon as anyone shouted anything, there was horror in the eyes of the others. They hugged their children to them as though the children were threatened, and the crowd broke into families. They couldn't understand anything, and every gesture, every sign, could signify a threat. Only members of the same family could still comprehend one another.

So this was it. The confusion of languages had made the world even more inhospitable than it already was. Incomprehension had caused a war to break out in the poor people's camp and I knew it could spread to all parts of the city. Where was Eber?

The women fled in all directions with their children, afraid of everyone else and afraid of this world they couldn't understand. They shrieked like startled herons in the night.

I yelled for Eber but he did not reply. I frantically began climbing the tower, up shaky ladders and wobbly scaffolding. I suspected he was high on the tower looking for Zippor the birdman. I finally found him on the fourth ring, huddled on the ground with something in his lap that at first glance resembled a pile of rags.

"Eber," I said. "We have to go."

He looked up with a wild expression on his face. Only then did I see what he was clutching in his hands: Zippor's head. I kneeled beside him and looked into Zippor's staring eyes. "Come on, Eber," I said again. "We have to go."

Eber stood up with Zippor in his arms.

"Leave him here," I said.

"No," said Eber. "We have to bury him. He's light as a baby bird."

We walked down, taking turns carrying Zippor's body, which was bleeding from a wound in the side. The idiots' "holy war" had claimed its first victim.

When we reached the bottom, we walked around the tower to a place where no one could see us and we buried him.

"Father," said Eber, "was building the tower the right thing to do?"

"No," I said. "But there will come a time when the power of the gods has waned and then people will build towers even higher than this one." I picked up a pebble, held it high in the air, and dropped it. "They will remember Zippor's question: Why does this small stone fall down but the vast moon still hangs in the sky? They will make discoveries we cannot even dream of, because our tower was only the beginning. Now people will scatter all over the earth because they no longer understand one another. The gods are defeating themselves, because people will end up in places where gods are thin on the ground, and so they'll be free to use all their powers of reason."

We walked toward our tent, but as we drew closer we saw that all was lost. The tents that were not on fire were being looted by angry youths, and some people were attacking each other with knives, though most were fleeing with their few possessions on their backs.

The exodus had begun.

"Father," said Eber, "I see Mother in the distance."

I could see a fluttering robe, a woman, and indeed, as she came closer, I recognized Milcah. She ran toward us. When she reached us, she fell to her knees and cried, "My lord and my son, do not leave me here alone. Take me away from here, for Shinar is in flames."

"You may come with us if you leave your gods behind," I growled.

She raised her head and looked at me beseechingly.

"Father," said Eber, "let my mother have her gods."

We took her with us.

I realized that the battle between the obedient humans and the rebels would continue for some time to come.

The Story of Sarai

I'll be honest: I loved my husband, but the idea of going to bed with a god was quite a thrill. I'd never seen a god in the flesh before, but I was sure he would be dazzling and a wonderful lover. For once I wanted to experience something other than the listless pounding to which most men subject us. I had experience with only one man, but all my slave girls told me the same sorry tale. Now, quite unexpectedly, the prospect of a divine lover had presented itself! And who had driven me into his arms? My own husband!

But let me start at the beginning and tell you how we got from Shelah to me, or at least to my husband, because, as you know, a woman's family history counts for nothing. In my case that's irrelevant, because I am my husband's half-sister, so we share the same ancestors. Here goes: Shelah begat Eber, Eber begat Peleg, Peleg begat Reu, Reu begat Serug, Serug begat Nachor, Nachor begat Terah, and Terah begat Abram, my husband, and, last but not least, me, albeit with another woman. I would appreciate if you could learn to recite these names by heart—in reverse order too. You should also remember that Abram had two brothers: Nachor and Haran. Haran begat Lot and two daughters, Milcah and Iscah, who play no further part in my story. Haran died before his father, Terah. So Lot was an orphan from a young age and Abram looked after Lot as if he were his son.

My father, Terah, who is also my father-in-law, originally lived in Ur, the city of the Chaldees, some hours to the southwest of the Euphrates River, not far from Shinar, which was soon rebuilt after the disaster with the tower. He decided one day to leave Ur, because we lived among strangers there who did not always see us as equals. He planned to take us to Canaan, the land of Ham and his descendants, because our forefather Noah had placed a curse on Canaan, which meant the Canaanites had to be subservient to us. That was a pleasing prospect. So he set off with Abram, Lot, and me, but when we were about halfway there, we received such a warm welcome in Haran that Terah decided to put up his tents in that place. Haran lies in northern Mesopotamia, on the left bank of the Balikh, a tributary of the Euphrates.

I enjoyed living there. The people were cheerful and laughed easily and often, like me, but I noticed from the start that Abram was unhappy that Terah had not gone through with his plan. In Haran he felt like a guest who was dependent on the kindness of his hosts, but who had no rights at all. We had never known any other situation, though, and I, who as a woman suffered a twofold lack of rights, thought he was making a fuss about nothing.

After a few years of living in Haran, Abram came to me one day and said, "Listen, the Almighty has spoken to me. He said: Depart from your land, leave your family, even your close kin, and go to the land I will show you."

I burst out laughing because I recognized the words. Of course I did. Everyone in our family knew that formulation, since it had been devised by our ancestors to allow a son to withdraw from his father's authority without any bloodshed.

"Why are you laughing?" asked Abram.

I could tell from his face that I had to be careful. He was apparently being serious.

"If I laughed, I was laughing with joy," I said. "We are going to Canaan!"

"I do not know which land the Almighty will show me," said Abram brusquely.

I understood. Of course we were going to Canaan, but Abram knew better than to confront his father about the unfinished business he'd saddled us with. In Canaan we could acquire rights; in Haran we could not.

So, when Abram told his father what God had commanded him to do, Terah immediately said, "You are going to Canaan."

"I am going to the land the Almighty will show me," said Abram.

"And that land is Canaan," said Terah.

"I do not know that," said Abram. "All I know is the Almighty said this to me: 'Depart from your land, leave your family, even your close kin, and go to the land I will show you.'"

"And you can take it from me, that land will be Canaan," said Terah obstinately.

"Father, please."

"What other land could it be?" asked Terah.

"Listen, Father. Listen. No matter where I end up, this is what the Almighty said:

> I will make you a great nation,
> I will bless you, I will make your name great,
> you will be a blessing.
> I will bless those who bless you,
> and curse those who mock you.
> All people on earth will be blessed through you.

Terah was speechless and I was trying hard not to laugh. I'm a bit of a giggler, I'll admit it, but I had no idea where Abram was supposed to get this "great nation" from. He was seventy-five and I was at least fifty. I knew that my monthly cycle had left me, and we had no children.

After a long silence, Terah said, "Well, good for you." I could see from his face that he believed none of Abram's words. "You are free to go but I have my own thoughts about the future of our people," he said. "We will be persecuted yet survive, we will be scattered across the face of the earth yet survive, we will be massacred yet survive. No one will envy our fate, but we will survive."

Abram embraced his father and said, "Father, I have too much respect for you to contradict you but perhaps that is why we need to part. Your gods speak differently from mine."

That was the end of the conversation; the decision was made. The future would show which of the two men had listened to the right god. Abram and I, Lot and his family, we all packed our belongings, herded together the livestock and the slaves, and left.

An endless caravan, a vast herd of animals, and an army of slaves created a cloud of dust so large that all of Haran disappeared like a mountain in the mist. Perhaps this was already a "nation," a group of people from many different backgrounds but all led by Abram, the shepherd prince. Maybe we didn't need any children to become a nation, since we already were one. Indeed we were so numerous that it felt like a mass migration when we moved off. Now that I was free from my father's authority, I wore my pride like a crown on my head, because next to my lord I felt like a queen: never before had I had any notion of the extent of our riches, but now that I could take stock of all our belongings—goods, people, and animals—I realized we were kings in search of a country.

From Ur, our father Terah had followed the river to the north. We left the river behind and went to the south. A risky undertaking, because a person can go for a long time without food but thirst will finish him within a few days. We filled all our waterskins and put everyone on strict rations. I didn't count the days, but the journey was long and hard. We repelled attacks from desert raiders with the army that Abram made from our slaves, but we had little defense against the sandstorms, the stinging flies, and the heat. Lot's wife began to weep. She wanted to return to the river and the good life in the city. Her life was all about looking back at what had been and could never come again. I avoided her whenever I could and chose my Egyptian slave Hagar as company. Hagar was young, strong, and cheerful; nothing was too much trouble for her.

Finally we arrived. The land that God wanted to show us was—oh, wonder of wonders!—the land of the Canaanites.

The descendants of Canaan, the son of Ham, had been cursed by our forefather Noah and should have been subservient to us, but we were to be disappointed. They possessed a beautiful, fertile land and had no intention of handing over even one square cubit. They made Abram pay a high price for passage and grazing. In short, we had just as few rights as when we were in the fields of Haran, which made me think it was perhaps better to be cursed than blessed. It was time to consult the gods about their plans for us in this place.

We crossed the land until we came to Shechem, where a holy tree grew outside the walls. The Canaanites often consulted this "tree of Moreh" because it could predict the future. The oak tree spoke to the people through the rustling of its leaves. Abram was impressed by the prosperity of the Canaanites, and he believed they must have built up a good relationship with their gods, so good that they had nullified Noah's curse. He therefore decided to consult the holy prophetic tree, because if you want to feel at home in a country, you need to make friends with the local gods.

So we sat beneath the tree and listened to the rustling of its leaves. And they rustled and rustled and rustled, and all I heard was rustling.

"Do you hear that?" said Abram. "It is not the gods of the Canaanites who are speaking. It is the Almighty."

I heard nothing, and I was surprised that it was not the local gods speaking to Abram, but the god he'd brought with him from Haran. I giggled nervously.

"Why are you laughing?" Abram asked with a frown.

"Because I'm worried," I said. "If the gods of Canaan reject us, we are far from home."

"Do not worry," said Abram. "For he has spoken: I shall give this land to your descendants."

I clapped my hand to my mouth, hoping not to burst out laughing.

"We have no descendants," I said through my fingers. "And we will never have descendants."

At that moment we saw a group of armed thugs coming toward us through the gate of Shechem and we knew we should make ourselves scarce.

The area around Shechem with its rolling hills and green valleys was a suitable place for a people of herdsmen like our people to stay for some time, but of course there were also local herders employed by the rich gentlemen who lived a life of luxury in the city. As usual, we were driven away. We had grown accustomed to it.

So we moved on and the farther south we went, the more barren the soil, until finally we came to the Negev, a desert of stones where hardly anything grew, and which teemed with predators in both human and animal form. Lot's wife wailed and wept salty tears, and I wished her tears would transform her into one great lump of salt, as fate is fate and complaining about it doesn't change a thing. Hagar, though, my lovely slave, was delighted because she'd heard that Egypt was now so close that every bird flying over from the west had breathed in the air of her homeland. She gazed at the horizon and sighed.

"The land of God."

"Which god?" I asked.

"There is only one god," she said. "Montu. He is the eternal one who created himself."

"Only one god?" I asked in surprise.

"One God in many forms," she said. "For each of his aspects, he takes a different shape: a woman, a man, an animal. Even the pharaoh is one of his forms."

"The pharaoh is god?" I asked.

"God is the pharaoh and a hundred more things besides."

I thought it a strange concept, but I felt a deep desire in me, one day, to see this god with my own eyes, in the form of the king of Egypt.

"Is he a human being too?" I asked. "Can you touch him?"

"Of course!" laughed Hagar. "All his queens touch him—and how!"

I was shocked, and I caught Hagar's giggles, yet I felt so bewildered that my laughter gave me a stomachache. How could a god be so earthly that he occupied himself with the pleasures of the flesh?

"You could call the pharaoh a human son of God," said Hagar. She was serious again, since she could see she had alarmed me. "He is both fully human and fully God."

"Oh," I said. "I see."

I was accustomed to seeing the god of Adam as a word, a name, but not as a form. The idea of meeting him in the shape of a person took my breath away and awakened a desire within me that made my body tingle. Imagine being touched by a god, or holding a god in your arms. It could only be supreme ecstasy!

Meanwhile we were desperately trudging across a rather ungodly desert. There was no sign we would ever own land on which we could survive. The god of Abram breathed not a word while our animals died of starvation before our eyes or had to be slaughtered to satisfy our hunger. Was Canaan perhaps not the promised land, but instead the land of our death? I saw Abram was wrestling with this question. To comfort him I whispered into his ear at night that maybe the promised land lay farther to the west, and that we were not yet at the end of our search.

Abram decided with a heavy heart to leave the land of the Canaanites and go to the west because there, somewhere far beyond the horizon, should be fertile land beside a river, the river of the Egyptians. We traveled to Beersheba and from there headed into Sinai. We followed a route not far from the coast, where the desert is less mountainous, but even so we suffered hardship, and beasts and humans perished along the way from exhaustion and hunger. As we approached the Egyptian border, we met Egyptian troops who treated us with great suspicion, believing we were Canaanites. The Canaanites were notorious for plunder and conquest deep into Mesopotamia, and Egypt too had often been their target. But the Egyptian linguists who accompanied the border troops soon heard that we were Mesopotamians, and Hagar solemnly declared that she was my sister and explained we were fleeing starvation and seeking protection from the pharaoh. It struck me even then that the Egyptians were all talking about me and staring at me as if I were some rare breed of animal.

I later asked Hagar, "What were those men saying about me?"

Hagar gave me a mischievous look and said, "I won't translate it literally since it would be too coarse for your ears. What they said, more or less, is they find you desirable."

I burst out laughing. Just imagine: If Abram was now seventy-seven and I was fifty, how could I be desirable in the eyes of such young men?

Abram had apparently noticed that the Egyptians found me pleasing to look at. When we were alone, he said, "Listen, Sarai, I know very well that you are a beautiful woman. When we enter Egypt and the Egyptians see you, they will think: That is his wife. And they will let you live, but they will kill me. So you must say you are my sister, and then perhaps, with your help, I will be treated well and my life will not be in danger."

I consented, but I wondered if Abram realized I was without a husband now and therefore eligible for marriage.

"Egyptians understand what beauty is," said Hagar. "You will be amazed."

She was right. When we entered Egypt and traveled south along the Nile, I was amazed by everything I saw. The people were beautiful in their looks and clothing, the ships on the Nile were a delight to the eye, the houses and the temples were marvels of ingenuity, and the land along both banks was so abundantly green that I thought: This is the land that God promised to show us.

I had heard that the pharaoh who ruled this divine land from the city of Waset was called Mentuhotep, and Hagar told me the meaning of his name: God is satisfied. A fitting name for the king of this land—for who would not be satisfied with such a beautiful sight?

The local rulers honored us with a visit; we exchanged gifts and feasted together. They were curious about stories from Mesopotamia, about our gods, our habits and customs, and, I must admit, also about me. Even these mighty men could not keep their eyes off me, which was flattering, but Abram grew uneasy. He said, "Desire can turn men into brutes, no matter how civilized they seem." The closer we came to Waset, the more worried he grew, because he knew just how powerful the pharaoh was—like a god whose wishes were commands. He told Hagar to spread the rumor that I was about eighty-five years old, though she didn't know exactly, that I was promised to a king in Canaan, and that I looked so young because I was an enchantress skilled in the arts of deception.

Nothing helped.

The rumors about my spectacular beauty must have reached Waset, because the pharaoh sent his emissaries to ask "my brother" Abram for my hand. I stood with my ear to the cloth that separated our private quarters from the reception room, and I couldn't contain my laughter. The funny thing was that Abram hadn't lied—he was my brother—but he'd concealed the fact that he was also my husband.

Abram called me in and asked, "Why were you laughing?"

I shook my head as if to deny it.

"Oh yes. You were laughing. Explain to the pharaoh's emissaries why you were laughing."

I looked furtively at the men in the circle. I could see they were wealthy and important, accustomed to luxury, civilized, and learned, but at the same time I saw they were viewing me with unabashed covetousness as if I were an expensive cow being haggled for at the market.

"Yes, brother, I laughed," I said. "Which woman would not laugh with joy if the pharaoh asked for her hand in marriage?"

"I have already promised you to King Raksok of Ai in Canaan," said Abram.

"Ah, my brother," I laughed, "even he will understand how the pharaoh's wish blows away such a promise like a foolish feather in the wind."

Abram looked at me aghast.

"But sadly I must disappoint the pharaoh. Appearances can be deceptive. I am an old woman of around fifty and my fertile years are over. I do not want the pharaoh to feel cheated and waste his precious time on me. Please tell him that I humbly ask him to withdraw his proposal and that I offer him my wondrously beautiful sister, Hagar, for she is young and full of life."

The room was silent for a long time, and the tension rose. I didn't know what I was hoping for. Did I want the emissaries to accept my offer or to pay me no heed? Later I realized that in my folly I was longing for an adventure, for an intimate encounter with a god, for glamour and glory. I had lived in tents all my life. What would it be like to live as a queen in a palace?

It did not occur to me that my separation from Abram would be permanent. I was foolish enough to see my meeting with the pharaoh as a trip from which I would return in a few days, as if I were going to someone else's wedding, not my own. I think my mind was also clouded by the ease with which Abram had put me in that situation. What is a woman to think of her husband's love when he is prepared to risk her honor in such a way? As well as my longing for adventure, I believe I was also harboring a desire for revenge in my heart. Whatever the case, I did not have to choose between my emotions, since others chose for me.

"We appreciate your modesty," said one of the emissaries, "but it is better to allow the pharaoh to judge for himself. We are here to fetch you, not to enter into a discussion. Your brother surely knows that in this country we refuse the pharaoh nothing. You will, of course, receive ample compensation."

I remained silent because I didn't want to continue feigning reluctance. I saw the despair on Abram's face and I took pleasure in it. He didn't want to lose me, but what could he do? He didn't dare expose himself as a liar.

So I packed my belongings, took Hagar and two other slaves with me, and climbed up onto the camel that was waiting for me. A messenger hurried ahead of us to inform the palace of my imminent arrival and I later heard that from that moment on Abram was showered with gifts. He received sheep and goats, cattle, male donkeys, male and female slaves, female donkeys, and camels.

Compared to the cities I'd seen before, Waset was breathtaking. It was laid out in an orderly fashion, and its streets were clean, its buildings majestic, its people beautiful and dignified. I felt inelegant and clumsy in my desert garb, but my appearance was apparently so exotic that the men turned and stared as I passed by, without even saying a word, let alone shouting after me, as had happened in cities outside Egypt.

The pharaoh's palace was simple on the outside but richly decorated within. There was an atmosphere of serious joy, a calm sort of vitality, expressed in the careful creation of beauty in everyday objects. In those halls, with their rhythmic successions of columns, softly colored wall paintings, and splashing water, the soul found rest and the eyes saw more clearly.

As I entered, I was instantly surrounded by chattering female slaves who took me by both hands and led me to a room where several women were gathered. A dense cloud of fragrance wafted toward me.

I was bathed, massaged, and rubbed with oil, but I protested fiercely when they threatened to shave my head.

"Stop it! Get off!" I screamed, but no one could understand me. "Where is Hagar? Bring Hagar here! Keep your hands off my hair!"

Hagar must have heard me, because she suddenly appeared beside me and I realized she had never seen me naked before. I blushed bright red.

"It's because of the lice," she said. "They'll give you a wig."

"I don't have lice," I screamed.

"But just in case."

"No! Not even just in case. Tell them to stay away from my hair."

I saw the slave girls whispering together and looking disapprovingly at my hair, but they put down their blades and scissors. I was taken to bed and allowed to rest after my long journey.

I don't know how long I slept but when I awoke, busy hands

dressed me. It felt more like putting on a disguise, because they made me look just like an Egyptian woman. The fabrics were light and thin and revealed the contours of my body.

"You are going to meet the pharaoh," said Hagar. "When you are standing before his throne, you must prostrate yourself on the floor. I'll tell you when to stand again."

I was led through long corridors, my heart thumping wildly in my chest. Which woman would not be excited about meeting a god for the first time? I was both afraid and curious. I wanted to go to him, but the urge to flee was almost as strong.

They took me into a dimly lit room packed with people. My eyes had barely become accustomed to the gloom when Hagar whispered, "Now."

"What do you mean?"

"Now!" she said. She was lying flat on the floor, right next to my feet.

What? Were we already standing before the throne? I quickly lay down on the floor next to Hagar, with my face in my hands.

Nothing happened. The buzz I had heard as I entered died away. "Now," said Hagar.

We stood up at the same time. The people had lined up along the walls, and now I could see a throne in the distance. There was definitely someone sitting on it, but he was so immobile and so decked out in strange ornaments and insignia that he looked more like some kind of dummy or doll. The silence rang in my ears. I knew I was being examined and judged. It lasted a long time and I felt an urgent need for fresh air.

Then the doll made a small gesture with its hand and the room began to buzz again. A man beside the throne spoke a few words in a loud voice and everyone cheered. Hagar took my hand and indicated the ceremony was over. She led me from the room and whispered, "The pharaoh has taken you as his wife."

Once again I couldn't help myself. I began laughing uncontrollably.

Nervously glancing around, Hagar quickly led me along the

corridors. My laugh bounced off the walls and returned to me as the cry of a braying she-ass. The whole situation was absurd, I was absurd, the god of Egypt was ridiculously absurd, and my poor Abram was the victim of the absurdity of the world and himself.

Once again I was bathed and powdered, and my face was painted until I looked like an Egyptian goddess carved in stone. The slaves did not let me go until evening fell and I glowed in the light of the moon. They threw themselves to the ground and cried, "Make the god happy, sister of Aburahana, queen of Egypt." Aburahana was their name for Abram.

Fear seized my heart, for I had known no other man than Abram, and now that it came down to it I realized I had no desire to know another man, even if he happened to be a god. Whatever had possessed me? To what did I owe this folly? Why had I not immediately rejected Abram's ridiculous idea?

As I walked along the dimly lit corridors with Hagar and half a dozen slave girls, on my way to the royal chambers, I felt my body stiffen and knew I would not be capable of love. Indeed, the pharaoh would be better off taking a dead crocodile to bed than me. What good was I to a young god?

We entered an almost empty room lit only by oil lamps. Hagar pointed at a chair and I sat down. I realized we were in an antechamber of the royal bedroom. The slaves were all gazing at a door, which would apparently open at some point.

We waited. We waited forever. The oil lamps cast strange shadows on the painted walls, the only distraction in the gloomy room. I longed for our tent, for the smell of the animals, for Abram's voice, for everything that meant life to me. My mind went blank; there was nothing left inside me but a white-hot fear of the future.

It must have been long after midnight when the door finally opened. An ancient woman appeared in the doorway and beckoned to me. When I was beside her, she began to whisper, but I didn't understand what she said.

"She said she has tried to prepare her husband for your arrival," Hagar translated, "but that it did not help."

I did not know what the woman meant.

"She asks if you are at fault somehow, if you have perhaps displeased the gods."

Had I displeased the gods? I was ice-cold inside. Of course I had displeased the gods by keeping silent about being not just Abram's sister, but also his wife! I did not dare to confess.

"Tell her," I said to Hagar, "that I am a simple woman who is not familiar with the moods of the gods."

The old queen shook her head skeptically, but gestured at me to enter the bedchamber. Alone. She closed the door behind me.

Dragging my feet, I entered the room like a dog that's scared of a beating. I stared at the floor, afraid to behold the god. It was only when I heard the sound of someone clearing his throat, followed by a hacking cough, that I forgot my fear and looked up.

I saw a wooden bed, with a wrinkled old man in a nightshirt standing beside it. When he had finished coughing, he beckoned me over and gave me a friendly, toothless smile. I looked around. Where was the king, where was the god?

Everyone would immediately have known that this decrepit old man was the divine pharaoh Mentuhotep—everyone, that is, except me. I was too wrapped up in my dream full of wonder, adventure, and revenge on my beloved "Aburahana."

What happened between me and the pharaoh belongs to the secrets of the bedchamber. I will tell you only of the disaster that had befallen Egypt: the deity was no longer able to get his thingy up. This apparently had consequences for the fertility of the land, which is why the queen kept dragging in new wives, in the hope they would be able to bring the king's manhood back to life.

But it was no good.

The king and I couldn't speak to each other and I cursed Shelah for calling down the confusion of languages upon us. But we did sit together for hours on the bed next to each other, holding hands. The god was lonely and sad, and I sang softly to him and stroked his bald head. We understood each other without words. He was a friendly old god and I rocked him in my arms like a child, because he was tired but could not sleep.

In the morning, when the sun's chariot began its journey through the day, I called Hagar to me. She prostrated herself before the pharaoh and kissed his feet. I said, "Tell the king it was a night I shall never forget as long as I live. Tell him that Egypt should think itself lucky to have a king who loves so selflessly. But tell him, too, that he must let me go or all the gods of Mesopotamia will turn against him. Tell him he has shared his bed with a woman who is indeed the sister of Aburahana the Mesopotamian, but also his wife. Tell him he must expel Aburahana from his land, along with me, Sarai his wife, but that he should let him keep his gifts."

The pharaoh listened with increasing amazement to Hagar's translation of my words, but he gently squeezed my hand to reassure me. He looked me right in the eyes as he began to speak through Hagar's mouth: "Why did that villain not say that you are his wife?"

"Forgive him, my lord," I said. "He was afraid."

"Afraid? Of what?"

"Of death."

"His fear of death made him give his wife to another?" cried the old man with the voice of a youth. "My lady, for your sake, I swear I would go gladly to my grave. I would praise the gods if they made a sacrifice of me to preserve your honor. Be wary of Aburahana, my lady. If he is capable of sacrificing his wife for his own benefit, who can be safe with him? But I shall respect your wish to return to the man. He must appear before my throne, so that he may receive you from my own hands."

After those words, I knew for certain the old man was a god, so merciful and wise was he. I held his hands to my bosom to show I would carry him in my heart until the end of my days.

Egypt! Blessed land! How dearly Abram would like to live on your abundant riverbanks, but how just it is that you sent him into the wilderness to teach him to live in the face of death!

Messengers were dispatched to fetch Abram. Trembling, he

appeared before the pharaoh's throne and prostrated himself at his feet.

Mentuhotep, attired in his royal robes, with painted face and finery, looked nothing like the sweet old man with whom I'd spent the night. Even I, who had seen him in all his impotence, shook at the sight of him. I realized that a god may reside in both the playful body of a child and in a body that is ancient and worn out.

The king told Abram to rise and then looked him in the face.

"Aburahana," said Mentuhotep in his powerful voice. "What have you done to me? Why did you not tell me that she is your wife? Why did you tell me she was only your sister? Now I have taken her as my wife. But I return her to you. Take her and go, but protect her from now on, even at the cost of your own life."

The pharaoh did not give Abram the opportunity to say even one word, but dismissed him as if he were shooing away a fly. I bowed to him and quickly went after my husband. I could feel the pharaoh's loving eyes on my back. He was not angry with me; I do not believe he was angry even with Abram.

We were expelled from the land, with our livestock and belongings, under the escort of an Egyptian battalion, and ordered never to return.

Abram tried to remain silent about what had happened and to leave the past be, but he couldn't manage it for longer than a day. He was concerned about me and my feelings; he wondered if I still loved him but didn't dare ask directly, so he approached the subject obliquely.

"What exactly happened?" he asked.

"It's a secret," I said. "I can't talk about it."

Wasn't it enough that I'd returned to him?

"How did the pharaoh find out you're my wife?"

"The gods told him."

"How?"

"They gave him a serious affliction."

"What sort of affliction?"

"That's a secret. I can't talk about it."

Why didn't he ask if I loved him? Was he afraid to hear my answer?

"Do you love the pharaoh?"

"The pharaoh is a god and a lovable man."

After a few weeks, when I had sufficiently demonstrated my loyalty to him, only one question remained.

"Can a man be a god?"

"A god may appear in the form of a man," I said.

And that thought took hold of Abram and did not let him go.

All the gifts from the pharaoh had made us very wealthy in livestock, silver, and gold. We set off again for the Negev—by "we," I mean Abram and I, Lot and his wife, and our formidable army of slaves, both male and female. From the Negev, we gradually moved onward toward Bethel, to the place between Bethel and Ai where our tent had stood before, and where Abram had built an altar. It was by that altar that Abram began to call upon the name of his god: El Shaddai, the Almighty, because nothing less would do. I had told him that according to the Egyptians there is but one god, who made himself and the world, the same god Adam met in Paradise, but who can take on any shape, human or animal, or who can even appear as a flaming fire, a whirlwind, or a column of smoke, and in all those forms he remains his own eternal self. Abram obviously wanted to give this god a name and so he was attempting to find out if the god would accept the name El Shaddai. I do not believe he received an answer to that question and so he tried other names too, such as El Olam, "the Everlasting One," but perhaps he would have done better to stick to the simple "El," the name by which the highest god was known throughout all of Canaan.

I know that when he called upon those divine names Abram was fervently hoping for the god to appear in some form so he could meet him as I had done in Egypt. I occasionally fanned the flames by whispering "Mentuhotep" in his ear and groaning, "Oh! God is satisfied, God is so very satisfied!"

Of course he had to swallow his twofold jealousy, but when he managed to do so, his curiosity eagerly reemerged.

"What was he like?" he sometimes asked, looking longingly into my eyes.

"Overwhelming," I would reply. "Regal. Dazzling." I was certain that was how Abram wanted to see his god and not as a wizened old man, while I myself had taken into my heart a god who needed my comfort.

Where we lived, on the edge of the wilderness in the land between Bethel and Ai, was greener than the Negev but still too arid to feed the huge herds of Abram and Lot. I never counted our animals but in that flat land they formed one moving mass all the way to the horizon, and between the hills they filled the valleys. From the time they were boys, neither Abram nor Lot had taken care of their own livestock; they had always had serfs to do that for them. Abram's herders and Lot's came to blows as they vied for pastureland. I was surprised by the fights since they were so unnecessary. If Lot and Abram had viewed their animals as one single herd, no animosity would have developed between the herders. Abram was quite prepared to do so, at my insistence, but Lot was not. He insisted their affairs should be kept strictly separate, and I knew instinctively who was behind it: his wife. I will not mention her name, because she does not deserve any memorial in our history. I will allow her to be lost in time since she was a despicable woman with only one desire: to live in wealth and opulence, preferably in a big city, far from the smell of manure and the bleating of sheep. She was trying to create a rift between Lot and Abram and she fired up her herders against ours. I have no proof, but everything indicated that she did not appreciate our simple nomadic existence, that she cursed our tents and longed for a city, where she could settle in a house made of stone. Had she not learned from the stories of our forefathers that our god hates city dwellers? Did she not understand that only people who travel the world with their tents are pleasing to his sight?

When the herders ended up wounded and even dead, Abram ran out of patience and he came up with a solution, one that Lot's wife must have surely had in mind.

Abram said, "Why should we quarrel, you and I, your herders and mine? We're family, aren't we? It's better if we go our separate ways. The whole land lies open to you. If you go left, I shall go right; if you go right, I shall go left."

Lot and his wife had, of course, been keeping their eyes open and they had seen how fertile the Jordan Valley was, just as plentiful in water as Paradise and as fertile as the Nile Valley. So naturally that's why Lot chose the Jordan Valley, but also—and I'm certain of this—to satisfy that wife of his. Now they could settle in Sodom, the big city famous for its lavish lifestyle, its luxurious houses and palaces. Why should a shepherd prince like Lot have to live in a tent if he could manage his herders from the city?

And so Lot chose the Jordan Valley and Sodom, where he and his wife settled and where they lived like kings.

We watched them go, somewhat surprised at the ease with which Lot had chosen the best land for himself, leaving behind his uncle, who had cared for him like a father, in the tough land between Bethel and Ai. But Abram was not discouraged, for Lot and his wife had not even passed beyond the horizon when the Lord began to speak to him. He said, "Take a good look around you. Look from the place where you are now standing to the north, the south, the east, and the west. All the land you see I give to you and your descendants forevermore. And I shall give you as many descendants as there is dust on the earth; they will be as numerous as all the motes of dust. Travel the land in all its length and breadth, for to you I will give it."

Thus spake the Almighty, or at least that's how Abram told it to me. I have to confess I had my doubts. The land belonged to the Canaanites from north to south, from east to west. We had not a single piece of land to call our own, not even a piece the size of a woman's hand. We had to pay for grazing rights and when we put up our tents we were dependent on the kindness of whoever owned the land. I could tolerate that uncertainty, because I was happy with our existence, but the word "descendants" gave me the hee-bie-jeebies. We did not have one single descendant and we couldn't make any either. What was God's intention? Or was it not God but Abram who was trying to tell me something?

Then my eye fell on Hagar the Egyptian, who was herself no spring chicken but certainly still fertile. I trusted her; she was more like a friend than slave. She was obliging and loyal, and if I asked her to carry a child of Abram's for me she would surely do it. The thought was painful, not because I was still troubled by jealousy in my old age, but because the child would not truly be mine.

But on the other hand: it's the seed of the man that makes children grow in the belly of the woman. The woman is only the warm oven in which the seed germinates. So what does it matter which oven the man chooses to let his child grow inside?

After plenty of brooding, I put my pain behind me and I asked her to do it.

She said, "I don't know if that's a good idea."

I didn't know if it was a good idea either, but we had to give the Almighty a hand. If Abram did not beget any descendants, God would be seen as a liar—and who can live with a god who lies?

I said, "I can see no other way, Hagar."

I saw her hesitate and thought that perhaps she dreaded sharing a bed with a man who had always been a father figure to her. But that wasn't it.

She said, "I am afraid you will hate me for it."

I was baffled. That possibility had not occurred to me for a moment. I cried, "Of course not! I will be eternally grateful to you!"

I realized only after my outburst that Hagar's fear had hit me so hard because it meant she must see me as someone who was capable of hatred. I realized that a slave can never truly trust her mistress and that our friendship would never be true as long as she was not a free woman.

"Listen, Hagar," I said. "As soon as you give me a son, you will be freed, I promise you that."

It was an impulse. I didn't know if I could keep my promise, since I had not consulted with Abram. I broke out in a cold sweat because I saw my own untrustworthiness as in a dark mirror before me.

"Mistress," said Hagar. "Even if I am free, I will remain your prisoner for the sake of your child, because I will be bound to him by an invisible umbilical cord."

It had been years since Hagar had called me "mistress." It upset and angered me. Why did Hagar react so unlovingly to my request? Why did she not show any understanding for my situation? Had I not treated her like a daughter all those years?

"I want an answer now," I snapped. "Are you willing to sleep with my husband and to carry my child for me?"

"Yes, mistress," said Hagar.

I could have hit her for that stubbornly persistent "mistress" she kept throwing at me.

"You may go," I said. I heard my voice betraying my bitterness and thought I saw silent triumph in Hagar's eyes as she turned and left the tent.

The most difficult hurdle was yet to come: Abram. I was afraid he would be furious when he heard my idea. I was sure he would berate me for my lack of faith in God, though I believe that God Most High is omnipotent, and yet he needs our help, just as a new-born has its mother in its power but would piteously starve to death without her. Or like the pharaoh who reigns supreme and yet is still needy.

My heart thumping, I entered his tent and said, "Listen, Abram, the Lord has sealed my womb. You must sleep with my slave Hagar, and perhaps I can have descendants with her help."

I waited breathlessly for his response, but I did not have to wait long.

"Fine," he said.

That horny old goat! He was eighty-five by then, but without any hesitation agreed to take a woman to his bed who could have been his granddaughter! No discussion about God and his omnipotence, not a single doubt about the piety of my plan—no, he consented with obvious satisfaction and without a moment's thought. A sickening wave of jealousy sent the contents of my stomach rushing to my throat. I thought I was going to choke. I was about sixty by then, or thereabouts, but my body was voluptuous and as smooth as marble, and men still turned their heads to look at me with lust in their eyes. Why was I not enough for Abram?

In my jealous rage, I forgot that he had never asked for Hagar, but that I had offered her to him. Yet, for the sake of form, could he not have protested a tiny little bit?

In blind fury I left Abram in his tent and went to hide in mine. I threw myself onto my bed and sobbed like a little girl. I didn't recognize myself in that foolish creature that felt so very sorry for itself, but I let it have its way, hoping it would leave me in peace once its rage was spent.

And so it came to pass. I recovered my composure. I dried my ridiculous tears, washed myself, and combed my hair to boost my returning confidence. Determined not to tolerate any more arguments from Hagar, I went to her and said, "Make yourself ready for my husband's bed. Go to him, make love with him, be sure that you receive his seed, and then never show your face near his tent again."

When I saw that Hagar was about to reply, I raised my hand to silence her. "When you have given birth to my child, you will be free, but not until then. Go to your tent and do as I have ordered you."

Hagar bowed to me but I sensed mockery in her servility. I thought at the time that I had kept my cool, but I know now that everything inside me was raging, that every dry straw within me was about burst into flame at the slightest provocation.

The hellish night came when Hagar left her tent and came to call on me.

"I want to ask your forgiveness for what I am about to do," she said.

Rather than embracing her and reassuring her, I asked coldly if she was certain she was at the peak of her fertility and when she confirmed that she was, I said, "Go, and make sure it works the first time. My husband is not a young man."

She went. I watched her go and was irritated by everything about her: the way she walked, hips swaying, hair flowing, her dainty feet, her ankle bracelets. My maternal feelings had been ripped to shreds and lay around my heart like unwashed rags. For the first time in my life, I felt like an ugly old woman and it was unbearable. I knew very well that I had brought this ugliness upon myself and that Hagar was not to blame, but that didn't help me deal with the hatred inside me.

The night was long. I didn't sleep a wink. I tortured myself with the terrible thought that Abram would take Hagar as his wife and downgrade me to wife number two. I feared her revenge for all those years she'd spent in servitude if she came to rule over me from Abram's tent. I clenched my fists and my jaw. I would kill her before I allowed that to happen!

Hagar became pregnant and began to behave insufferably. Fiddling with her hair, rubbing her stomach, the faraway look, the blissful look, the kittenish look, the longing look . . . it was enough to drive anyone crazy. She "accidentally" dropped fragile things, vomited over the rug, massaged her breasts in public, hollowed her back to push forward her bulging belly, but the most insufferable thing was that she no longer did whatever I said. She was always too queasy or her legs felt weak or her head was spinning. In short, she didn't do a stroke of work.

I complained to Abram about her behavior, but he just shrugged his shoulders.

"I am not in charge of your slave girls," he said. "Deal with it yourself."

I was all alone, as if I no longer had a husband to watch over me! Perhaps he loved Hagar, perhaps he had already started to banish me from his life. My mouth turned dry as if I'd eaten sand and the blood rushed to my head. I was going to tackle that she-devil and thrash the arrogance out of her pregnant body! I took hold of the stick I used to drive my donkey and headed for her tent. Swishing the stick through the air, I screamed, "Hagar, you Egyptian slut, get yourself out here!"

She rushed from her tent, fell to the ground before me, and grasped my feet.

"Mistress," she wheedled. "What have I done wrong? What have I done to arouse your anger?"

Her questions took me by surprise. What exactly had aroused my anger? Frantically I searched for words but found none.

"Get up," I snarled. "Fetch water from the well. I want five pitchers full before the sun has reached its highest point."

"But, mistress . . ." she began.

"Silence!" I screamed. "Not another word. Do as I say."

I turned my back on her and, trembling, returned to my tent. What had I done? I knew very well that five pitchers full, within the time that was left to Hagar, was an almost impossible task even for a strong, robust woman. What did I want from her?

Exhausted, I lay down on my bed. I knew that my mind was disturbed, that I could no longer control my feelings, but the realization didn't help me. It didn't calm my rage. I was breathing fire; steam came pouring from my nose.

I heard Hagar groan as she placed the first pitcher before my tent, but I felt not a spark of compassion.

"Hurry up, woman!" I screamed. "Or do you want to feel my stick?"

The sound of my own voice disgusted me, and I couldn't imagine that there was anyone in the world who loved me. "Hagar!" I hissed. "You have turned me into a witch. And I am going to teach you a lesson!"

Where had the venom come from that had transformed my heart into such a pit of snakes? I did not know then, but I know now. I myself had brewed the poison that was proving fatal to my spirit: jealousy.

I can still hear myself raging, "You harlot from Egypt, you had to go and sleep with my husband, didn't you?" To which Hagar replied, "Yes, but you asked me to . . ."

"Yes, I did, but you could have refused, couldn't you, you hussy?"

I am deeply ashamed at my shameless irrationality, but that's how it happened. I can't deny it.

Hagar brought me the five pitchers and dropped to the ground in front of the tent, exhausted. I heard the dull thud of her body in the sand, and I heaved myself up from my bed. My heart was pounding away deep inside me. I walked over to Hagar and looked down at her. I was sorry that she had completed her task so I had no reason to flog her. I said, "I have no need for your child. You may keep it." I knew what I was doing. I was releasing myself from the obligation to let her go free in exchange for the descendants she would give me. I wanted her to remain my slave so I could continue to make her life a misery. She did not react and that too inflamed my fury. Had she never believed my promise? Did she feel she had any right to doubt her mistress's promise? Who did she think she was?

"Get out of my sight," I hissed.

But she didn't move.

"Go away!" I screamed. "I cannot stand the sight of you!"

Only then did it dawn on me that she was unconscious, but my heart was so hardened that her condition did not bother me. I beckoned over two men who were milking the goats and told them to drag Hagar to her tent.

I knew there was something seriously wrong with me, but I was powerless against the evil forces that had taken up residence in my heart. When Hagar recovered, I dreamed up a hundred more provocations to try to incite her to disobedience, which sometimes worked but usually did not. I was so disgusted with myself that, in my despair, I turned to Abram.

"You're responsible for the injustice that has been done to me, for it is you who made her pregnant! I placed my slave at your disposal. Now that she knows she's pregnant, she shows no respect for me at all. That's your fault, so you must solve the problem, or let the Lord be the judge of who is in the right: you or me."

As I screamed these words, I knew they made no sense. What

did I mean by "right"? Had I been "right" to torment Hagar? Or "right" to blame Abram for my insanity? I was shrieking like an animal being slaughtered, in panic and with no shred of sense.

I could see from Abram's dazed expression that he didn't know what to do with me and, even though my soul was in a frenzy, I could understand that. I didn't know what to do with myself either, which is why I'd sought his help.

He said, "She's your slave. Do as you see fit."

I fell silent. Of all the possible answers, that was exactly the wrong one, but the wickedness within me smiled triumphantly: Abram had given me free rein. I could do as I pleased. I did not have to restrain my rage.

Drunk with power, I strutted out of Abram's tent and screamed for Hagar.

"Come here, you pregnant she-dog, I am going to whip that whelp out of your bulging belly!"

I looked around, but she did not appear. Her tent was empty. No one knew where she was, or they pretended not to. There was a strange silence in the camp, an emptiness; the world filled up with absence. My rage collapsed like bread that has failed to rise and lay in my stomach, a motionless lump. What had I done?

For around sixty years, I had been under the impression that I knew myself: a friendly woman, always ready to laugh, and with little harm in her. How mistaken I had been! I was a person no one could trust, least of all myself.

Hagar was not there.

The woman I had welcomed into my heart as a daughter years ago was gone. I crept to my tent without asking anyone about her, because I knew the answer no one would speak aloud. Hagar had fled from my bestial cruelty.

She could not be far away and yet I didn't send any men after her as I normally did with runaway slaves. I let her go because I thought she was right to try to escape from an ugly horror like me. I threw myself onto my bed and cried bitter tears. I had lost my daughter and Abram his son.

She was surely fleeing for her homeland, but between here and there lay a desert that would slowly devour her, piece by piece, unborn child and all.

God, my god, why did you forsake me? Where was your help? Where was your punishment? Were you not paying attention to me or did you not want to see me? What good is your omnipotence to me if you do not reach out even a finger to help me?

I did my utmost to place my sins upon God and to send him into the wilderness like a useless goat, but it did not work. I did not become one ounce lighter. I didn't dare to face anyone, but hid in my tent, and if someone asked for me, I cried out: "Unclean!" so that no one would come in and see me in my misery. I was unclean. I had so deeply sullied myself that no water could ever wash me clean.

I don't know for how many days or weeks I lay there like that. I remember water was sometimes pushed under the tent cloth and that I drank, but I did not eat. Just the thought of food was enough to make me retch. Maybe I wanted to die. In any case I did not want to be there, so great was my shame.

I ended up in a state where I felt no more hunger and began to see things that were not there. When I heard Hagar's voice, I thought at first I was dreaming and when I saw her appear beside my bed I believed I was inside one of my visions.

It was incredible, but it really was her. She was emaciated and tanned by the sun, but the joy shining from her eyes lit up my darkness.

She stroked my hair and whispered, "Mistress, Mother, please do not be angry with me any longer. I do not want to be free. I belong with you. I'm your obedient slave."

She covered my hands with kisses, removing all the guilt I had heaped upon my soul with my foolish behavior. I did not deserve it, but it helped.

My heart was as small and as soft as a newborn bird. Hagar caressed it with her words, filling it with tenderness. Maybe I would get my daughter back; I had a second chance.

"Where were you, Hagar? What happened to you?" I managed to say.

"I was in the desert by a spring, the spring on the road to Shur. An angel came and spoke to me."

"An angel, an angel," I murmured. "What's an angel?"

I had never heard the word before.

"Don't you know what an angel is? I heard people talking about them when I was a child and we lived in Ur, the city of the Chaldees. They said angels are God's messengers, creatures like us, but immortal."

It took me a moment to imagine what she might mean, because why would God not appear himself if he had some message to impart?

"But I'm not entirely certain it wasn't God himself," Hagar said.

I looked at her in astonishment. Had she read my mind?

"The pharaoh?" I asked.

"In a very different form," said Hagar. "A man in the prime of his life. He said, 'Hagar, slave of Sarai, where did you come from and where are you going?' 'I fled from Sarai, my mistress,' I replied. 'Return to your mistress,' he said, 'and obey her once more.'"

Hagar fell silent and looked at me and looked at me.

"Did he not ask you why you fled from me?" I said.

She shook her head.

"Did you not tell him?"

Again she shook her head.

I was deeply grateful to her. I concluded from the words of the "angel" that God was not aware of my misbehavior. I could tell from her face that more had been said and she was dying to tell me.

"Go on," I told her.

"The angel said, 'To reward you, I will give you many descendants, so many they cannot be counted. You are pregnant now and will bring a son into the world. You must call him Ishmael, because the Lord has heard how much you have suffered.'"

I was taken aback, because "Ishmael" means "God has heard of her misery." So he *did* know! What was in store for me now? Sickness, death, widowhood? I shook my fearful thoughts from my head. Whatever would come, would come. For now, I was being undeservedly rewarded by Hagar's return.

She continued her story.

"'Ishmael will be a wild donkey of a man,' said the angel. 'He will wander restlessly and lash out at everyone, just as everyone will lash out at him. He will live in hostility with all his kin, for he will be stubborn and free from all ties.' Then I cried, 'You are a god who knows how to see! The god I have seen here has seen my needs!' And so, beside the road to Shur, I named the spring Beer Lahai Roi, 'the well of him that lives and sees.'"

That was the end of Hagar's tale. And for anyone who wants to find that well, it lies between Kadesh and Bered.

What mattered most to me was that my love for Hagar had returned and that I did not begrudge her the son I couldn't have.

I told Abram what had happened to Hagar in the desert and he said, "How is it that you women see God wherever you want, but I still know him only by name?"

I laughed at his overstatement, which amused me. "Perhaps he likes women better than men," I replied, doubting it was true.

Abram had to wait thirteen years after Hagar before he got to see the Lord with his own eyes. I do not have to count the years, since it happened when Ishmael was thirteen years old.

It was a sweltering day. The scorching sunlight hurt our eyes. Animals and people sought the cool of the shade, and even the lizards and snakes hid themselves away. Abram was sitting in the doorway of his tent when he saw three men nearby, whose gleaming white robes appeared to be giving off light. Abram leapt to his feet and said to me, "That must be him."

We weren't expecting any guests. I didn't know who he meant, but I could tell it must be someone important.

So I said, "Who?"

"God, of course," cried Abram and he rushed out into the burning heat.

I peered out of the dark tent at the three men in the bright light and wondered which of the three was God. Or were all three of them God? They were handsome strong men, men I'd certainly have fallen for in my younger years, but I couldn't see them as gods because, unlike the pharaoh, they weren't surrounded by the symbols of their power.

The men were already quite close to the tent when Abram fell to his knees and bowed so deeply before them that his forehead touched the ground. "Lord," he said, "please be so kind as not to pass your servant by."

"Do not be afraid," said the man on the left. "We will stay a while."

Abram leapt up and pointed at me inside the dark tent. I knew he was about to start giving me orders. Water to wash their feet, food, drink ... I knew exactly what needed to be done when we had guests to welcome.

But the man in the middle raised his hand to silence Abram. "We do not need anything, we will return another time to eat and drink with you. We cannot dine at the table of an uncircumcised man."

Of course, I did not know at the time what that meant, but I knew the unfamiliar word somehow referred to Abram.

"We promised you the land of Canaan," said the man on the right this time, "and countless descendants. We will make a covenant with you and all the generations that follow, but in return you have this obligation: circumcision."

Abram waited for an explanation, but it was not forthcoming.

"Lord?" he asked. "Circumcision, what is that?"

The question appeared to cause some embarrassment among the three men. They held their heads close together and talked in whispers.

Then the man in the middle said, "You will have to cut off part of your body as a sign of our covenant."

That sounded familiar. I'd seen tribes that carved symbols into their faces, some that made a hole in the flesh between their nostrils to hold amulets, and others that cut their arms, chests, and legs during ritual dances, irrigating the fields with their blood.

"Which part would you like?" asked Abram. "How about an earlobe?"

The men gave embarrassed smiles and there was another whispered discussion.

"No," the man in the middle said. "It has to be your foreskin."

Who can blame us for never having heard of a foreskin? A foreskin? A skin before what? Abram gaped at the men. If he felt as dumb as I did, then he felt like an ass.

"Come here," said the man on the right.

Abram took a few steps forward and the man put a hand to his ear, whispering into it. I saw Abram's face turn pale, and when the man had finished speaking he reeled back as if he'd been thumped in the face.

"Do you understand?" asked the man in the middle.

Speechless, Abram just nodded.

"Not only you, but all the men and boys have to be circumcised," he continued. "Everyone who was born among you or bought by you must be circumcised. That will be the sign of our covenant. When that has happened, you must call yourself Abraham, and your wife will be called not Sarai but Sarah. I will bless you and give you a son by her."

That's right! Abram was ninety-nine years old and I was about seventy-five, and again we'd been promised a son. What kind of gods were these? Did they think we were stupid?

The men took their leave and said, "We will return when you are circumcised, for then we can eat and drink with you."

When Abram returned to the tent, dripping with sweat, I asked him, "What is it? What do you have to cut off?"

Now, I apologize for using this word, but it was the word we used together and the one that came most naturally to us.

He said, "A bit of my dick has to come off."

I thought I was going crazy. After a moment of stunned silence, I started to scream.

"Absolutely no way!" I shrieked. "That's out of the question! As long as I am alive, not a single man or boy in our camp is going to cut off a bit of his dick!"

But Abram had seen his god, and there was not the slightest protest in him.

"Was it really God?" I yelled. "There were three men. So, if I might ask, which of the three was it?"

"Why should God not be able to appear as a trio?" Abram mumbled.

I calmed down. I wondered why I was interfering. If a man wanted to cut off a piece of his penis, it was his own business. What annoyed me was his unquestioning obedience.

"Listen, Abram," I said. "There are gods living in this land who ask people to sacrifice their firstborn sons. Did you know that? And sacrifice is just a polite word for slaughter. They slit the child's throat and then they burn it. What do you think of that? Would you meekly slaughter your own child?"

"My god would not ask such a thing of me," muttered Abram as he rummaged around in my cooking utensils.

He was looking for the meat knife. I knew where it was, but I didn't say anything. I didn't want to play any part in his folly. I thought: When people don't speak back to the gods, the gods just get crazier and crazier.

He found the meat knife.

"Leave me for a moment," he said. "It'll be over in no time." He looked at me with the eyes of a frightened and desperate child.

"No!" I screamed. "How are we ever going to have a son if you cut off your dick?!"

"It's just a small piece of skin, that's all," said Abram, the sweat falling from his forehead. "But I'd look the other way for a moment if I were you."

I ran out of the tent, because I wanted nothing to do with Abram's self-mutilation. At the same time I wanted to stay close to him, because I loved him in spite of his insanity and didn't want to forsake him. I heard a shriek of pain and then a moan like that of a dying animal.

"Abram?" I asked. "Are you all right?"

"My name is Abraham now," he groaned.

He'd changed his name because he'd cut off a piece of his dick!

"Come, Sarah," he said. "Bring me a clean cloth to bind up my wound."

I went inside, fetched him a strip of white linen, and said, "My name is Sarai."

I could see he was bleeding like a stuck pig, but he didn't appear to have done himself too much damage.

"What does 'A-bra-ham' actually mean?" I asked.

"By God, I don't know," he replied. "But if my god says I'm called Abraham, then I'm called Abraham."

I kneeled down and helped him to bandage his wound. When I was done, I stood up and was about to go drink some water because I felt sick, but Abraham said, "Call Ishmael."

Enough was enough. I ran outside and screamed, "Hagar! Hide Ishmael! Abram wants to cut off a bit of his dick!"

There was no one around since they were all hiding in their tents from the heat, but still a deep silence seemed to descend upon the camp like a cloud of dust. I was a voice crying in the wilderness. I felt like a madwoman spewing obscenities because her mind was unhinged. Is it typical of women to bear upon their shoulders the burden of the insanity of gods and men?

My screaming did not help. When Hagar heard about Abram's divine mission, she went to him like an obedient cow and handed over her calf. We heard the boy's desperate screams as Abraham set to work on him in his tent. Hagar turned pale but didn't move a muscle. I realized that people were at the mercy of the gods, with no will of their own, that they were possessed and incapable of resisting. I was the one who was different; I was the crazy woman. If I was not careful, I would become a stranger among people. I had to learn to hold my tongue; my mockery and laughter must no longer escape my lips.

After he had circumcised Ishmael and the poor boy left the tent bent over in pain, Abraham called together all his male slaves and free herders.

"Men," he said. "God has made a covenant with me and, as a sign of that covenant, all the men in my household must be circumcised. That means a piece of skin will be removed from your penis. When that has happened, I will have many descendants. God has promised this to me." He raised his bloody knife in the air to show the men what he meant to do.

The men looked at Abraham with glassy eyes and I had to bite my tongue to stop myself from laughing.

Serug, a free herder who was as thin as the branch of a tree, stepped forward and asked, "If we allow ourselves to be circumcised, will God make a covenant with us, too? Will we then belong to the same people as you?"

Abraham frowned and wrinkled his brow, because he had to think.

"No," he said finally.

"So why should we allow ourselves to be circumcised if it is no benefit to us?" asked Serug.

"I do not know," said Abraham testily. "That is none of my concern. God says it must happen, and so it must happen."

The men continued to look at him in silence as if expecting some further explanation, but none was forthcoming.

"Who wants to go first?" asked Abraham.

No one stepped forward.

"What kind of men are you?" Abraham cried angrily. "Scared of a little pain? Do you wish to defy the orders of the gods for the sake of a tiny piece of skin? Do you have no thought for your spiritual well-being?"

A deep silence followed; no one seemed to see any connection between their spiritual well-being and cutting off their foreskins.

"Fine, then. Don't bother," grumbled Abraham. "I shall send my herders packing and sell off my slaves, because I do not wish to live with the uncircumcised. They are an abomination to me. Get out of my sight. I cannot look at you any longer." He turned around and walked into his tent. He let down the tent flaps so no one could see even a glimpse of him.

I have to confess I hadn't expected that, and I realized it was a smart move. For miles around there was no better boss for free herders than Abraham and, as far as the slaves were concerned, being sold would definitely mean a change for the worse.

The men stood there, staring at Abraham's closed tent. When they had waited a long while and the tent flaps still didn't move, they knew it was decision time.

Again, Serug stepped forward, but now he said nothing. He began to gather stones and to pile them in front of Abraham's tent. The crowd started to move and many people gave him a helping hand. They seemed to know what they were doing. It was only when the pile of stones began to look like a table or an altar and had reached about the height of a man's hip that I grasped their intention.

When the altar was ready, the men stood in a long line. Serug called his master and Abraham came out with his knife.

I ran away and hid in my tent. I covered my ears with my hands, but the screaming of the men, one by one, laying their penises on the sacrificial altar, went through my flesh and bones and hit me deep in my stomach.

I wondered how a man so possessed could gain such power over others that they would lay their most vulnerable part on the altar for him.

The weather remained sweltering hot. I didn't count the weeks but not many had passed before the three gods reappeared, surrounded by the gleaming light of the sun. I thought: This time they've come for the women. Which bit of us do they want to cut off?

Abraham ran to the gods and said, "My lords, please be so kind as not to pass your servant by. I shall have some water fetched for you so you may wash your feet. Make yourselves comfortable beneath this tree in the meantime. I'll bring you something to eat as well, so you may regain your strength before you continue your journey. That's why you've come to visit your servant, is it not?"

The gods replied, "We are pleased to accept your invitation."

Abraham waited in silence, as if expecting some other unpleasant command, and I too held my breath. I would not allow my body to be cut, not by anyone. I was prepared to take my own life before that happened.

But they said nothing on the subject. Abraham turned around and I saw the incredulous expression on his face. The gods were staying to eat! He hurried to his tent and said, "Sarah, quickly, three measures of fine flour! Make dough! Bake bread!" Then he hurried to the herd, chose a handsome calf that looked nice and tender, and gave it to a serf, who quickly prepared it. He fetched butter and milk, took the roasted calf, and served it all up to his guests. As they ate, he stood with them beneath the tree.

"Where is Sarah, your wife?" they asked him.

"In the tent over there," he replied.

Then one of the gods said, "I will return to you in exactly a year and by then your wife Sarah will have a son."

I clapped my hand to my mouth. Abraham was ninety-nine years old and I was seventy-five or so. Can you imagine how hard it was for me not to laugh? But I was determined that no one would ever notice my rebelliousness, mockery, or disbelief again, and so I clenched my jaw tightly together.

Then one of the gods asked, "Why is Sarah laughing?"

I was scared out of my wits, thinking the gods could see right through me. But then I realized they must have known their promise was ridiculous, and would therefore assume it might make me laugh.

"Why is she wondering if at her age she can still bring a child into the world?" asked another god.

I wasn't wondering, I *knew* I couldn't give birth to a child at my age, and the gods knew it too. I wasn't going to let them make a fool out of me; they weren't going to put silly ideas in my head.

"Is anything impossible for God? At the appointed time, in exactly a year, we will return to you, and Sarah will have a son."

I stopped laughing. Is anything impossible for the gods? Oh

yes! They cannot make the sun stand still or walk upon water. It is impossible for them to make a woman pregnant when her child-bearing years are over. I left the tent, planted my hands on my hips, and said, "I did not laugh."

Then the three gods said at the same time, "Yes, you did laugh."

"Did not," I cried furiously.

"Did so," said the gods.

Abraham looked sternly at me, so I held my tongue.

Otherwise, the visit from the three gods went pretty well. Abraham and the three nameless gods talked about this and that, as men do when they're together. I watched them from a distance, because I was not supposed to join their conversation. When men are in conversation, women remain silent. I have never understood why, but that's one of our customs. She watches over her household and does not eat the bread of idleness.

While I provided the men with food and drink, I kept my ears open since I was hungry for knowledge. I heard the word "Sodom" mentioned at a certain point. So I took a pitcher of water and went to stand behind Abraham as if ready to top up their cups, because everything that was said about that city interested me and not only because Lot lived there. The city! My slave girls spoke of it in hushed tones, as if nothing that happened there could be spoken out loud. I think most of it was about lust and love, about depravity and wickedness, but the way they spoke suggested secret longings. Scandalmongers' gossip often betrays their own dark desires.

"We need to talk about Sodom," said one of the gods. "Why should I keep my plans secret from Abraham?"

"No, there's no need," said the second god.

"But he has to know how to teach his son to act with justice and goodness," said the third.

Forewarned is forearmed.

At the mention of Abraham's nonexistent son, I felt a stab in my heart. What would happen when I did not give him that son?

Would I be accused of disobeying the gods? Would I be cast out? I decided at that moment that Abraham would have his son, no matter what it took.

"Well then, Abraham," said the first god. "Serious accusations have been made against Sodom. Its sins are said to be unparalleled in their gravity. I mean to go to that place to find out if the complaints I have heard are justified and if they have indeed called down destruction upon themselves. That is what I want to know."

The food was finished, the fun was over.

The first god had said he was going to look at Sodom, but to my surprise the other two bid us farewell and went on their way, while the first stayed with Abraham. I did not know what to make of it then, but now I realize the "I" of the gods can just as easily mean "we" or "they." I thought back to what I'd learned in Egypt: all appearances of the divine are manifestations of the same single and eternal God, even if he presents himself as a trio, which was handy in this case, because two of them could go look around in Sodom while one stayed behind to talk to Abraham. I wouldn't mind being a trio myself when I find I'm shorthanded.

"I will go look," said the god who stayed behind, "but I know the outcome already. Sodom must be destroyed."

I could tell something was bothering Abraham. I saw that defiant thoughts were brewing within him and I fervently hoped he would have the courage to speak them. He moved a little closer to the god and asked, "Will you take the lives of the innocent as well as the guilty?"

My heart soared. This was unheard of! My own husband, who had not always been so brave in the past, dared to criticize his god's intentions! My elderly heart filled with love and pride. I saw the god was taken aback. He couldn't have been expecting it, but what good is a covenant between men and gods if all man may do is bow down? The god stood in perplexed silence.

"There are perhaps fifty innocents in that city," said Abraham. "Would you snatch them out of life too, rather than granting the entire city forgiveness for the sake of those fifty?"

Magnificent! And yet I knew Abraham had left out an important argument. So I said, "And besides," but I got no further than that.

"Be quiet, Sarah," said Abraham. "I'm talking."

So I was quiet. I thought: He'll come up with it himself. I'm sure he will.

He turned back to the god and said, "You cannot do that. You cannot allow them to perish with the guilty! That lumps the innocent in with them. You just can't do that! He who is the judge of all the earth must do what is right, mustn't he?"

My husband, my hero! And yet there was something missing from his argument. Once again, I couldn't contain myself and I said, "And besides—"

"Sarah!"

So I said nothing. I thought: He knows, he's just saving it for later. I'm sure he is.

The god said, "If I find fifty innocents in Sodom, I will forgive the entire city for their sake."

I looked at Abraham expectantly. I thought: there are so many more innocents in Sodom. Go on, tell him. But to my dismay, Abraham made a different move. He said, "Now that I have been so bold as to speak to the Lord, although I am nothing but dust, what if the number of innocents falls five short, would you then destroy the entire city for the sake of those five?"

It was as if he were haggling at the market! That wasn't the way to go at all! I opened my mouth but the god spoke first. He said, "No, I will not destroy it if I find forty-five innocents there."

Abraham bargained him down to forty, to thirty, to twenty, to ten, before giving up.

I was almost bursting with impatience.

"But!" I screamed. Tears of fury filled my eyes.

"Quiet, Sarah," said Abraham. "We must no longer try the patience of the Lord."

The god turned around and disappeared into thin air, like a cloud burnt off by the heat of the sun.

"But, Abraham, there are hundreds of innocent children living in that city!"

My husband, my hero, he looked at me blankly as if he did not understand my words.

"Children!" I cried. "Do you understand me? Thousands of children who are entirely innocent!"

"Oh, yes," said Abraham, falling to his knees in despair.

I held his hands and tried to pull him to his feet, but he was too heavy for me.

"Get up. Go after the god and tell him."

"It's too late," said Abraham. "The Lord's mind is made up."

I looked at him in astonishment. How could he be so resigned in the face of such terrible cruelty? What do the gods do to the hearts and the minds of men?

My whole being was aflame. Things between me and the gods would never be right, I knew that for sure. I felt a deep disgust for life. I longed for the realm of the dead, where I would forever be free of them.

I watched from afar what happened to Sodom, and the rest was told to me. I don't know if I should believe all the stories, but I pass them on in the hope that posterity will be better able than I to judge their truth.

I have already mentioned Lot's wife, whose name I will not say, for she does not deserve to live on in history. She and her husband occasionally visited us, even after they'd been living in Sodom for years. They came riding in on their ridiculously rigged-out camels, followed by a procession of slaves, male and female, who looked as if they were there just for show. Madame herself couldn't take a step without jangling like a flock of sheep, as she was so hung about with jewelry and other ornaments. She turned our herders' heads with her painted lips and coal-black eyelids and was interested only in flattery.

I loathed that woman, but to my surprise she had produced two daughters who were not only stunningly beautiful but also exceptionally sweet and intelligent. They were called Adina and Ayala, because they were as slender and kind as deer.

While their mother sat looking down her nose at us tent-dwellers, the two sisters immediately rolled up their sleeves and set to work. They helped me to pour wine and to share out the bread. When everyone had eaten enough, they went outside and played with the children and helped feed the lambs. They felt at home with us, while in Sodom they would always remain strangers, no matter how hard their mother tried to be a real Sodomite.

I mention Adina and Ayala because they ended up playing an unenviable role in the story of Sodom's destruction. I shall say again that I don't know how much slander is hidden in this story. I'm telling you what I heard myself, and if I doubt the truth of the scenes I describe, I will not keep those doubts from you.

All right then, here goes. The two gods arrived in Sodom by evening. I don't know where the third god had gotten to, but he'd probably returned to the assembly of the gods to report on his conversation with Abraham. Anyway, two of the three headed to the city gate, where Lot happened to be chatting with his friends. It will not surprise you that Lot immediately recognized the two men as gods, because that's something the men of our family are very good at. He approached them, bowed deeply, and said, "My lords, please come with me. Your servant's house is open to you. Spend the night here and wash your feet. Then tomorrow morning you can continue your journey."

But the gods said, "No, thank you. We will spend the night in the town square."

I find that response quite surprising: Did the gods really want to spend the night in the open air like a couple of vagrants? Or could they have been referring to a guesthouse in the square? There are plenty such ambiguities in this story to start a person thinking.

Lot must have thought it odd too, because he kept insisting the square could be a dangerous place at night, there were all sorts of bad characters wandering around, there weren't enough guards, and so on and so on. You were better off inside.

So the gods decided to take up Lot's offer of hospitality after all. They went into his house. Lot prepared a meal for them and baked bread, because his wife was, of course, too lazy and his daughters were already in bed.

As Lot and his guests were about to go to bed, a huge commotion broke out in the street. Lot went to his bedroom window, still in his pajamas, and saw to his horror that all of Sodom had gathered outside his door—at least, all the men, young and old. They were shouting and bawling, but Lot couldn't understand what they were saying. His wife sat up in bed, terrified, and said, "Do something, go talk to them, before they break down our door." Knees trembling, Lot walked to the front door, opened it a crack, and put his head out.

"Where are the men who are staying with you?" they shouted. "Bring them out here because we want to fuck them."

I'm sorry, but I can't help it—that's what they said. It's the coarse kind of language that men use when their wives aren't around. What else can I say? It's widely known that men sometimes want each other—women too, for that matter—so it's no surprise to anyone, but it is the custom kindly to request such labors of love and not to demand them as if it were your right.

So Lot said, "Wait just one moment. I shall inquire if my guests are willing to satisfy your needs." He closed the door and waited, heart pounding, to see if the crowd would calm down. Of course, he certainly didn't intend to consult the gods about the demands of the crowd. In the meantime, his wife had come downstairs and stood beside him, shivering in her nightclothes. The door shook in its frame as the men outside kicked it furiously.

"Do something!" she sobbed. "Get those men out of bed and send them out there. The crowd is going to murder us."

Lot gaped at her. "They are our guests! Any man who does not protect his guests loses his honor forevermore!"

"Honor?! Honor?! What damn good is honor to me?!" his wife screamed. "I don't want to die! I want to live, even if it's without honor!"

The door groaned as if pounded by a battering ram. It couldn't be long before it would give way. And it was not hard to guess what would happen when the frenzied crowd invaded the house.

Lot's wife wrung her hands in mortal terror and screamed, "Give them Adina and Ayala! Your daughters belong to you! They could save our lives!"

According to the stories I've been told, Lot did as his wife asked, but I don't believe that. It can only be based on wicked gossip, since I don't think a father could do such a thing. I'm writing it down, but I hope you'll agree with me that it's a lie. It simply cannot have happened.

The house shook, and the baying of the crowd sounded like a violent storm. Both the two guests and the girls had been standing behind them in the living room for some time without Lot and his wife noticing. The girls had heard what their mother said and from that terrible moment they lost her forever. For if a woman is prepared to sacrifice her daughters to save her own life, can she still be called their mother?

But what really amazes me is the attitude of the gods. They stood there without saying a word. That's what makes this story so unlikely. Could they not have intervened before the girls lost their mother for good?

Lot went outside and closed the door behind him. That was brave, but listen to the words he is said to have spoken: "My friends," he said to the crowd, "you cannot do this. My guests are unwilling, they are not in the mood, they are tired from their journey and want to sleep. But I have two daughters who have not yet slept with a man. I shall bring them to you. Do with them what you will, but leave these men in peace. I have offered them a safe place to stay."

I hope Adina and Ayala didn't hear those words, because then they would have lost their father too. It cannot be true. Don't believe these lies! The men of my family are not capable of such shameful deeds.

The story goes that the crowd did not accept Lot's offer. They

did not want girls. They wanted men, perhaps not so much to satisfy their own lusts as to humiliate the strangers.

"Get away from that door!" they shouted. And, "Who do you
think you are, you stupid foreigner, trying to lay down the law to
us? Just you wait, we'll soon sort you out and we'll treat you even
worse than those two good-looking guys."

So that was what it came down to: Lot and his wife were outsiders in Sodom and the Sodomites' entire gruesome display was
prompted by their irrational hatred of foreigners. Abraham and I
were only too well aware of this notion: we were strangers in the
land that had been promised to us, dependent on the whims of the
people who had lived there longer. Most of them treated us with
respect, but we knew we had no rights at all.

If this is the sin for which the gods wanted to punish Sodom, I
have some understanding, for if such injustice is allowed even once,
there's no stopping it.

The seething Sodomites grabbed Lot and dragged him away
from the door, preparing to break it down. Some men arrived with
a beam and set it up as a battering ram. Just as they were about to
begin their assault, the door swung open and the two gods stood
in the doorway. Their sudden appearance made the crowd fall
silent for a moment and the gods seized the opportunity to pull Lot
inside and close the door.

It strikes me again that gods, when they pretend to be men, cannot have all their powers at their disposal. Or let me put it this way,
when they appear as men, they not do always go for the most obvious solution. With all their omnipotence, the gods didn't even need
to leave their beds to prevent the Sodomites from entering Lot's
street. So why did they not do that? It's because there would have
been no story to pass on. The iniquity of Sodom had to be demonstrated, so that we human beings would understand why it needed
to be destroyed. But unfortunately it was a bad story, conceived in
the brains of gods who were none too bright. There must surely
have been repercussions for them at the assembly of the gods!

The Sodomites didn't take it lying down, but bashed the door with their battering ram until it crashed into the house with a thunderous bang. But then—oh, miracle of miracles!—the Sodomites suddenly found themselves in the dark. They had forced the door but couldn't find a way in, as they'd all been struck blind!

First Lot's wife had to betray her daughters, then they had to be threatened with rape, and then Lot had to risk his life before, finally, the gods decided it was time to show their powers. And all that just to create a rather dubious story!

The Sodomites slunk off, groping their way along the streets, looking for their homes. I think this punishment would have been sufficient; even if it was only temporary, their sudden blindness must have made the scales fall from their eyes.

But the gods didn't know when to stop. They asked Lot, "Do you have other relatives here? Sons, daughters, sons-in-law, take everyone who belongs to you and leave Sodom. We are about to lay waste to the city."

"Oh," said Lot, "it's good of you to mention it. I'll warn my future sons-in-law."

For Adina and Ayala had been promised to two young Sodomites. So off Lot went, passing a group of Sodomites who had lost their way in their blind confusion, and finally finding his sons-in-law in the town square. He took them aside and said, "Quick! You must leave the city, for God Almighty is about to destroy it."

His future sons-in-law thought he'd gone stark raving mad and said, "We have no business being outside the city. Besides, Sodom is a city that will never fall."

So, mission unaccomplished, Lot returned home and told them what had happened. Adina and Ayala burst into tears, since they had really been looking forward to their weddings, and their mother was also overcome by her emotions. She had hoped these marriages would mean that she would finally be accepted by the locals as a Sodomite.

"The boys are right!" she cried. "This city is eternal. It will never fall!"

It was getting light and the gods were becoming restless.

"Quickly! Take your wife and your two daughters and leave this place."

But Lot's wife sobbed and tugged at her husband's arm because she didn't want to leave Sodom. Then the gods grasped him, his wife, and Adina and Ayala by the hands and dragged them out of the city. The earth shook as if it were about to burst apart.

The gods stood still and said, "It has already begun. Flee, for your lives are in danger! Do not look back and stop nowhere in the valley. Flee into the mountains or you will perish."

Then the gods went their own way or vanished into thin air, the story doesn't say. But, anyway, Lot was suddenly left to his own devices.

Lot thought it was a bad idea to go into the mountains. He was sensible enough not to follow the gods' advice. He knew the mountains; he could hear them rumbling and knew they were about to start spewing fire. He pulled his wife and daughters along with him, through the valley, toward the town of Zoar, a little place that was too insignificant to arouse the fury of the gods.

The earth began to shake wildly and they could clearly hear the crashes as the buildings collapsed. Lot put his arms around his daughters' shoulders and covered their ears with his hands.

"Don't look back!" he cried.

Sounds of weeping and wailing rose from behind the city walls, but Lot forced his daughters to keep on walking. The mountains around them began to smoke.

He looked to one side and saw that his wife was not beside him. "Wife!" he called. "Don't look back! Don't look back!"

But it was too late. She had looked back, unable to leave the city behind. Apparently as punishment, she was transformed into the pillar of salt she had always been. But there were no witnesses to that metamorphosis, as neither Lot nor his daughters looked back at her.

Abraham and I felt the earth shake beneath our tents, too. We saw the black smoke on the horizon. Abraham wept. He must have been thinking about the thousands of innocent children of Sodom.

Suddenly it became too much for him to bear. He clung on to me, as a child to his mother, and said, "Is Almighty God, who made heaven and earth, not allowed to destroy what he himself created?"

"No," I said. "He is not."

I realized that the gods, as soon as they become human, pile one mistake on top of another, cause one disaster after another, before retreating, self-satisfied, to the mountains. It would not surprise me if in the future a prophet should arise and urge the gods never again to appear in the form of man, so they forever remain invisible and we have no image of them. That is the only way we will be able to keep them sacred and uncontaminated by unjust behavior.

I had no confidence whatsoever in their prediction that I would have a son in my old age. I didn't hold this against them, for no one is bound by the impossible. I saw their promise more as an instruction: I had to ensure that, one way or another, Abraham would have a son from me. Hagar's son did not count. So three months after the fall of Sodom, I told him I was pregnant.

Abraham was beside himself with joy and everyone who heard the news rejoiced in the miracle—everyone, that is, except for my slave Hagar. She went around with a mocking smile and tried to ridicule me.

"Sarah's child is going to come falling from the sky, not from her belly," she said to anyone who would listen. Some of them laughed and others grew angry, afraid of their own doubts.

I was seething, not because Hagar had seen through me—there probably wasn't one single woman in the camp who believed for even a second that I could bear a child at my age—but because she had shamelessly betrayed the female bond of solidarity that requires us to remain silent. We had long been living together as mother and daughter once again, but her behavior reignited my hatred and my blood burned. I vowed that, as soon as I had given Abraham his son, I would deal with her once and for all.

I should not have worried, because either Hagar's nonsense

didn't reach Abraham or he turned a deaf ear. His faith in the promise the gods had made was so great that he would have believed in my pregnancy even if I had stubbornly denied it. The gods had said it would come to pass and so it must be true.

Abraham was almost one hundred years old, and we had lived together as man and wife, but also as brother and sister, so we were connected twice over. We glowed with intimacy even in our old age, but I have to confess that Abraham's faith somewhat alienated me from him. There are those who see blind faith in the wisdom, justice, and goodness of the gods as the highest virtue, but I am not one of them. The unfortunate children of Sodom had opened my eyes, but Abraham believed that his wits fell short of understanding the infinite wisdom of the gods. This is a position that surprises me, because injustice is unjust, no matter the motive.

Among our people, pregnancy and childbirth are women's matters. The men keep out of the way until the child has been born and washed. They know nothing of the pangs of labor, of pain and blood, of fear and anguish during the birth, and yet still they take possession of the child as if it were theirs alone. Women have no say about the children they have brought into the world with so much pain and effort, and among the Canaanites it sometimes even happens that a father decides the child must be sacrificed to the gods. The woman can do nothing but surrender her baby to the priest's knife. She is even required to do it without so much as batting an eyelash.

Everything in me rebels against such behavior. Down with the gods who devour children and mangle the mother's heart as if it's some lump of dead meat!

When an old woman is required to give her husband a son, when it's actually seen as a divine command, it's important for that woman to understand the ways of the world. So she must know that not all children are welcome, that some are abandoned in the wilderness, that others are consigned to the river in a basket of reeds, and that in the best case such a child is handed over to a childless woman who receives it with joy and considers it her own, even if she cannot put it to her own breast and must find a wet nurse for it.

There are many women in the world who unexpectedly have a child at an advanced age. Their husband struts around like a peacock, full of this miracle that has been granted to him in his old age. Of course, he too knows the stories about rejected infants, about unmarried mothers who do not want to live in shame, or about mothers who have already given birth to so many children that they are afraid they will not be able to bring up a fifteenth one. But the need to believe in the miracle is so strong that it makes a hearing man deaf and a seeing man blind.

When a man doubts and wonders if his child really has come from his seed and been conceived within his wife's womb, his wife does well not to take him into her confidence but instead to tell him a perfectly plausible story and to have a trustworthy midwife at hand who will confirm that story. But, most importantly, she needs to be highly indignant about any suspicion from the husband to whom she has been faithful all her life. Think of the descendants! Ensure they need never doubt their origins.

I myself needed no such cunning and deception, for I became pregnant and gave birth to a son, whom we called Isaac, and we welcomed him with great joy and were able to laugh again. So, after all, Abraham had a child by his own wife on his one-hundredth birthday. I breastfed Isaac in the privacy of my tent and he grew up healthy and strong. No one doubted the miracle of my late blooming; only Hagar kept whispering that my child had fallen from the sky and not from my belly. Ishmael was probably the only one who eagerly believed her gossip, because he thought his inheritance was at risk. When the day came that little Isaac was weaned from the breast, Abraham threw a big party. Everyone came, the free herders, the slaves, some Canaanite friends, and, of course, Hagar and Ishmael. Their presence at the party was displeasing to me because I knew Hagar's sharp tongue and feared Ishmael's jealousy. My fears turned out to be legitimate: Ishmael, incited by his mother, openly began to joke about where our beloved Isaac had come from. I saw some of the slave girls giggling at his gossip, but fortunately he stayed far away from Abraham, so his vicious words did not disturb my husband's good cheer.

"Sometimes fruit grows on a dried-up tree," mocked Ishmael. "However can that be? Did someone hang the fruit up there to make fools of us? Does someone want to make us believe that a tree whose sap dried up long ago can still bear fruit?"

I went to Abraham in a rage and hissed in his ear, "Send Hagar and her son away, for I do not want my son Isaac to have to share his inheritance with that slave's son one day."

Abraham looked at me in surprise, smiled, and said, "Absolutely not. Ishmael is my son. Don't talk such nonsense."

It was like a slap in the face. I felt humiliated, particularly because I sensed that he had seen through me. It's not wise to show your vulnerability. Reveal your weak spot and you can be sure someone will stab a knife right into it.

So I remained silent, held my head up, and endured the presence of Hagar and Ishmael as if it were no effort. I forced myself to seek out their company and to look them straight in the eye with a superior smile frozen onto my face. Why had I not done that before? They seemed to cower under my gaze and not another inappropriate word crossed their lips.

Why does it take humiliation to find out who you really are? I felt strong and knew I had nothing to fear from Hagar or Ishmael as long as I kept my fear hidden from them. As far as I was concerned, there was no more need to send them away, since I now had an attitude that would silence anyone who threatened me.

But to my surprise Abraham came to me the next day and said, "Listen, Sarah. I have spoken to God. He said that I don't need to worry about the boy or the slave woman. He said, 'You must do whatever Sarah asks.'"

His words took a moment to sink in: "You must do whatever Sarah asks." Praise the Lord! What a glorious, wonderful God we have! Whatever Sarah asks! That does indeed seem to me to be the very best thing that my man—what am I saying?—that *man-kind* could do! I hope womankind takes good heed of this divine message.

But I must confess that, in this one instance, Abraham should not have done as I asked. It cast a shadow over my life and burdened me with guilt.

Early the next morning, Abraham took bread and a skin of water, hung them from Hagar's shoulders, gave her the boy, and sent her away. She headed into the desert of Beersheba, where she would wander.

For the second time, Hagar had been sent into the desert because of my actions, this time with her son, who was also Abraham's son. I knew the two of them would starve out there, and that was an abomination to me. I, who had been so concerned about the children of Sodom, was now sending a child and his mother to their deaths. So unnecessary! My poisonous words had been so unthinking! And those were the very words to which God had consented! Why, God? Why? You are a mystery to me, but I am an even greater mystery to myself. Why did I not stop Abraham? Why did I let him do what I'd asked of him? A crime is a crime, even if the gods approve of it. They grant no forgiveness for the crimes you commit at their command. They demand disobedience, while wanting you to place what is right above all else, even above them. It must be something like that, because listen to what happened next.

I have been told that Ishmael was dying of thirst. Hagar put him down in the shade beneath a bush. She herself went to sit elsewhere, about a bowshot away, because she couldn't watch her child dying. And as she sat there, she cried bitter tears.

But God heard the boy whimpering, and an "angel" called to Hagar from heaven that she should help her son to his feet. Then God opened her eyes and she suddenly saw a well to which she had apparently been blind before. She filled the waterskin and gave water to the boy. Ishmael should not have mocked me, but his death would have been far too harsh a punishment. I have long since forgiven him.

They survived and grew accustomed to life in the desert.

Ishmael became skilled in the use of a bow. I imagine it was for hunting. They went to live in the desert of Paran, and Hagar chose an Egyptian wife for her son.

I hope Ishmael's descendants do not remember my misdeeds and that our peoples can live in peace. That is my hope, but my heart tells me that it will be a long time before we're reconciled.

I'll finish my story here. I have lived a good life in spite of the mistakes I made. I have given my husband the son he wanted for so long. The gods have shown themselves to be merciful and have not punished me for my rebellious nature and for giggling at the wrong moment. My husband and I are old. We do not have long to live, but all of our wishes have been granted. I hope that in the time remaining to us nothing happens to mar our love, since there have been enough tricky moments. I pray to the gods to let us live in peace, so that we may enjoy our last days. Finally, I pray they will protect Isaac, his whole life long.

The Story of Isaac

My father was my hero, and he still is, even though he's no longer alive. He was too great to comprehend. He rose up before me like a mountain of granite that yet held so much fertile soil it flourished like an orchard. He was already one hundred years old when I was born, but I never knew him as anything other than a poker-straight man who took in the world with the eyes of an eagle and ruled his people with the natural ease of a lion.

Abraham! His name resounded over mountains and valleys, carried by the wind; his fame was like fruitful seed scattered all over the land of Canaan. God asked him for advice and, even though he was not a king and we were strangers without our own land, kings recognized him as their peer.

I shall give an example of my father's equal standing with the kings. I was about ten years old when the Philistine king of Gerar paid a visit to Abraham. He was accompanied by his general, Phicol, who was a great orator, but whom alas I did not hear say anything. As we were then living just outside the borders of Philistia, the general led a battalion of Philistine soldiers to protect the king.

I was deeply impressed. The Philistines were a people of warriors who excelled in military ingenuity. Their armor showed they came from afar; no tribe in Canaan had such shields, helmets, or spears. Everything the Philistines carried into battle looked exotic, strange, and therefore terrifying. Their name showed they were once a nomadic tribe like us, that they were once outsiders like us. But now they owned land, constructed cities with impressive temples and palaces, and maintained a strictly disciplined army whose armor shone dazzlingly in the sun. Even my mother, who poked fun at everything and found even the most sublime things ridiculous, was speechless when Abimelech and his men rode into our camp.

What prompted the Philistine king to visit my father outside the borders of his own land? It was this: my father's holdings of livestock and slaves were growing by the year. We regularly crossed the border and grazed our animals on Philistine soil, partly because we felt safer in Philistia than in Canaan. The Philistines were a seafaring people who lived from trade, so the presence of our herds hardly troubled them. The king was increasingly well disposed to our grazing his land, since we spent our money in his cities, but the people Abraham brought with him grew so numerous in some regions they were now the majority. So the king wanted to assure himself of Abraham's loyalty to the Philistine kingdom, or in other words: the king wanted to be certain that Abraham would obey the laws of the land.

After the king and my father had exchanged pleasantries, the king spoke as follows: "The gods appear to stand by you in all your undertakings. So swear to me by the gods, here in this place, that you will never deceive me, my children, or my children's children, but that you will show just as much loyalty to me and to the land where you enjoy such hospitality as I have shown to you."

Even as a ten-year-old boy, I knew this was a reasonable request. When you enjoy someone's hospitality, you should not deceive your host and it's only natural that you should follow the rules of his house.

So Abraham answered immediately and said, "I swear this to you."

They embraced each other and swore eternal friendship but, during the feast that followed, Abraham said, "I'm sorry to have to trouble you with this, but your men in Philistia have taken possession of a well I dug."

I held my breath, because I wasn't sure you could make an accusation like that directly to a king's face. But the king looked helplessly at Abraham and stammered, "I don't know who did that. You have never mentioned this to me before. This is the first I've heard of it."

That was the effect my father had on the great men of the earth. He said what was on his mind and feared no one, and so he grew to be a man of authority, even in the eyes of those who were seldom contradicted and who were not accustomed to criticism.

Abimelech immediately ordered that Abraham's well should be returned to him, confirming that the covenant they had made was not about unilateral subjection but mutual obligation.

Who would not wish to have such an impressive man as a father? As a child I took delight in pleasing him and obeying him in every respect. I would do anything to earn his smile of satisfaction. My mother, though, annoyed me because she always treated him with sullen defiance, and even after he had explained to us that there was only one God, the creator of heaven and earth, that all other gods were idols, statues of wood or stone with no meaning, still she stubbornly spoke about "the gods." How was it possible that she didn't accept the authority of a man who conversed with God as if he were his big brother?

I felt no need to rebel against him; on the contrary, I enjoyed my absolute obedience, because this too can be a pleasure: completely submitting to someone else's authority, surrendering your own will, being devoted to someone who is greater than you. For me, my father and God were one and the same, because God spoke to me through Abraham's mouth, and my ears did not hear God's voice directly. Who would not wish to be the son of a prophet? He shows you the way, he knows how to live, he explains the words God has spoken to him.

My half-brother Ishmael came by now and then, a big, rough man who smelled of wild animals. He drank wine like it was water, he used coarse language, he barked at his father. I could not understand how such people existed. How is it possible to live without respect? Is that not the same as living without food? How can you find your way if you don't ask anyone for directions? I had the distinct impression that he looked down on me because I was not rebellious and because I honored our father. Whenever I meekly said, "Yes, Father," Ishmael burst out laughing as if I were terribly funny, a fool, a buffoon who existed only to entertain him. I was still just a child, and I didn't understand what was wrong with him. I still don't understand, but I know that some people are unable to follow because they're leaders. It was impossible for Ishmael to see his father as his leader, since he desired to be his father's leader. So, such sons also exist: sons who deny they are subordinate.

It surprised me that Ishmael's character was more like my mother's than mine. My mother loved my father, that's for sure, and she was also capable of obeying him and seeing him as her leader, but this was always accompanied by ridicule, sometimes sly and sometimes even overt, as if she constantly wanted to point out that men are comical creatures who cannot be taken seriously. That was something else I found hard to understand, because Abraham's wisdom came directly from God and so it was anything but comical. Her mockery scared me because I feared God. He had crushed the children of Sodom because their parents had done wrong, so he could squeeze me to death between thumb and forefinger to repay my mother's mockery. As I say these words, I can imagine the incomprehension among those who listen to my story. They will say, "Isaac was an unhappy man because he was afraid of God." The opposite is true: I feared God and I rejoiced in my fear, like a bird that happily darts about in the sky, knowing that a bird of prey stalks it high above. My sense of dread made me feel alive; the fear of death danced a lively jig inside my head.

I'm saying this in the hope that you'll understand when I tell you about the event that shaped the rest of my life, that marked me and made me who I am. I was born again, this time not from my mother but from my father, who remade me in his image and likeness.

I was fifteen when my father called me to him one day. He said, "Tomorrow we are going on a journey because God has commanded it. Do not mention it to your mother, for we do not want her to worry. Saddle your donkey and pack your things. We're leaving before sunrise."

It was still dark when two of my father's men woke me. It was Obil, who was in charge of the camels, and Ebal, a man with a face of stone who could tell the most terrible stories without batting an eyelash.

I was surprised my father had chosen these two men as our traveling companions, because they were incorrigible gossips who blabbed about everything, so you could tell them nothing in confidence.

I found my father at the edge of the camp, beside a pack mule laden with firewood. When he saw me looking at the strange load, he said, "We are going to make a sacrifice to God."

It felt as if I had suddenly become a lot taller; my pride made me grow. My father had built various altars throughout the land and had planted sacred trees, but so far he had always visited these places alone. I'm sure he had never taken Ishmael, but now I was allowed to accompany him on his way to God. I was being rewarded for my obedience and for my deep reverence for the god who spoke to me through my father's mouth.

We headed off together, my father and I on our donkeys, with the mule tied to mine, and Obil and Ebal on their camels behind us. The sun rose and began to warm the earth. I tried to control my curiosity and to keep silent until my father spoke, but I couldn't keep it up for long. I asked, "Father, where are we going?"

"To the land of Moriah," said Abraham. "God will show us a mountain there."

I had no idea where Moriah was, but we were riding toward the sun, so I thought it must be somewhere in the east.

The two of us rode on together.

We were silent for a long time. I could see that Abraham was thinking about difficult matters. He looked as if life were weighing heavily on him; his age was painfully visible. I was filled with compassion and the hope that I could do something to comfort him.

"My son," he said, when the sun was already at its highest point. "I waited a long time for you. Know that you are the dearest thing I have."

I saw tears in his eyes, but did not understand where his sadness came from. I was the dearest thing he had and I was with him. Was he saying farewell? Could he feel his death approaching?

On the third day, Abraham pointed at the horizon and said, "There's Moriah."

We rode onward to the foot of a mountain, where we dismounted.

Abraham loaded the firewood onto my back and said to Obil and Ebal, "You stay here with the animals and wait for us. I'll walk on with my son to kneel over there. Then we will return to you."

He took a knife and a burning taper, but nothing else. Something was missing, but at first I didn't know exactly what. My mind was occupied with other thoughts: Abraham had said "then *we* will return to you." That was a relief because I had been afraid that he meant to depart this life on that strange mountain.

We began climbing. The burden on my back grew heavier and heavier, but it lay as light as a feather on my spirit; any yoke that Abraham placed upon me was soft, and I wanted to carry everything for him. If only he would live, if only he would stay with me and not die until I was an old man myself.

We were halfway up the mountain before I finally realized what was missing. My burden should have been much heavier.

"Father?" I said.

"What do you want to say to me, my son?" replied Abraham.

"We have fire and wood," I said. "But where is the lamb for the sacrifice?"

Abraham answered, "God will provide a sacrificial lamb for himself, my son."

We climbed onward. I was delighted by my father's reply. I was going to see a miracle with my own eyes, a divine intervention. God's almighty hand would deliver a sacrificial animal to us so that we didn't have to haul it up the mountain ourselves.

When we had reached the top of the mountain, we worked together to build an altar and arranged the wood on it. After we finished, a silence descended that made my ears hum. I looked around but there was no sign of an animal to sacrifice.

"Father?" I whispered. "Where is the lamb?"

I looked at him longingly, because I wanted to see the miracle occur, but his face was somber; never before had I seen such sadness gathered within him. Again I feared that he was the sacrifice, that he was going to die. Then he finally opened his mouth and said, "Forgive me, my son. You are the lamb."

It took a moment for his words to sink in and for me to decipher them, word by word. I was the lamb that God had chosen to be sacrificed to him. I looked at my father and saw the terrible pain dripping down his cheeks as streams of sweat.

What I felt then is almost impossible to explain to those who come after me. I felt a wild joy flow into my body like a river bursting its banks after a cloudburst. My father, the prophet who talked with God as if he were his big brother, was now being scourged by God as no other man before him. It seemed that he would be crushed under the weight of God, but I, his son, who had never heard a single word from God's mouth, could stand by him and ease his pain with my obedience! I realized that I didn't want to go on living if it meant I would have to be disobedient. My will to live had never been very strong. I lived because I happened to have been born.

I climbed onto the altar, lay down on my back upon the firewood, and said, "Father, tie me up so I cannot escape."

My head was reeling. My longing for total surrender, to give myself up for something that was bigger than me, had unexpectedly been fulfilled, and in such a dramatic way that it felt as if I had ascended high above the mountain and was swooping around in circles up there like a stork. The world was far away, a small and miserable place I would leave in a glorious manner.

My father tied me up. With every turn of the rope my body was bound more tightly to the bed of wood. The more deeply it cut into my skin, the freer I felt.

Abraham took ahold of the knife, clutched it with both hands, and, trembling, raised it into the air, right above my chest. He was sweating blood. He stood there, the very image of terror; he didn't want to do it but he had to. My God, how could I help him?

"Was it you, God?" screamed Abraham. "Was it really you?"

I heard his doubt in the unfamiliar harshness of his voice, so I called, "Father, even if it is not God's will but yours alone, I still want to be your sacrifice!"

But still the knife hovered in the air like a falcon.

"Was it you, God?" screamed Abraham again. "Or was it Satan?"

His sweat and his blood dripped into my eyes, blinding me.

"Do not doubt, Father," I cried. "Have you ever mistaken Satan's voice for God's? Stab me! I beg you!"

And still the knife did not descend. For how long would I be able to face death with joy? When would I too start to doubt? I desperately clung to my death in the hope that being was good, but being a dead man was better.

A deep silence descended.

"Did you hear something?" whispered Abraham.

"No, Father, I heard nothing and there is nothing," I said.

"Yes, there is. Listen carefully. I heard something."

I could see he was all ears, and it was driving me to despair.

"Father," I said. "God has spoken. Obey! I cannot take this any longer, I am the sacrifice, I want to be the sacrifice. The doubt comes from Satan. Do not doubt!"

But the knife would not fall.

"Listen," whispered Abraham. "Listen carefully."

I didn't want to listen, but I obeyed. I could hear rustling in the bushes.

"God is calling me," said Abraham and he lowered the knife until it hung by his knees.

"It's a rustling sound, that's all!" I cried.

My father was listening not to me, but to a voice I couldn't hear. He sank down until he was on his knees and pressed his forehead to the ground.

He stayed there for a long time, time that passed in painful deafness. Then he kneeled back up. He screamed, "Thank you, Lord, but never do that to me again!"

He stood and untied me, still sweating and bleeding, but now his face was so intensely radiant that it actually seemed to be giving off light.

He helped me down from the altar, but I collapsed when I tried to stand. My legs were so resigned to death that they were not yet willing to come back to life. In my mind I had already died, and now I had risen from the dead. I felt an unquenchable anger rise in me as I realized one day I would have to die all over again, even though I'd already suffered those mortal agonies.

"Father!" I groaned. "What are you doing? Have you forsaken God?"

Abraham smiled beatifically.

"No, my son," he said.

His bliss irritated me beyond measure. Had it all been for show? Had my father just wanted to make the point that I was nothing compared to him?

"Come, get up," he said. "A miracle has occurred."

He pointed at the rustling bush.

I scrambled to my feet and leaned on his arm. I looked. I saw a ram whose horns had become entangled in the bushes. The sacrifice. I remembered that during our climb to the top of the mountain I'd been hoping for such a miracle, but now that it was happening before my eyes, I didn't care. I would rather have been the miracle myself, the boy who sacrificed himself to make his father's piety known to the whole world.

Abraham grabbed the animal, bound it to the altar, and sacrificed it in my stead.

He said, "The Lord has provided a sacrificial animal. He does not want any child sacrifices."

"Oh," I said. I didn't know what else to say. As much as I wanted to submit to my father's god, I couldn't help thinking he could just as easily have made that known when we were at the foot of the mountain.

As the smoke from the burnt offering rose to the heavens, we descended the mountain. My confusion gradually cleared, until I was relatively capable of thinking again. I realized that my father had already lowered his knife even before he'd seen the ram in the bushes. What had been going on in his mind?

When we reached Obil and Ebal, Abraham said, "Before we leave, I want to tell you what happened, but you must promise not to tell anyone else."

I almost burst out laughing—an inheritance from my mother—because Obil and Ebal were such notorious blabbermouths; there really were no bigger gossips to be found among the slaves. Their vow of silence would be worth nothing and I couldn't imagine that my father didn't know that. Unlike my mother, though, I can keep a straight face, so no one noticed my amusement.

Abraham told the eagerly listening serfs about God's terrible command, about the altar on the mountain, about the raised knife. "But then," said Abraham, "I heard someone calling my name: 'Abraham, Abraham!' And I said: 'I am listening.' I knew that I had heard God's voice. 'Do not touch that boy,' said God. 'Do not harm him! For now I know that you fear me: you did not wish to withhold your son from me.' So I lowered the knife."

Then he told them about the ram in the bushes, the miracle that spared his son. "This is God's message to the world," he concluded. "He does not want child sacrifices."

Neither Obil nor Ebal spoke a word, but I could see they were itching to tell Abraham's story to anyone who would listen. And then suddenly I realized that had been Abraham's intention. He wanted the story to be spread among the people. All of Canaan had to know that God did not want child sacrifices.

Unfortunately he'd overlooked one terrible flaw in his plan: the story would also reach my mother.

"Is it true what people are saying?"

I heard my mother's shriek of rage all the way through several layers of tent cloth. I ran inside because I knew what it was about. She stood in front of my father, who was sitting on the ground, and her body was bent over him like a drawn bow: "Is it true? Is it true?" she asked.

My father nodded, but he didn't dare look at her.

"You laid your son on an altar to slaughter him?"

My father nodded helplessly.

"But, Mother," I protested.

She flashed me a look like a lightning strike.

"And you let him lead you like a lamb to the slaughter, you idiot?"

I was silent. I knew she would not understand, no matter what I said. We lived in different worlds. I couldn't understand her defiance and she couldn't fathom my obedience.

She called Abraham all the wicked and ugly names under the sun. He suffered it with resignation, like a villain being flogged. He had no defense.

I cannot understand anyone thinking they can oppose God. He is almighty, he decides what is right and what is not. He punishes us without our understanding why. He is everything to us; we are nothing to him.

"God said this, God said that," snorted Sarah. "What kind of loser are you? I'm glad God didn't try that on me. What were you thinking, you lump of chicken shit? What fool would obey a command so criminal? Have you gone insane?"

And she went on and on. The curses tumbled over and over one another like stones in a rockslide. Abraham let them come down upon his head without defending himself.

"Are you the man who dared to say to God, 'You just can't do that!' when you wanted to save Sodom? How is it that in your old age you've become such a brown-nosed coward? Huh? Explain that to me! Were you truly willing to slaughter your own son for God? Tell me, were you?"

Abraham nodded as the tears trickled down his cheeks.

I could bear it no longer. I pushed Sarah away from Abraham, stood in front of her, and said, "Not another word, Mother. That's enough."

Fleetingly, she looked into my eyes, and then she turned around and ran weeping from the tent.

I kneeled beside Abraham and put my arm around his shoulders. He looked up and said, "Love your mother, my son."

How could I love her when she was cursing my father, the prophet who heard God's voice while the rest of humankind turned a deaf ear!

"Listen carefully to me," said Abraham. "What would you have thought of a mother who rejoiced in our sacrifice? Wouldn't you rather have a mother who protects her child like a lioness? Sarah is such a mother. Do you think God doesn't understand her? God himself didn't want our sacrifice, did he? Was he not like a mother when he sent us a ram that became entangled in the bushes? Love your mother and be the comfort of her old age."

I did my best but a deep gulf had opened up between the two of us. Things were never the same again between my mother and father either. Sarah silently did her duty, but she never reached out to my father again. She stayed with him because she could not live without him, but at the same time she could barely put up with him. Silence hung about her like armor, and everything she did showed that she had had enough, that she no longer wanted to live. That was the sacrifice my father and I had unwittingly made: a woman's heart. The knife that spared me left Sarah's heart too wounded to beat for anyone or anything ever again.

She died that same year. My father was inconsolable, and I was powerless in the face of his grief. All I could do for him was rouse him from his deep mourning and point out that we had no grave where we could bury my mother. We were still strangers in a strange land, where we had no right to own our own ground.

We were close to Hebron in Canaan, at a time when the city was in the hands of the Hittites. The city lay far beyond the borders of Hatti, their homeland, and was surrounded by hostile Canaanite tribes. I suspected they would be well disposed toward my father, who could mobilize a large army. So we went to Hebron to meet them. They welcomed us warmly and we met with a large number of landowners at the city gate.

Abraham spoke, stammering with grief. He said, "I live as a stranger among you. Please give me a grave of my own here, so that I may carry my deceased wife from her tent and bury her."

The Hittites replied, "My lord, we regard you as a prince favored by the gods. Bury your wife in the best grave we have. None of us will refuse you his grave and prevent you from burying her there."

The Hittites were right: my father was not just some nomadic herdsman. His possessions had multiplied, year after year, and with the number of people in his service he could easily have filled a small city. If he stayed near Hebron, he and his armed men would be able to offer the city and surrounding land protection from the bands of Canaanite robbers and marauders. The Hittites did well to give him a foothold on their land.

To my surprise, my father already had a grave in mind. The cave of Machpelah. I had never heard of it, but the name rolled off my father's tongue with the ease of a man to whom the word was familiar.

Abraham bowed deeply to the Hittites and said, "So if you agree that I may carry my wife from her tent and bury her, please be so kind as to urge Ephron, the son of Zohar, to relinquish the cave of Machpelah to me."

Ephron! The son of Zohar! How did my father know these Hittite men? He must have had his ear to the ground long before my mother had passed away. Like a real prince, he wanted to know all about everything that happened around him and to be aware of every important man in the region. Those without land are safe nowhere; we have no walls to hide behind, no powerful king to protect us. I learned then, in Hebron among the Hittites, how important it is to keep informed, to gather knowledge, all throughout our lives. I shall later give the right of the firstborn to the son who is willing to learn, even if he is not the eldest, because my tribe must be educated if it wishes to survive.

Oh, happy chance! This Ephron, son of Zohar, was present at the meeting at the city gate! Abraham was aware of that, of course. They knew each other and had apparently met before. I understood later that this was also part of my father's strategy: know your neighbors, show interest and respect, even if they speak a different language, have different customs, and worship different gods.

"Listen, my lord," said Ephron. He looked at my father, his eyes soft and velvet like a deer's. "I give you the cave of Machpelah and the field that surrounds it. With these men of my tribe as my witnesses, I give it to you so that you may bury your wife there."

My mother would surely have chuckled at Ephron's words and I too felt the urge, knowing Ephron's "gift" would prove to be an expensive one. Accepting Ephron's generous gesture without payment would not please the Hittites, for Abraham was known as a wealthy man. Our problem was also one of urgency: my mother had to be buried that same day. We were in need and Ephron knew it.

"I want to pay the price the field is worth," said Abraham. "Please accept the money from me and allow me to bury my wife there."

"All right, then," said Ephron. And again I was struck by the softness of his gaze. "You are rich. Four hundred silver shekels are nothing to you."

What a swindler! For one silver shekel you could buy a thousand square yards of ground! I didn't know exactly how big Ephron's field was, but it was certainly nowhere near eighty acres.

Abraham acted as if four hundred shekels was the current market value for Ephron's little field and paid him in pieces of silver.

That bought him not only his first piece of land in Canaan, but also the continuing friendship of the Hittites. When you are a minority in a strange land, friendship is expensive.

So in just one day I learned several lessons that I knew had to be passed on to my descendants. We tell stories to hand on the wisdom our ancestors have acquired. Sometimes we add a little wisdom of our own, and so the accumulation of knowledge grows and enables us to lead a good life.

We returned to our camp outside the city, took my mother's body from her tent, and laid her on a bier that was carried by four slaves. My father and I followed behind, and as we approached the cave we set foot on our own land for the first time. My father made everyone stop for a moment to allow his dead wife to experience this great moment, even though her spirit had already departed. Never before had we owned land, never before had we been able to say: This belongs to us. Sarah had died too soon, she had surrendered too early to her resentment of what God had asked from us, for behold what he had now given us: the ground beneath our feet.

When I had reached a marriageable age, my very elderly father took the decision that a wife should be found for me. It could not be a Canaanite, since the Canaanite women stubbornly worshiped the wrong gods and my father also found them no good in other respects. So he ordered Eliezer, his senior servant, to travel to Mesopotamia, the land whence Abraham came, and specifically to the city of Haran, where his family had remained.

Before he left, Eliezer had to swear an oath of allegiance. The manner in which he did this might puzzle future generations, because Abraham dusted off an ancient tradition whose meaning he probably no longer understood himself. Eliezer had to place his hand "under the thigh" of Abraham, but you can take it from me that the expression is a euphemism. Old Eliezer hesitated because he didn't know exactly where to put his hand. He held it out, trembling.

"Lower," said Abraham.

Eliezer's hand went lower.

"To the side," said Abraham.

Aha, so that's where Eliezer was supposed to be: with his hand on Abraham's member, or to put it in my mother's mischievous words: he had to swear with his hand on his part. It sounds rather comical or even inappropriate to us now, but I can assure you the ritual was carried out with due ceremony and that both old men were full of the solemnity of the moment. I saw it myself, for I was there.

Abraham said, "I want you to go to the land I come from, to my family, and to search there for a wife for my son Isaac."

"Can I go with him?" I asked. I thought it would be good to see my future bride myself before I married her. Besides, I was curious about distant Mesopotamia, about which I'd heard so many tales.

"No," said Abraham sternly. "You're staying here."

I didn't understand at the time why my father would not even consider my request, but I do now. He had left his land and his family, and he was scared that I would do the same, but in the opposite direction.

Eliezer understood what I wanted. He said, "Perhaps the woman will refuse to come with me to this country. If that's the case, should I take your son back to the land you left behind?" I saw through the old fox's cunning: if necessary, he'd make sure the woman refused to go with him, so allowing me to go fetch her myself.

But my father did not want me to leave Canaan.

"No," he said, "under no circumstances are you to take my son back there. If the woman refuses to come with you, you're released from your vow."

I was troubled by his suspicion and for the first time I felt a certain estrangement from him. I had always been obedient and subservient to him, so I didn't understand why he would give me so little freedom. I came to the decision that there should be more distance between us, and that I should separate my herd from his and begin my own household. While Eliezer readied himself for the journey, I took down my tents and set off for the Negev with my herd. It was hard for me to say farewell to my father, particularly because I saw sadness in his elderly eyes, but I had no choice. Obedience is good, but captivity kills the soul. I departed. I took my mother's tent with me as a memory of her, and so I would have a place to mourn her. I ordered the slave Keturah to take care of my father, secretly hoping he would take her as his wife so that he wouldn't have to spend his old age alone.

It took forever for Eliezer to return. In the beginning I counted the days, then the weeks, and finally the months. When his caravan eventually appeared, I ran toward him. A girl was riding beside him. She slipped down from her camel and covered herself with her veil, because I was not permitted to see her until we were married. I don't know where this peculiar custom comes from: my father had known Sarah since she was a young girl, and I couldn't understand why there should be any objection. "I want to see you!" screamed a voice inside me, but I had to be patient, so I just kissed her hand and asked for her name.

"Rebekah," she said.

Rebekah! I'd never before heard a girl's name that sounded so melodious. How many girls in the future would want to be called Rebekah? Countless, I should think. Her name sounded like health, like being well fed, like a lust for life, like everything I was lacking. How wisely Eliezer had chosen!

We gave her into the care of the slave girls and of Deborah, the nurse who had traveled with her. I hastily pulled Eliezer with me to my tent, because I wanted to hear all about his journey and especially about her, Rebekah, my bride.

"Is she beautiful?" I asked before even sitting down. Not a very intelligent question, but ah, I'm only human.

"She is the most beautiful girl I have ever seen," said Eliezer.

That was good news. I could feel life flowing into me as if I were rising from the dead.

"Tell me," I said eagerly, "how did you find her?"

"When I arrived in the land your father comes from, I knew I needed help to find the right girl," said Eliezer. "Then I thought about my master's god, because he seems to be powerful and more helpful than all the other gods. I sat down beside a spring and said, 'If you really wish my undertaking to succeed . . .' I had to stop and think about what I wanted to ask of God. I said, 'If a young woman comes from the city to draw water and I say to her, Will you please give me a little water from your pitcher? and if she replies, Drink, and I'll draw some water for your camels as well, then let that be the woman you have chosen for my master's son.'"

"And?" I asked. "Is that how it happened?"

I could see Eliezer was embarrassed and didn't want to answer. He bowed his head as if ashamed.

"What's wrong?" I asked. "Don't worry. This is just between the two of us."

Eliezer looked up. "Are you sure you won't give me away when your father questions you?"

I put my hand "under his thigh" and said, "I swear."

"All right, then," said Eliezer. "I didn't think the first girl who gave me water and drew water for the camels was very, um . . . suitable."

I couldn't help myself: a grin appeared on my face, a smile that stretched from ear to ear.

"So I said to myself, 'Lord God, this surely cannot be her? This girl is ugly and fat.'"

I burst out laughing—an inheritance from my mother. I had kept my laughter on a leash for a long time, but it had pulled itself free now and was darting around inside me.

Eliezer was shocked and said, "You're laughing, but no one must hear of this. And that includes Rebekah."

I vigorously shook my head and said, "I shall be as silent as the grave."

"A second girl came along," Eliezer told me shyly, "but she was too, um . . ."

"Not very suitable?" I asked. I managed to keep a straight face. Eliezer nodded.

"But listen now to God's mysterious ways. The third girl was amazingly beautiful and I thought, 'This one will surely be too conceited to give me a drink and she certainly won't draw water for the camels.' But she smiled sweetly and gave me a drink and drew water for the camels. And that's not all. Here's the real miracle: she turned out to be your uncle Nachor's granddaughter!"

I am telling you this story because it taught me that my father's god trusts in us to use our own good sense, not to think everything will work out by itself, not to believe we don't have to make any decisions of our own. I owed Rebekah to Eliezer's good judgment; with God's help, he'd used his own good sense. I was not to tell my father, since he would not be sure Rebekah was the woman God intended for me. So I was silent. But now I am an old man, my father died long ago, and Eliezer is no more. For me there is no question that Rebekah was God's choice; it was her, because she gave me new life. What is life? It is guessing what is good and what is bad, guessing which path is best to follow, and guessing at God's will.

I took Rebekah to my mother's tent, which from that moment on belonged to her. After we married, I saw her without a veil. Eliezer was right: she was beautiful.

To my delight, Abraham took the slave Keturah as his wife. My father had apparently found his appetite again, because to my surprise Keturah bore one child after another: Zimran, Jokshan, Medan, Midian, Ishbak, and Shuah. I would appreciate it if you could learn to recite these names by heart—in reverse order too. Only after my father's death did I discover that he had also had a considerable number of children with his concubines, but he sent all of them away, having showered them with gifts, to the land of the east, far from me. I do not know their names.

Abraham turned 175 years old. When he died, I sent a large number of scouts into the desert to track down Ishmael. I anticipated difficulties if I excluded him from my father's funeral.

Ishmael was found. We buried Abraham in the cave of Machpelah, next to my mother. Then Ishmael and I solemnly said farewell. All that had connected us was our father. Now that he had died, we knew we would not see each other again. I have to confess the farewell was a relief, since Ishmael was a ruffian who stank of the blood of wild animals, a man who had not learned another thing since he mastered the bow. I thought I was rid of him for good, but around the time I'd almost forgotten him, much to my dismay, I had a son who looked just like him. It seems that nothing ever really disappears, and no problem is ever truly solved.

We had to wait twenty years for Rebekah to become pregnant. I began to fear that she was facing the same fate as my mother: that she would bear a child only through a miracle of God. But it didn't come to that. She became pregnant at an age that did not suggest divine intervention. She was just a girl when I married her, she could afford to wait twenty years, and besides she bore not one fruit in her womb, but two, which I feel more than compensated for those lost years. Rebekah knew even before the birth that she was going to have twins, because she could feel a fight going on inside her belly. There was such kicking and shoving that she despaired, and said, "If it's going to be like this, why should I live?" She foresaw jealousy and strife between her children, a violent rift within our family, murder and mayhem. It drove her to despair even before they were born.

The idea is that people should learn from their experiences. That's why we tell stories. I knew what jealousy could do: it was because of jealousy that Cain killed Abel and Hagar was driven into the desert, and jealousy flared up within Ishmael whenever he saw me. The children inside Rebekah's belly already seemed to be consumed by jealousy.

One day Rebekah came to me in my tent and said, "Listen. God has told me something."

I have to confess I wasn't pleased, since God seemed to talk to everyone except me, but before my jealousy could ignite, I thought of Cain, who had also suffered because of God's silence, and it had led him to murder.

I said, "Tell me what he said, Rebekah."

"He said, 'Two nations are within your belly, two peoples who have parted before you have even given birth. One will be more powerful than the other; the elder will serve the younger.'"

Rebekah laid her hands upon her belly as if trying to defuse the little war that was going on in there.

I was speechless for a long time, because if those truly were God's words, he was announcing that he was going to break his own law. We understood it was a divine law for the elder son to rule over the younger one, and not the other way around. It seemed that I was being told to choose the younger one as my heir and to disinherit the elder. I knew this would only fan the flames of the jealousy that burned between my children even before their birth and turn it into a raging inferno, and I thought: This command is so foolish that it cannot have come from God. I refuse to carry it out. My firstborn son will be my heir, and no one but him.

For this is our most important task, to let good sense prevail over the prophetic word.

Rebekah was right. She gave birth to twins, and two boys who could not have been more different. The elder was a redhead with hair all over his body, as if he were wearing a coat made of hair. We called him Esau, which means "the hairy one." When his little brother appeared, he was holding onto Esau's heel. We called him Jacob, which means "he who grasps the heel." Jacob was an ordinary infant, smooth and hairless.

The two boys developed as their infant physiques predicted. Esau became a big-mouthed bruiser who loved the outdoors, while Jacob was a quiet and gentle boy who preferred to stay close to the tents. Esau irritated me because he was so like my half-brother Ishmael in every respect, but I forced myself not to show any sign of my dislike. On the contrary, because Jacob was clearly Rebekah's favorite, I encouraged Esau to believe that I preferred him to his brother. I really did everything I could to ensure Esau had no reason for jealousy.

Esau learned to use the bow, just like Ishmael, and he became a hunter, just like Ishmael, and as soon as he was a great marksman, he learned nothing more, just like Ishmael. I began to understand why God did not see Esau as the right heir, but I didn't understand why he, who is all-powerful, had allowed him to be born first. Sometimes I wonder why God thrusts conflict upon humans; it's almost as if he doesn't wish us to live in peace with one another. What could his intention be? Or does he have no intention? I hope one day to find the answer, but I doubt one exists.

To please Esau I pretended to have a particular fondness for wild game, and I stuffed my face with the birds and small animals that he shot for me. It even reached the point where Rebekah accused me of favoring Esau over Jacob, so I knew I was playing my part well. The very opposite was true: Jacob was my favorite because he was thoughtful and eager to learn. He listened attentively to the stories of our forefathers, while Esau, tired from the hunt, fell asleep at the first words. I felt that the great tribe born of Abraham should not be made up of thoughtless hunters, but of contemplative herders who ruminated upon the world as their animals grazed around them. Ours should not be a tribe that sought out excitement, but insight.

My dilemma hung above my head like a thundercloud. No matter how hard I tried to convince Esau of my love, a day would come when I would have to deprive him of his right as my firstborn son. How was I to do that without his knowing he'd been deceived by his own loving father? To my relief, Jacob came to my assistance.

This is what Rebekah told me: Jacob had been cooking lentil soup when Esau came home exhausted from the hunt. He was a man whose needs had to be satisfied immediately. When he was tired, he slept; when he was thirsty, he drank; when he wanted a woman, he jumped on one. When Esau came to Jacob's tent he was hungry. He said, "Quick, give me some of that red stew you're cooking." For that reason, Esau is sometimes called "Edom," because that means "red."

Jacob knew the smell of his soup would prove irresistible to such an impulsive man as Esau and so he seized the opportunity with both hands. He said, "I will give you food if you sell me your birthright."

No one would pay such a ridiculously high price for a bowl of soup—no one except Esau. He said, "If I don't eat now, I'll die of hunger, and if I am dead what good is my birthright to me?" And he reached out his hand for the bowl that Jacob held out to him.

"Swear it to me right now," said Jacob.

So Esau did. He sold his birthright for a bowl of soup and some bread.

Have you ever heard anything like it?

Esau ate and drank and then left without a word, as if nothing had happened. I loved him, but that indifference made him completely unfit to be the forefather of the tribe that had been promised to Abraham.

There was something else. When Esau was forty, he married Judith and the fragrant Basemath, both of whom were Hittite women. This was an abomination both to Rebekah and to me, for they worshiped the wrong gods. Esau was completely indifferent about that as well. He did not follow in his forefathers' footsteps because he had never listened to the stories I told about them. Rebekah and I resolved not to show any sign of our displeasure, because we knew Esau's fiery nature and were afraid that in his fury he could commit a crime.

There was one problem remaining. The right of the firstborn concerns the legacy and the transfer of property. The firstborn is entitled to a double share and Esau had thrown it away. He had only himself to blame and I think he was well aware of that, because he didn't appear to hold a grudge. But I knew I had to give my paternal blessing to my elder son before my death, as Abraham had done to me. That blessing would confirm that my son was my successor, my spiritual heir, the head of the family, and that only *his* children would be seen as the descendants of Abraham and Isaac.

But I could not give Esau the blessing, since he was not the right recipient. This problem had occurred before, for I was not Abraham's firstborn son. Abraham had passed over his firstborn Ishmael in my favor, not only because I was born to Sarah, but also because Ishmael's character was unsuitable for the nation that

Abraham had in mind. He too broke a divine law in order to please God.

Two things combined: my age and Rebekah's love for Jacob. In my old age, my eyesight declined rapidly and Rebekah saw it as a sign that my end was approaching. She feared I would die before giving Jacob my blessing. I too had the sense that my days were numbered. I always searched for opportunities to make Esau feel that he was my favorite, so I said one day, "Listen, Esau, I am old and any day could be my last. Take your quiver and your bow, go into the field and hunt some wild game for me. Prepare it for me in the way that I like and bring it to me to eat."

Esau asked, "Then will you give me your blessing?"

His question pained me. I should have told him the truth, but I didn't dare. I was afraid he would go out and kill Jacob. I said, "The roast meat will give me the strength to bless you before I die."

It was a terrible lie and I desperately wondered how I was going to get myself out of this awful dilemma.

Delighted, Esau leapt to his feet and ran out of my tent. The sound of his footsteps quickly disappeared and, when all was quiet, I heard some movement at the side of the tent. I knew someone had been eavesdropping and I could guess who it was: Rebekah. I heard her running off to her tent. Soon after that I smelled roasting meat and I thought: That cannot be Esau's wild game, because he can't possibly be back from the hunt yet. I began to suspect what Rebekah was planning and a deep gratitude filled my heart. That woman really knew what she was doing! She was my rock and my comfort.

My heart pounding, I waited for the events that would follow. There was a storm inside my head, and my thoughts hopped and skipped around like wild rabbits. How could I know what was the right thing to do? Did God want me to deceive a fellow human being, my own son? Was I to build a nation based on lies and deceit? Did the god of Abraham, the Righteous One, want me to sin for him?

Parts of the stories that had been told to me raced through my head. Who had tempted Eve to eat the forbidden fruit? The snake or God himself? Who had provoked Cain to murder his brother? Who had challenged Shelah to build a tower that reached to the heavens? Who had ordered Abraham to become his son's murderer? Am I saying too much if I say that God is a mystery? Was it God's voice that told Rebekah to allow the younger son to rule over the elder?

God alone knows.

I am blind, but still I see. I can see the good, just as clearly as the bad. Rebekah, Jacob, and I were going to do something wicked in order to please God. Or rather: to please the god we believed to be God, because it's also possible that we had followed our own wicked urges, without god or command. Who can say?

Someone was approaching, along with the scent of roasted meat. I could tell it was a man from the footsteps. He came into the tent and I immediately knew who it was. I am blind, but still I see. Although the man smelled like Esau, I knew it was Jacob. The meal he had brought in a cooking pan was roast meat, but it didn't come from a wild animal. The deception was cleverly done; they'd thought of everything.

"Father?" he said.

"Yes, my son," I replied. "Which one are you?"

Oh yes, I confess, I wanted to make him drink the cup of his deceit right down to the last drop. I wanted to hear him speak the lie loud and clear, not to remove the blame from myself, but to let God hear the depths to which man must sink in order to do his will.

"I am Esau," said Jacob, "your firstborn son. I have done as you asked of me. Come, sit up and eat some of what I've killed, for it will give you strength to bless me."

He could at least have made more of an effort to imitate Esau's voice, because it sounded nothing like him. Esau suddenly had the voice of a smooth-cheeked boy! I had the urge to tease him a little, I don't know exactly why, but maybe it's simply this: rogues like me like a good laugh. I asked, "How were you able to find something so quickly, my son?"

I heard his breathing become faster. He must have had an answer prepared, but saying it seemed to be a struggle. I could smell his sweat.

"Because the Lord, your god, ensured my success."

So that was the answer Rebekah and Jacob had come up with. They had invented an Esau who had suddenly become incredibly pious. It was God himself who had helped Esau to find his game so quickly!

I still hadn't had enough. I wanted more sweat from my "Esau." I wanted to wallow in wickedness as a bird delights in a sand bath.

I said, "Come a little closer, my son, so that I may feel whether you are truly Esau."

Jacob came and stood beside me and I touched his hands. They'd even thought of that! They were as hairy as Esau's! It clearly wasn't human hair but what did that matter? I imagined Jacob was wearing some sort of gloves made of goatskin, the knave! I mumbled, loud enough to be understood, "It's Jacob's voice, but Esau's hands."

Jacob was shaking.

"Are you truly my son Esau?" I asked.

"Yes," replied Jacob.

So the lie was complete. I took no pleasure in it; life was bitter. "Then bring the meat closer to me," I said, "so that I may eat." I ate the meat and drank the wine and the bitter taste disappeared. I wondered how many lies and deceits men swallow along with their food and drink.

Just one more thing, I thought. I wanted him to feel the full weight of his betrayal one more time. I said, "Come closer, my son, and kiss me."

The kiss is an expression of affection, of trust, of connection, but it can also be an instrument of treachery and deceit. How deep man falls when he employs his most tender gesture in the service of a lie!

Jacob came closer and kissed me. His clothes smelled of blood and meat, of animals' mortal fear. In other words, they smelled of Esau. In the future, "donning Esau's clothes" would become an expression signifying artful deceit. Oh, Rebekah, where did you learn to clothe your lie so well, right down to the smallest of details? When did you turn into a plotter who would use any means to get her own way? I know where, I know when. You were a sweet and innocent girl until you became pregnant, here in the Negev, and God confused your mind with his strange command.

Both Rebekah and I thought we were doing evil at God's behest and maybe that was true, but at the same time our badness was also goodness, because Esau was not worthy to become the forefather of our tribe. If one can do right by doing wrong, is it not also possible to do wrong by doing right? I don't know the answer. I add it as a question to the experiences my ancestors and I are handing down to our descendants as our life story.

I had to give Jacob my blessing, but before I began to recite the formula, I gave him one last venomous sting. I said, "The smell of my son is like the smell of the field."

Then I blessed him:

> May God give you the dew of the heaven
> and rich, fertile earth,
> and an abundance of grain and wine.
> May nations serve you,
> and people bow down before you.
> May you be master above your brothers,
> and have power over your mothers' sons.
> Cursed be he who curses you,
> blessed he who blesses you.

By speaking those words, I made Jacob the master and Esau the slave of his brother. The evil had been done.

Jacob slipped out of the tent and I knew the worst was yet to come. When Esau came I would have to bear my own feigned innocence and his grief. I would have to keep up my playacting because it was better for Esau to remain unaware that his father and mother were part of the conspiracy that had been forged against him.

Jacob had only just left when Esau returned from the hunt. He made a tasty dish of his wild game and brought it into the tent. He said, "Sit up, Father, sit up and eat some of what your son has killed, for it will give you strength to bless me."

This was the big moment. I asked in an anxious voice: "Who are you?"

"It's me, Esau, your son, your firstborn."

I let a long silence fall. It was meant to show my horror. Then I cried out with a voice like that of a sheep being slaughtered: "So who was it that just brought me food and to whom I gave my blessing?"

I took advantage of Esau's stupefied silence to add, "And that blessing will remain upon him forever!" Because a blessing is a blessing, even if it is taken from a father by deceit. Which is actually pretty strange now that I come to think about it. Why can't a blessing be undone?

Once Esau had grasped the meaning of my words, he immediately knew who had played the trick on him. He uttered a wild, desperate cry that cut through my soul like a knife. He begged me, "Bless me, bless me too, Father!"

But I had nothing left for him.

I loved Esau. I loved his roughness, his zest for life, and his courage, particularly because I didn't possess those qualities myself. And yet I felt akin to Jacob, while with Esau I'd always wondered how in God's name I'd come to have such a child.

My hands were empty; I had nothing to offer Esau. I knew he had sought out the company of Ishmael in the desert and that seemed perfectly natural to me. Esau had been born into the wrong family.

"That heel-grabber has cheated me twice now!" roared Esau. "First he took my birthright and now he has taken my blessing! Do you truly have no blessing left for me?"

No, I did not. I said, "I have made him lord and master over you. So what is there that I can do for you, my son?"

"Do you have only one blessing, Father?"

That was a good question. Why should a father have only one blessing to give? Couldn't I give Esau a kind of secondhand blessing, a consolation prize? I knew no formula for a blessing that placed a son in a position of subservience while also offering him some consolation, so I quickly cobbled together a creation of my own.

"All right, then," I said. "Because it's you."

I laid my hand on his head and said:

> You will live far from the fertile ground,
> far from the heavenly dew.
> You will live by your sword
> and serve your brother.
> But once you tear yourself free,
> you will cast his yoke from your neck.

Those last two lines were the only consolation I could offer. I could do no more, and yet it was clearly not enough for Esau.

He leapt furiously to his feet and screamed, "I do not want to cause you grief and so I will not kill Jacob until after you are dead, but one thing is certain, he will not outlive his father by even a single day!"

He ran out of the tent and left camp with his two wives. I was fairly certain that he'd gone to seek consolation from Ishmael.

He'd shouted his threat so loudly that it didn't surprise me the whole camp had heard, and anyone who had not heard found out about it soon enough. It wasn't long before Rebekah came scuttling into the tent, scared as a wounded rabbit, with Jacob trailing behind her.

"I heard that Esau wants to murder the son you blessed," said Rebekah.

I said nothing for a long time. I heard both Jacob and Rebekah panting anxiously.

"That has not escaped my attention," I said finally.

Rebekah was evidently expecting me to say something more, but I said nothing. I thought the conspirators should solve their problem themselves.

"Jacob must leave," said Rebekah.

"Oh," I said.

I'd had enough. Esau would live out the rest of his days in the desert; Jacob would have to take refuge in strange lands. I found life tiring. It had not brought me what I'd hoped. It would have been better if Abraham's knife had actually struck home, then I wouldn't have had to live through this.

"He must go to Haran, to my brother Laban, for he will be safe there," said Rebekah.

I did not agree and I did not disagree. I was empty inside and found nothing but despondency in my heart.

"And besides," said Rebekah, "what if Jacob also takes a Hittite bride? We already have enough misery with those wives of Esau and their grisly gods! Jacob has to marry a girl from my family."

Then I awoke from my lethargy because that sounded to me like a divine command. I had made the right son my successor but what would my decision be worth if Jacob married the wrong woman? I wanted my people to inherit the god of Adam, Noah, and Abraham, and no other deity. I wanted a mother for my grandchildren who would pass on our stories intact, and where better to find such a person than in our own family?

I said to Jacob, "Leave this place, go to Haran and marry one of the daughters of Laban, your mother's brother."

Those are the last words I spoke to my chosen son. I heard that he left the next day. Rebekah cried but I did not, because I had cried all my tears years before.

I never saw Esau again either. I heard he took a third wife, a daughter of Ishmael, probably because he thought he would find favor with me, since she was a girl from our family, but all it confirmed was his kinship with Ishmael, the man rightly cast out by my father.

I don't have much longer to live; my time is up. I can't complain: Rebekah was a good wife to me and I've grown rich. My possessions are so numerous I am unable to count them, but I really have no need for it all. My will to live has always remained a tender shoot within me; death has called to me from an early age. When I am dead, I will be rewarded with eternal oblivion. Nothing else can touch me in that realm, and I will finally have peace. I thank God for having made our lives finite.

The Story of Ben-Oni

I am Ben-Oni, the youngest of my brothers and yet the only one to recognize the vizier of Egypt as soon as I saw him. I knew who he was but said nothing to my half-brothers, so it seemed that I, too, was willfully blind. But I recognized him, believe me, because I saw my mother's smile in his. I never knew my mother—she died at my birth—but my father said to me, "If you want to see your mother, just look at your brother's smile." I am the youngest, and, since people rarely listen to the youngest, also the quietest son.

I rarely spoke up, but my head was full of stories, because I am good at both listening and remembering. I soaked up conversations, events, and experiences like a sponge. It would have taken only a squeeze for a torrent of words to come pouring out, but no one ever squeezed. I had to wait until I had children of my own before my stories could emerge and find a home in their wide-open ears.

As I had been brooding on my words for so long, without allowing them to hatch like eggs, I had plenty of time to consider their meaning. What were the stories I had been told actually about? What was their message?

I came to the conclusion that much of what I had heard was about jealousy. Wasn't Eve jealous of Adam because of the easy relationship he had with his creator? Wasn't Adam jealous of Eve for her open curiosity about the forbidden? Was it not jealousy that made Cain kill his brother? And what about the jealousy of Sarah, who drove Hagar into the desert, or the treacherous jealousy of Jacob and Esau? I learned from all those stories that jealousy is an all-destructive force, a toxic source of evil, a pool of misery that never seems to dry up. And, in all of this, "God" played a role, a god who did not seem free from jealousy himself; after all, where did my parents' dislike of the Canaanite gods come from? Are people not free to worship the gods they love best? I had the distinct impression that my parents' god found the existence of other gods a nuisance and wanted to expel them from the minds of men. I wonder, too, if the god of Abraham, Isaac, and Jacob was plagued by jealousy just as humans are—or perhaps I should phrase it differently and wonder if God, in fact, is human. Does he have the same qualities as human beings? Does he know vindictiveness, jealousy, blind rage, as humans do? It is possible to reach that conclusion on the basis of the stories about the Flood and the destruction of Sodom. Was God not a little jealous of Eve for taking Adam's attention away from him? Was he not jealous of Isaac because Abraham loved him above all else? For now, I shall just say that God is a mystery to me.

I was brought up in a household that seethed with jealousy. A chasm full of hissing snakes yawned between the children of my father's two wives. Where did all that jealousy come from?

My father told me that my mother Rachel was a playful little lamb and that her sister was a dull worker bee. They were my father's two wives, sisters, who in their childhood had had no reason to compete with each other. Leah, as the elder of the two, would be first to marry, and Rachel could marry only after that, but then Jacob came along and chose Rachel, the younger sister, over Leah. That's when the seed was planted. Jealousy grew rampant in the minds of both sisters, who before had known nothing of envy and resentment.

When Jacob took the firstborn's blessing from his father by means of deceit, he ignited a furious jealousy in his brother Esau's heart. According to Jacob, this was part of a divine plan: he had to flee Esau's fury, and that prevented him from taking a Canaanite bride, like Esau, who served the wrong gods. So it could be said that it was God's aversion to the gods of Canaan that set this whole story in motion.

Jacob fled to Haran, where his uncle Laban lived, the brother of Rebekah, his mother. One day he came to a well, where three flocks of sheep were lying nearby.

"Where do you come from, my friends?" he asked the shepherds.

"From Haran," they replied.

"So then do you perhaps know Laban, the grandson of Nachor?"

Oh yes, they knew him. And that was no surprise; all the herders who farmed the pastures that belonged to the city landlords knew one another. I do not know the area around Haran, but there cannot have been too many of them.

"Look," they said. "Here comes his daughter Rachel now, with the sheep."

What a coincidence! For it was the middle of the day and nowhere near the time to gather the sheep together at the well. It was better to lift the lid of the well after the sun had gone down.

Jacob saw the girl approaching and was deeply moved. Overwhelmed by strong emotion, he forgot all the rules of decency. He ran up to her and kissed her, even before introducing himself. Rachel was about twelve, and she was horrified. The shame! A strange man had kissed her and everyone had seen! Leah told me that Rachel's shame spread like a wildfire within her and she thought she was going to die.

When Rachel saw that the stranger had started to cry, she realized something out of the ordinary was happening. His tears calmed her and so she was able to ask him who he was.

"I am the son of Rebekah, your father's sister," said Jacob.

Without saying another word, Rachel turned around and ran home to tell her father the big news. It wasn't long before Laban came running, delirious with joy, for he had not heard anything from his family in Canaan for a very long time. He kissed Jacob and took him home.

"Tell me," he said. "Tell me everything."

And so Jacob told his whole story to Laban, but he did not tell him the reason for his coming. He did not need to either, for Laban remembered how Rebekah had found her husband, and so he knew Jacob had come to Haran because he was looking for a wife. That was handy, because his elder daughter Leah was almost of a marriageable age.

To Laban's surprise, Jacob did not appear to be in any hurry. He didn't say a word about any marriage plans, but helped to look after Laban's flock as if he had all the time in the world and without asking for payment. Laban did not know that Jacob was fleeing from Esau and had found a safe shelter with him. It was wise of my father not to mention that to Laban; if your family find out that you are dependent on them, you might as well offer yourself up as a slave.

When a whole month had passed and Jacob had still not asked for Leah's hand, Laban ran out of patience. He wanted to know where he stood with this relative, who looked after his sheep silently and without payment.

"Listen, Jacob," he said, "you don't need to work for me for free just because you happen to be family. Tell me what you think your wages should be."

He was almost certain Jacob would ask for Leah's hand now.

But Jacob was in love with Rachel, because she was a playful lamb, a frolicsome filly with sparkling eyes, while Leah was a cow dozily ruminating with the expression of a creature who has seen it all. Jacob wanted Rachel, but he had nothing to offer Laban—and everything has a price. So he said, "I shall work for you for seven years for the hand of Rachel, your younger daughter."

Laban was baffled, not because of the seven years, since Rachel was more than worth seven years of work, but because Jacob had shamelessly passed over his elder daughter, flouting common practice and customs. He realized this was an unacceptable humiliation for Leah and that she would give him plenty of trouble if he couldn't find some way to satisfy her. He thought very quickly and because he was a wily man, a solution soon occurred to him.

He said, "I'm better off giving her to you than to someone else. You can stay."

Any man receiving that answer from his beloved's father would take it as a yes, but if you listen carefully you'll realize it's nothing more than an acknowledgment that Jacob would be the best husband for Rachel. That's all. I might have smelled a rat, but Jacob, who was so in love, fell blindly into the trap that had cunningly been set for him, just as his father Isaac had done.

So he went to work, for seven years in a row. That seems like a long time, but it felt like only a few days to Jacob because he loved Rachel so much.

Their love was mutual. Jacob was a strong man and a hard worker with a big heart. Rachel longed for him. She tried to let it show as little as possible so as not to hurt Leah, but Leah didn't miss the loving glances that Rachel and Jacob gave each other, and jealousy flared up within her like a fire from smoldering coals. Her bitterness made her vindictive and she was prepared to go along with her father's heartless ruse.

When the seven years had gone by, Rachel was a fine age to marry, nineteen or so. She was itching with impatience, but her father said nothing and Jacob said nothing. It seemed as if both men were too proud to be the first one to bring up the subject of the wedding. I can imagine how hard it must have been for Rachel to hold her tongue, but girls were not supposed to appear too keen. They had to act as if they would rather stay with their father and were leaving him with only the greatest reluctance.

I know my grandfather Isaac did not see his bride until after the wedding night, when she had removed her veil and morning had come. My father had the good fortune of being able to watch his beloved and everything she did for seven years. That had increased his certainty that he had not made a mistake: he wanted Rachel and no one else.

He waited one full month of the eighth year, and then he went to Laban and said, "It is time. Give my wife to me now. I want to take her to bed."

Everyone can understand why Jacob formulated his wishes so clearly. For seven years he had waited chastely for his Rachel! For seven years his love for her had burned within him!

Laban organized a big celebration and invited all his friends and acquaintances from the city. When evening came, Laban brought Jacob's veiled bride to him. Night fell and in the pitch darkness the couple found each other by touch.

Zilpah, Leah's slave, giggled when she told me that Jacob thought that first night a little disappointing. He had expected more enthusiasm, more passion, and more sweet words from his bride. Instead there was just silent and dutiful intercourse as if there were no life in the woman.

When Jacob awoke the next morning, he had the fright of his life when he found not Rachel lying in bed beside him, but Leah. She looked at him with big, terrified cow eyes because she feared his rage. But Jacob, who remembered the trick he had played on his father, realized he would have to bear Laban's deceit calmly. Once he was over the initial shock, he said, "Do not be afraid, Leah. You obeyed your father, nothing more. You are my wife."

He never regretted that statement, because Leah proved a conscientious wife, who was usually pregnant and bore him six sons and a daughter.

"But," Jacob added, "I cannot live without Rachel. I have worked seven years for her and I must have her."

He went to see Laban and cried, "Did I not work for you for the sake of Rachel? Why have you deceived me so?"

Then Laban told him that in his culture it was the custom for the eldest daughter to marry first, before the youngest could be given away. That may well be true, but still something about it wasn't right, because if Laban had said that beforehand, Jacob would probably have agreed to a double marriage: one with Leah and one with Rachel. The urge to swindle one another, to get our own way by means of cunning and intrigue, and by choosing lies over the truth, is apparently irresistible. Perhaps honesty is considered too risky when we want to achieve something, which is why the stories of my fathers and forefathers are full of traps and tricks. Behold the man.

"Wait until your wedding week with Leah is over," said Laban, "then you shall have Rachel too, on the condition that you work another seven years for me."

When my brother Joseph told me this, his smile was so bright that it was like the sun coming up, and so I could imagine how Rachel's smile must have looked when she heard Laban's words. It was that unique smile that I later saw again on the face of the vizier of Egypt, and by which I recognized him.

So Jacob had to go to bed with Leah for another six nights, while he was longing for Rachel. It was quite a chore, and I'm afraid that neither he nor Leah took much pleasure in it. But Leah became pregnant, because she always became pregnant.

And who was behind it all? God! Yes, I swear it. It was he who opened Leah's womb while Rachel remained childless for so long that it drove her to despair. God did so because Jacob loved Leah less than Rachel.

Now I ask you, Lord, was Leah not forced upon my father? Did Jacob not speak, from the very beginning, of his love for Rachel? Why is love punished? Where were you, Lord, when Leah was brought in a veil to Jacob's tent? Why did you remain silent?

The temptation is great to take other gods than you, because we do not understand you. I can see it all around me. The need to be faithful to the god of Abraham, Isaac, and Jacob is undermined by the mystery of your being. You are too complex for us. I know Canaanite and Egyptian gods who are more simple. So I ask you: be clear, explain yourself in greater detail, make your intentions known, because otherwise you will lose people.

For Rachel's sake, Jacob worked for Laban for seven more years. Leah gave birth, in order, to Ruben, Simeon, Levi, Judah, and, after a break of a few years, also Issachar, Zebulon, and, finally, Dinah, the only daughter. I would appreciate it if you could learn to recite these names by heart—in reverse order too.

They say my mother became jealous of Leah because she didn't have children while Leah did. I doubt that. My brother Joseph, who was apparently very much like Rachel, never showed the slightest hint of jealousy and I myself have just as little talent for it. I think she wanted children, nothing more, and she became desperate because of all the children Leah bore, while she waited and waited year after year and nothing happened. She ran out of patience, so one day she went to Jacob.

She said, "Give me children or I will die!"

Jacob became angry and cried, "Who do you think I am? God?"

I don't know if this conversation was passed on to me accurately, but isn't it wonderful? Does it not vividly encapsulate the despair of the two lovers in just two simple sentences?

They say my father did not like Leah; some even claim he hated her. I never saw any sign of that: he valued her, he treated her with respect, and he tried to be a good husband to her. But he was not ablaze with love for her as he was for Rachel. If God had wanted him to love Leah, why did he not have Leah appear at the well by Haran? Or was he planning to do so but other gods thwarted his plans? Why did he allow Esau to be the firstborn and not Jacob? All these events are not easy to understand unless there are other gods who have different plans for humankind and therefore create obstacles for one another.

Laban had given each of his daughters a slave upon the occasion of their marriages: Zilpah for Lea and Bilhah for Rachel. Such slave girls were not intended to toil in the fields with the sheep or to go to market with baskets of goods on their heads. They were handmaids who took care of their mistresses. They cut their hair, bathed, massaged, and dressed them. They served in every aspect of the lady's intimate life, even taking a mistress's place in her husband's bed if necessary.

"Take my slave, Bilhah," said Rachel, "and sleep with her. If she has children, she must give birth to them on my thighs while I kneel before her, so that they count as mine."

I don't exactly know what men think in such situations, but I have my suspicions. Bilhah was an exceptionally beautiful woman who seemed barely aware of her beauty, given the timid way she went about her work. So I'm not surprised that my father made no objection to Rachel's proposal.

Bilhah became pregnant and gave birth to her child on Rachel's lap. It was a boy. Rachel called him Dan, which means "judgment," because she felt that God had finally given her justice.

She thought one child was not enough for her to be respected among women, so Jacob spent another happy night with Bilhah. She became pregnant again—and again she bore a son on Rachel's lap. Rachel called him Naphtali, which means "my struggle." Some say she was referring to her struggle with Leah, but I think she had fought with God and chose that name because she wanted to rub his nose in her victory. We are not a people who allow ourselves to be browbeaten by a god who is unjust. Rachel told him the truth and God paid attention, as will soon become clear.

Leah was apparently not pleased that Rachel had succeeded in giving birth with Bilhah's help, particularly since it came at a time when it seemed she was no longer capable of allowing Jacob's seed to grow within her belly. She still hoped to win Jacob's love, because his care and appreciation were not enough for her, so she gave him Zilpah, her handmaid, to bear children in her place.

Zilpah became pregnant twice and two sons were born. Leah called the first one Gad, after the god of good fortune, and the second Asher, "happiness."

Rachel's longing for children to call her own, without the help of Bilhah, had not been appeased. One fine day in spring, Ruben, Leah's eldest son, picked some love apples, rare fruits of the mandrake, and took them to his mother. The juice of these fruits is known for its stimulant effect on the sexual organs of both men and woman, and for increasing the potency of the male seed. So Leah was grateful to receive them.

Rachel heard about this. She went to Leah and said, "Give me some of the love apples your son brought to you."

But Leah said, "Is it not enough for you that you have taken my husband from me?"

I swear it: that's how the conversation was passed down to me! Leah, who took her husband through her father's deceit and at her sister's expense, she who bore one son after another, accused my mother of having taken Jacob from her, and I think she meant it too. Jealousy corrupts the mind; it twists and turns itself in knots until even the most ridiculous lie becomes truth.

Rachel was not taken aback. She said, "In exchange for Ruben's love apples, Jacob may sleep with you tonight."

Leah must have thought this a fair exchange, because she gave Rachel a few love apples.

Whenever this story was told, I burst out laughing because I thought it was funny that the two women made use of Jacob as if he were their servant. And maybe he was. Perhaps, without realizing it, men are always the servants of their wives. Not my father, though; he must have been well aware of his place, because when he returned from the field that evening, Leah went to meet him and said, "You *must* sleep with me. I have *hired* you in exchange for my son's love apples."

She had paid for him! He had to sleep with her because she had paid for him! What does that sound like? It sounds like prostitution, with Rachel acting as Jacob's . . . I won't write that word down. I don't wish to besmirch my mother's name. Besides, it all seems rather comical to me, and I can't see any harm in it.

So Jacob obediently went to bed with Leah because Rachel had rented him out to her. This state of affairs was apparently in accordance with God's wishes. Leah became pregnant again and bore a son for the fifth time: Issachar, which means "recompense." It's said that Leah felt rewarded by God because she'd given Zilpah to Jacob, but I think that's a little far-fetched. She had Issachar because she had paid Rachel for a night with Jacob.

It didn't stop at that one night. She became pregnant again and gave birth to Zebulon, her sixth son, and a daughter, too, Dinah, and then it was finally over.

I don't know if it was because of the love apples or because God had stopped punishing love, but Rachel finally became pregnant too and gave birth to a son, whom she named Joseph. She hoped she would have another son, and indeed she had one: me, Ben-Oni. Sadly, my birth cost my mother her life, so I only know her from the stories that are told about her. I'm thankful to the storytellers who have kept my mother alive, since without them she would not have existed for me. I advise everyone to listen to storytellers, for if we do not listen, we do not know who has gone before us and what we can learn from them.

I was the only one of all my brothers to be born in Canaan. So my mother made the journey from Haran to the land that had been promised to Abraham. When Jacob had worked in Haran for twenty years, seven for Leah and seven for Rachel and six years for his animals, he wanted to return to Canaan to see his father Isaac again, but Laban did not wish him to go, because Jacob had brought him prosperity. Not only Jacob's flock but also Laban's had grown under Jacob's care to become one of the largest in Haran. His son-in-law had made him an important man. Like all shepherd princes, Laban had enough armed men to prevent Jacob from leaving. So Jacob decided to escape. He waited until Laban was with his flock, shearing the sheep, and then he ordered his wives and children to get ready to travel. Rachel was looking forward to the journey; she was happy finally to free herself from her father, who treated her husband like a slave and his daughters as goods for sale, but she was a pious woman who had always served the gods of her land with great devotion. She could not imagine a life without her gods, and so she crept into Laban's tent, stole her father's household gods and hid them in one of her saddlebags. She took the gods of her homeland with her so that she would not be without help in the distant land to which they were traveling. Jacob knew nothing about it then, but he found out later. He did not hold it against Rachel, but allowed her her gods, as befits a good husband. What right could a man have to decide to whom his wife directed her prayers? He loved her, so he also put up with her gods.

Rachel did not know how dangerous this theft would prove for her, and Jacob must have looked back in horror and trembling at his recklessness in putting Rachel's life at risk, but that strange event still lay ahead of them.

Jacob put his children and wives on camels, drove his herd, and took with him all the possessions he had earned in Haran. He fled with all he had and headed for the mountains of Gilead.

It was three days before Laban realized Jacob was gone. He was furious. His source of income had made a run for it! Of course, in front of his relatives he played the part of the offended father who had not even been able to say farewell to his beloved daughters. They fell for it. Many family members gathered around him, accompanied by their armed men, and Laban set off in pursuit with this fearsome troop, determined to capture Jacob and his daughters and to bring them back to Haran. For twenty years they had served him; he could no longer do without them. He was the head of the family. Family is all about belonging. And he was on his way to get back his belongings.

I listened carefully to the stories of my forefathers, so I know that whenever someone wishes to break away from their family, this must be sanctioned by God, since it cannot happen without his consent. I am the property of my father or, in his absence, my grandfather or uncle, or whoever happens to be the head of the family at that moment. So it doesn't surprise me that God had to get involved in order to cool Laban's overheated mind. God appeared to him in a dream (it's handy for the gods that people dream). He said to Laban, "Consider this: Jacob has not withdrawn from the authority of the head of the family. He is returning to Canaan to submit to the authority of his father, Isaac. When you catch up with him, there's no need to grovel, but you mustn't do him any harm either, for he's in the right."

There was nothing Laban could say to that, since a father's authority was greater than that of a father-in-law or uncle. He could have worked that out without a dream, but he was blinded by his fury, so God came to his assistance. Laban was none too pleased about it, though; he would rather have given free rein to his rage and taken his belongings back to Haran as captives. And so he desperately tried to work out how he might still have his way in spite of the dream.

After a journey of seven days, Laban reached the mountains of Gilead, where Jacob had pitched his tents. Because he was afraid of Jacob's god, he did not attack but set up his own tents nearby, beyond the reach of the archers.

The next day, Jacob saw him coming, on foot and alone, but behind him on a hill the silhouettes of his armed men stood out clearly against the blue sky. The women called their children back to their tents; the men crouched silently and stared at the ground.

Jacob respectfully kissed Laban's hands and held open the flaps of his tent for him. Slave girls brought water to wash his feet, while others offered him sweet fruits and drinks.

"How are you?" Laban asked finally.

"Fine, Father," said Jacob. "And you?"

"Not so great," said Laban.

"Oh, Father. What's wrong?"

"I'll give you three guesses."

Jacob acted as if he were thinking deeply. He frowned and wrinkled his forehead and pensively stroked his beard. Out of politeness, he allowed a little time to pass until he saw that his father-in-law had had enough. He said, "I cannot guess, Father. What's the problem?"

"You are the problem, of course, you wretch! For taking my daughters!" Laban growled. "What father's heart wouldn't break if his son-in-law silently stole away, taking his daughters like spoils of war? What a dirty trick! What in the name God did I do to deserve it?"

Jacob did not answer immediately since he needed time to get his anger under control.

"Father," he said then. "I worked seven years for Leah, seven years for Rachel, and six years for nothing. I told you several times that I wanted to return to my father in Canaan, but you wouldn't let me go."

"No!" screamed Laban. "Of course not, dummy! What father wouldn't protest if his son-in-law wanted to drag his daughters away to a distant land? What kind of father would I be if I had said, 'Go on, do as you will, take my daughters with you so that I may never see them again?' Do you have no feelings in that heart of yours? Did you really have to dishonor me by abducting my girls?"

"Father, you wouldn't let me go. I had no choice."

"Then understand that it's a father's place to refuse. You should have insisted, begged, burst into tears, twisted yourself in knots, threatened suicide. You should have given me and all my relatives a good reason to let you go. Then I would have personally seen you off with song and dance. I would have had my band turn out to play you a fine farewell. Now I haven't even had the opportunity to kiss my daughters and grandchildren goodbye, you piece of scum."

"Father," said Jacob. "Be reasonable. Maybe you would have let me go, but never your daughters. You would have taken them from me, since you consider them to be your property and not mine."

Laban leapt furiously to his feet and pointed his index finger at Jacob's eyes.

"And you kept telling me that story about desperately longing to see your father. If that's true, why did you steal my gods? Explain that to me! Does it not mean that you meant to steal the protection of the gods from me and make it your own? Does it not mean that you want to ruin my house?"

Jacob looked at him in horror. The news about the stolen gods came completely out of the blue, but he immediately understood the gravity of Laban's accusation. Taking away the household gods ripped out the heart of a tent, the spiritual center of a family, the anchor and support of a clan, the symbol of a tribe. Only the very strongest of measures could remove the sting of Laban's venomous accusation. Jacob was thinking of a slave when he said, "You and your relatives may search all our tents. If you find your gods with one of us, you may take them home and I will have the thief put to death."

He did not know that he was issuing Rachel's death sentence, and neither did Laban. All they knew was that Jacob's edict could not be revoked, even if that was what they both wanted. Once a word was given, it was as immutable as if carved from stone, but in exchange Jacob succeeded in making Laban surrender his daughters, so that all Laban now wanted was to restore his honor. The life of a thief seemed a small sacrifice if it brought peace between them.

Laban accepted Jacob's offer, and he headed outside and called his armed relatives down from the hilltop. Together they searched every tent in Jacob's camp, one by one. Leah screamed that it was outrageous that she should be suspected of theft: "I, who have always served my father like a dog that does not dare to look its master in the face, I who followed his orders before he even spoke them," and so on, and so forth. A litany of outrage, but still her relatives went into her tent and turned everything upside down. They found nothing. They searched the tents of Jacob, Bilhah, and Zilpah. They found nothing. They were about to burst into Rachel's tent, but Laban stopped them.

"I'll do this one," he said, "on my own."

This was the first sign that Laban was afraid of the promise Jacob had made. Laban had considered everything, except his own feelings. Rachel was not only Jacob's favorite, but also her father's. Even before he entered her tent, he realized that he'd been hunting for Jacob but his favorite daughter might turn out to be his quarry.

He went into Rachel's tent and saw her sitting on her camel saddle. She was silent and bowed her head to show she was still subservient to her father. As he looked at her, he felt his heart break. He was going to lose her one way or another, to Jacob's distant land or to death. This was the cruel day of farewell he had dreaded for so long.

He searched her tent while she remained seated on the saddle. He thought: She has hidden them in or under her saddle. Gods, help me, what should I do?

He rummaged through her belongings, his hands sweating. With a shameful face, he searched her clothing. He was invading her intimacy, and he knew a father should not do such things. He cursed himself. He found nothing; of course he found nothing. He stopped searching, turned around, walked up to his daughter, and looked at her imploringly. Think of something, he thought. Make it possible for me to leave without searching under that damned saddle.

Rachel looked up at him, calmly, like a daughter who knows she can trust her father. That was more than Laban deserved, so he could barely meet her eyes.

"Do not be angry, Father," she said.

Oh gods! Laban looked at her helplessly. His anger had long since melted into tears. He remembered that it was Rachel who had always looked after his gods. She had dressed them, made chains of beads for them, carried them around with her. She had held them to her bosom as if they were babes in arms; she had made his gods her own. What was to prevent him from buying new gods from the stores around the temple in Haran?

He remembered the girl in whose eyes he could do no wrong and who loved him above all else. He should have known that one day a man would come into her life whom she loved more than her father. He had not prepared himself; when it happened, it hit him like a sledgehammer. There was no sense to his anger; it was no more than a deep fear of the inevitable farewell. But it had to happen and he did not want her to die; he wanted her to live, even without him.

He didn't know how to go about saying farewell, so he did nothing. Clumsily, he turned around and walked out of Rachel's tent. When a cousin started to head inside to give the tent another quick search, Laban stopped him.

"Do not enter Rachel's tent," he said. "She is indisposed." For men may not set foot inside the tent of a menstruating woman.

Had she told him she had her period, or had he invented it? I don't know. In any case, it was enough to keep all the other men out of her tent.

Laban knew, now that his accusation had turned out to be false, that he would have to submit to humiliation from Jacob for

Rachel's sake. He considered it his punishment for putting her life in danger.

After all the tents had been searched, Jacob exploded with rage.

"What objects from your household have you found in our tents?" he snorted. "Lay them here before us so that we might see them. Well? Why do I see nothing? Did you find nothing at all? Do you know why that is? That's because I have taken only what belongs to me: my wives, my children, and my animals. For fourteen years I worked for my wives and during the six years I built up my own herd, I did not neglect yours. Even on scorching days and freezing nights I worked for you, and do you know what my reward would have been if I had not escaped? You would have taken everything from me, my wives, my children, and my animals. You would have driven me naked into the desert if God had not protected me. I long for my father, because what kind of father are you to begrudge his daughters their husband, to treat his son-in-law like a slave? Tell me: Who would not flee from you?"

Laban allowed Jacob's accusations to rain down upon him and waited patiently for him to finish. He felt such contentment flowing into his heart as he had never known before: he had been able to say farewell to his daughters and he had spared Rachel's life. Jacob was no longer the enemy who was robbing him of his daughters, but more like a younger brother who was lifting a heavy burden from his shoulders. It was time to make peace.

"You no longer need to flee," he said. "You may go in peace. Look around you, everything you see is mine: your wives, your children, and your animals. How could I do anything to hurt my own daughters, my own children, and my own animals?"

Jacob remained silent since, strictly speaking, Laban was right. The head of the family owns everything; the sons own nothing as long as the father lives. I hope that in the future someone with authority will reform family law, because it was not a good situation: everything Jacob was allowed to take was a gift from Laban. Jacob had no rights.

"So let us make a covenant," said Laban. "Then I will let you go."

Jacob thought that was a good plan and he immediately began to heave a stone upright. All his men gathered stones together and threw them into a pile. Laban called the heap of stones, in his language, Jegar Sahadutha; and Jacob, in his, Galeed. They felt they should be able to name the memorial in their own languages for posterity.

"This pile of stones is the sign that the gods are keeping watch on you and me," said Laban, "even when we are parted from each other. We shall never pass this pile of stones with ill intent."

When this ceremony was over, they enjoyed a meal together and drank to a fine future for everyone, but still Jacob didn't really relax until he saw his father-in-law disappearing over the horizon the next day.

All my life I've been curious about the gods my mother hid in or under her camel saddle. I asked my father about them.

"I disposed of them after her death," he told me.

"Why, Father?"

"They were her gods, not mine."

So gods existed that belonged to someone else, not to me.

"Why is there no image of our god?" I asked.

"Because the god of Adam is a word and not an image," said Jacob.

"So there are gods who are words and other gods who are images?" I asked.

"That's right," said Jacob.

"The gods who are images—are they false gods?"

"Whatever are you thinking of?!" Jacob exclaimed. "They were the gods of your mother! How can Rachel's gods be false gods?"

Ashamed, I fell silent, because I had not meant to insult the gods of my dead mother. I didn't dare to keep on asking, which was too bad. Because isn't getting rid of gods because they aren't yours the same as saying that they're false? Are you allowed just to toss other people's gods as if they're trash?

I understood that everything to do with the gods was extremely complex and that plenty more study would have to be devoted to the subject before we could ever begin to make sense of them.

My brother Joseph always said, "If you want an image of God, then look at the sun."

But that sounded more like an Egyptian notion.

The god of Abraham, Isaac, and Jacob was no sun, and most definitely not a ray of sunshine. He was more like a tyrant who did not know his own strength. That's why my forefathers attempted to bind him by the laws of a covenant, so that, for his own good, he could not just do whatever occurred to him. Had he not been sorry about the terrible flood? Had he not deeply regretted the deaths of the innocent children of Sodom?

I had seen that other people's gods demanded only subservience, but the god of my forefathers seemed willing to bind his omnipotence to laws. He didn't always succeed, but at least he tried to be just. When Rachel was punished with childlessness simply for loving Jacob, that was unjust, but he put it right in the end. Sometimes I feel that he's a giant child taking his first wobbly steps toward adulthood, when his temper tantrums will finally be overcome and his behavior will be dignified. I sense that the path will be long and that I will not live to see that day.

The story I am going to tell now will sound implausible, but I swear to you I heard it straight from my father's mouth. In the past he had sometimes distorted the truth to get his own way, but his way was his god's way: he had no choice. When he cheated his brother of his birthright and the paternal blessing, he ensured the tribe that would grow from Abraham was not rooted in the vagaries of fate, but was chosen by God.

When he told me the story of his encounter with God, he had no reason to lie, and so I believe it's true.

To reach Canaan, Jacob had to travel through Edom, the land of Esau. He stood at the northern border, which was formed by a tributary of the Jordan River: the Jabbok. He found a spot where he could wade through, then waited for night to fall so that no one would see him crossing into Edom. He first sent his wife and both handmaids across, then his children, and then he had his men drive the animals to the other side. Meanwhile, he stayed behind on his own in the pitch darkness. He was just about to wade across the river, as the last member of the party, when he heard something snorting like a roused, angry bull. At that moment he was attacked, but it was no animal; two hands grabbed him by the throat and tried to strangle him. He tore himself free and lashed out. At first he had no idea who he was dealing with, but it was a man, that much was certain, and not just any man but a real fighter who apparently wanted to stop him from crossing the river. Twenty years of hard work had made Jacob a force to be reckoned with; he had used his fists to settle many a fight between the herders, and had killed predators with his bare hands, so he knew how to defend himself. The men fought hard, kicking and punching away, holding each other in strangleholds; they sweated, spat, and bled. After they had been fighting for hours, beating each other black and blue, it dawned on Jacob that this was no ordinary man. In fact, it wasn't a man at all. He was wrestling with God himself! He couldn't explain how he knew, but it was as true as the sky. He realized how important it was for him not to lose this fight—important for him, but also for God. Because it was God, Jacob clenched his fists and delivered a well-aimed hit right on his nose and the blood spattered in every direction. It was time to teach God a proper lesson: humankind was not insignificant; unlike the immortal gods, humans possessed a phenomenal will to survive. Of course, God hit back. Jacob's right ear was torn to shreds, his eyebrows were bleeding, but he kept his wits about him. He used his good sense and carefully searched for God's most vulnerable place. He dished out a few little jabs, just to see if God was guarding the spot, and to his surprise Jacob saw the Creator was too focused on his attack. When he spotted his opportunity, Jacob lashed out and dealt God a devastating blow to the mouth, and a few teeth came tumbling out onto the ground. God teetered. Jacob waited to see if God could still come back after the blow that had taken his breath, and he did come back, but with less and less conviction in his blows. He's realized he can't win, thought Jacob, and he was right. God couldn't win, but he couldn't lose either. So they fought on, two hopeless, bleeding bundles of rags, until morning came.

Jacob told me this story on several occasions, always in more detail, and every time it gave me goose bumps. If God is a word, then he is an exceptionally muscular word, no doubt! But what kind of god thinks it's a good idea to go to the effort of fighting a brawl? What did "almighty" mean now that he'd proved incapable of beating Jacob? These are puzzles that will probably never be solved but there's one conclusion I dare to draw: God is human and humans are divine; in all their smallness and greatness they are very much alike.

"Father, what did God look like?" I asked Jacob several times.

His answer was always the same: "He looked awful."

When the sun had risen and God saw he couldn't win, he decided to play another dirty trick on Jacob. He lashed out and kicked him really hard on the hip, dislocating the joint. So I would never know my father without a limp. Furiously, Jacob grabbed hold of him, but God said, "Let me go now, for dawn has come." He was lisping a little because of the missing teeth.

"Oh no!" cried Jacob. "You're not getting away from me that easily. I won't let you go until you bless me."

Then God asked, "What's your name?" Which is a strange question for a god who knows everything, but he'd taken such a beating that maybe his memory had failed him.

Jacob said he was called Jacob because he'd grabbed his brother's heel at birth.

"Oh, I see," said God. "But that's no longer such an appropriate name for you. I shall give you another one. From now on you will be called Israel, because you have fought with God. For 'Israel' means: he who wrestles with God."

"Now that you know my name," said Jacob, "it would be nice if you could also introduce yourself to me, as is the custom."

"Do you mean you want to know my name?" asked God.

"Yes," said Jacob. "I think it's useful for a man to know the name of his god."

"Well, that's too bad," said God, "because I'm not telling you. Why should you know my name? Call me the Eternal One or something like that and be content. All the gods that reside in your tents have names, but I am here. That's the difference."

Jacob couldn't follow God's reasoning, but he was too exhausted to make a fuss. He kneeled to receive his blessing and it was given to him. When the ceremony was over, both men stumbled on their way, bleeding like pigs, but satisfied with their nocturnal encounter. It had been a refreshing fight.

Jacob gave that place by the Jabbok the name of Penuel, for he had faced God there and had not been defeated.

He said: "Our people will be called Israel after me, because we do not so much *have* a god as we wrestle with him."

It always seemed like a profound thought to me, but I worry this view might make us strangers on earth. The future will tell.

My father had God's blessing, but by no means did that mean he was safe from then on. His family would survive in one way or another, that was all God had assured him, but he could lose even that promise if he did something foolish. One might wonder exactly what such a blessing is worth, and so Jacob was terrified when Esau approached him with four hundred armed men. There's a big difference between a herder like Jacob who can mobilize a good number of men to protect his wives, children, and animals, and someone like Esau who lives on robbing and plundering, and does nothing but wage war. If Esau had malicious intentions, Jacob would be powerless against his well-trained troops, and what reason did Esau have to mean well? Did he not have every reason to be vengeful? Could it not be said that he had every right?

Jacob was wise not to set too much store by the benefits of God's blessing. He begged for help, fell whimpering to his knees and pretended to be a weakling, as if he had not just beaten God in single combat, for that is what the gods like to see: humans pretending to be more pathetic than they are, so the gods may feel great. Is that not the tactic children constantly use with their parents when they want to get something, by demonstrating how small and dependent they are with trickling tears and pleading voices? Just as it is smart of children to try to work out the needs of their parents, so we must study the gods so that we know how to find favor with them. Our stories describe the behavior of people and their gods so that we might learn.

Jacob had learned. He was not counting on anything but his own good sense. All he hoped to achieve by begging and groveling was that God would not act against him. He sent messengers out to gauge Esau's mood, and when they returned with the news that Esau was on his way with four hundred men, Jacob prepared himself for the worst, blessing or no blessing.

He divided his family, his slaves, and his animals into two groups, because if Esau made mincemeat out of one group, the other might still be able to escape. I imagine he kept Leah and her children with him, while he put Rachel and Joseph in the care of one of his most trusted men, with orders to run as soon as the blood began to flow. I think this was because he saw Joseph as the father of Israel, and not Ruben, Leah's eldest son. Jacob's preference for Joseph would also, with God's blessing, result in a great deal of misery, but more about that later.

Then he separated some animals from his herd: two hundred female goats and twenty males, two hundred ewes and twenty rams, thirty female camels with their young, forty cows and ten bulls, twenty female donkeys and ten males, all as a huge gift for Esau, and he sent them ahead, led by his slaves and divided into several herds.

"Go to meet Esau," he said, "and leave space between the herds."
He wanted Esau to encounter gift upon generous gift in the hope
that his heart would be won, little by little. He sent spies along to
see what Esau's reaction would be.

When the first herd reached Esau, he asked the slave in charge,
"Who are you, where are you going, and to whom do those animals
belong?"

The slave knew what he had to say. He said, "The animals
belong to your servant, Jacob. They are his gift to you. And he is
following behind."

"I see," said Esau. "That's nice of him. Is he perhaps trying to
make up for something?"

The slave had no answer to that, but he did not need one, for
Esau had spoken in jest—and more importantly he accepted the
gift.

The same happened with the second and third slaves. Jacob's
spies returned with favorable reports. The gifts appeared to be having the desired effect. It seemed that Esau had nothing malicious in
mind, and so Jacob changed his tactics, but he stayed on his guard.

He called the two groups of his people back together. When
he saw Esau approaching with his four hundred men, he sent his
wives and children ahead, Bilhah and Zilpah with their children in
the lead, then Leah and her children following at some distance,
and after that Rachel with Joseph. And he bravely went right at the
front, alone, unarmed, and with no one to protect him. Even before
he reached his brother, he threw himself to the ground seven times
as a sign of submission, but Esau ran to meet him, embraced him
and kissed him. Both men wept.

Life had treated Esau well. He was content. Even without his
birthright and his father's blessing, everything had turned out
nicely, and he no longer knew why he had been so upset.

He was pleased to meet Jacob's wives and children, because
they too were no reason for him to be jealous: like Jacob, he had an
abundance of wives and children. He was a wealthy man. His gods
had ignored Jacob's deceit and had treated him as the firstborn that

he was. What can be more wonderful than a brotherly reconcilia-
tion after jealousy has given way to prosperity?

They made a celebration of it, and yet both were wise enough to
realize they should part company as soon as possible. They were
too different.

And so it came to pass. Jacob traveled on to Canaan and set-
tled to the east of Shechem, where he bought a piece of land from
Hamor, the king of that city. Out of gratitude for his safe arrival in
Canaan, he set up an altar there and called it "The god of Israel is
God," which is undeniably true, just as it is also undeniably true
that the god of Shechem is God, because everyone has his own
God.

And so King Hamor took no offense at the name of Jacob's altar.

The relationship between Jacob's family and the people of Shechem
was a very friendly one. Dinah, Leah's daughter, made friends with
some girls in the city, including a few of King Hamor's daughters.
And Dinah went to the royal palace and enjoyed herself there with
the princesses. The crown prince, who was named Shechem like
the city, fell in love with her and she with him.

When Dinah said, "I'm going to see my friends," she always
received permission to go to the city, but those friends were increasingly used as a cover for meeting Prince Shechem. This went on
for a long time until the prince wanted more than just a few fleet-
ing kisses. The prince tried, with sweet words and gifts, to tempt
Dinah to do more, and one day they ended up fooling around on
his bed. He started kissing her, caressing and undressing her.

The undressing was a step too far.

"Stop it, my prince!" she cried. "I love you, but first you must
ask my father for my hand in marriage."

He didn't listen. When she struggled, he took her by force.
Then immediately after the deed was done, he deeply regretted it,
because he loved her. He realized that he had committed a terrible
crime and desperately sought for a way to put it right, first with

Dinah herself, then with her furious family. Rape is the most despicable thing a man can do to a woman and the very opposite of an act of love. Even so, with an ocean of tears and a deluge of apologies, he was able to convince Dinah of the sincerity of his love, and she agreed to marry him, but her brothers most certainly did not approve. They were out for revenge on the man who had dishonored their sister. They did not ask about Dinah's feelings, or Jacob's; they listened only to their own violent natures.

I am telling this story because it contains a warning against the sons of Leah, a warning that Joseph should have heeded. He did not do so because he was a dreamer who saw no evil in people.

I never found out exactly what role my father played. It seems that my brothers, or at least the sons of Leah, had more power in this matter than he did. It would appear that my father had absolutely no control over his sons and they could do as they wished, with disastrous consequences. Prompted by this tale, I took a good look at those around me and saw that girls have more to fear from their brothers than their father. I do not understand why that should be, but I have seen how brothers guard their sisters as if they are sheep and every man who so much as glances their way is deemed a wolf.

In this case Dinah's brothers had every reason to be angry. Shechem had raped their sister and such a thing should not be done. But the issue was complicated because the two people concerned loved each other and wanted to spend their lives together in spite of Shechem's crime.

Prince Shechem understood that he alone would not be able to calm the anger of Dinah's family, and so he asked his father to serve as a go-between. King Hamor went with Prince Shechem to visit Jacob. It turned out to be a large gathering, because Leah's sons were there too.

The king spoke up to say, "My son Shechem, the crown prince, loves your daughter with all his heart. Forgive him for what he has done and give him Dinah as his wife. Then we will become one family and that will strengthen our bond. Our sons and daughters can marry each other in the future; we will become one people and our land will be open to you. You will be free to move around or to settle wherever you wish."

This was a tremendous offer from the king, for it gave Jacob resident status on Hamor's land, with all the associated rights. We would no longer be strangers in Canaan but subjects and kin of the king of Shechem. I am surprised that my father remained silent, but perhaps he was waiting for Prince Shechem to speak up himself.

The prince said, "I can only hope you will forgive me and offer me your friendship. For my part, I will do everything to deserve Dinah. Whatever you ask of me, no matter how high the price, I will pay it, just as long as you give me my girl as my wife."

Then it was not Jacob who spoke but one of my brothers. That is strange. I cannot see it as anything other than gross impertinence, because my brothers bypassed Dinah's father as if he were some minor figure in this matter. They said, "We cannot give Dinah to a man who is uncircumcised, because that would be a disgrace to us."

So cunning! So terribly cunning! Not another word was said about the rape, because the two lovers had made up with each other, so the uncircumcised penis was probably the only remaining obstacle to this marriage as far as Jacob was concerned, but he did not know what wicked ulterior motives the brothers had.

This is what they said next: "We can only agree to this marriage if you become like us by having all the men of your tribe circumcised. Only then will we give our daughters to you and take your daughters for ourselves. Only then will we be one people."

How well my brothers had judged the prince's boundless love! He immediately agreed to their condition, even though he must have known that circumcision did not feel pleasant to a grown man and was also not without risk. What was even more curious is that all the male inhabitants of Shechem immediately agreed. They must have loved their prince very much indeed to allow their flesh to be cut so grievously for his sake!

When the man with the knife came, the city was no doubt so full of the sound of shrieks and moaning that the birds became frightened and flew off to seek refuge in the surrounding fields.

It is known that for adult men the third day after the circumcision is the critical one. Weakened by the loss of blood or feverish from infection, newly circumcised men are capable of doing very little. Sometimes their condition is so painful that they have to stay in bed and be nursed.

So Dinah's brothers waited until the third day. Then two of them, Simeon and Levi, took up their swords and went into the city with their men. They chopped all the male residents into pieces, including Prince Shechem and King Hamor; they fetched Dinah from the palace and took her back to Jacob's camp. When the other brothers heard that the men of Shechem had been defeated, they went into the city to loot: they took all the livestock, carried away and enslaved all the women and children, and stole all the goods they could find in the houses.

They had taken the ritual that Abraham had introduced to sanctify his people for God and abused it as a weapon of war. By being circumcised, the men of Shechem had recognized the god of Israel as one of their own, but they were rewarded with death. It is hardly possible to imagine a greater blasphemy.

Jacob was deeply shocked by his sons' crime. He also realized that he and his family were in grave danger.

He said: "You have brought misfortune upon me, because now no one in this land will trust us and everyone will see us as their worst enemy. If they conspire against me, they will surely destroy us. There are too few of us to raise a defense."

My brothers were not only criminals but also inconceivable idiots. They simply did not understand.

They said, "Should we have allowed them to treat our sister like a prostitute?" Which is a strange thing to say, since prostitution is not the same as rape.

Unfortunately Jacob did not punish them, which gave them the idea they could do as they pleased, and again my father would pay dearly for that later.

And what about Dinah? I have never known her as anything other than an embittered, sorry mess of a human being who had to live among the men who killed her beloved and enslaved her friends. Whenever her brothers came with a potential suitor for her, she ran screaming from her tent to Joseph or me to comfort her. No man ever touched her again.

The word "family" has such a sweet ring to it. But you can't fool me: relatives are just as strange as strangers; there's no difference. Or maybe it's worse; maybe the men of Shechem, though I never knew them personally, were more akin to me than my own brothers.

We could not stay near Shechem, because the surrounding tribes had heard about our crime. Jacob decreed that we must leave and so we abandoned Shechem, where we had forfeited our chance to become citizens and instead made enemies out of everyone. We headed south, toward the desert.

Soon after setting off, Jacob stopped beside an impressive oak tree. He called his men together and said, "Now that we have lost the favor of humankind, their gods are going to cause us all kinds of misery. We can only hope for the favor of the god of Israel. So cast aside all the foreign gods you have with you and remove the amulets from your ears so that they can do us no harm."

No one protested because everyone could see we had made enemies of the gods of every land.

Jacob had a hole dug beside the oak tree of Shechem and solemnly committed the gods to the earth, along with the amulets the people had worn in their noses and ears. Only Rachel's gods were spared, for she was heavily pregnant. She clasped her gods to her breasts as if her life depended on it. They were the dolls of her childhood, the gods of the house where she was born. Jacob could refuse her nothing; he would not take her gods from her.

They were near Ephrath, also known as Bethlehem, when Rachel went into labor. They halted to put up her tent and to wait for the birth. The midwife who was with Rachel felt that the child was lying the wrong way and the birth might put her life at risk. Unfortunately, she was proven right. Rachel survived my birth for just long enough to give me a name: Ben-Oni, but my father called me Benjamin.

Rachel died on the road to Bethlehem. She was buried there, together with the gods from her father's house.

Jacob put up a stone for her and said, "This woman, whom I loved, is the mother of Israel." He mourned her for the rest of his life.

I never knew her, so I shall not be sentimental about her loss. There were plenty of women around to make a fuss over me. But it was a boy who took care of me like a real mother: my beloved brother, Joseph.

I've known many good-looking men, but girls can be so beautiful that it's startling. Joseph was the only boy who was just as star-tlingly beautiful as girls can be. So girls reacted to him as if he were one of them. They did not lower their eyes as they did with other boys, but looked at him openly and beamed with joy. My father said Joseph had inherited my mother's smile, and if that's true she must have been irresistible. When Joseph smiled at people, they had but-terflies in their stomachs and a song in their hearts.

It seldom happens that exceptionally beautiful people are also kind and caring, but that was true of Joseph. He was hardly even aware of his beauty; he wasn't full of himself, but filled with something greater than he was. He could be deep in thought, but whenever I needed his attention he gave it to me, as if he could jump out of his thoughts with the ease of a frog leaping out of a bowl of water.

Jacob loved Joseph as he had loved Rachel. He loved him above all others—and he made it obvious. That did not bother me, because I too loved him above everything that walked the earth, and he returned my love so generously it overflowed.

Because Joseph was so often sunk in thought, and our broth-ers did not know what thoughts were, they called him a dreamer. Whenever anything came into their heads, they just followed their emotions, without any thought, as we had seen in Shechem. They had never gone into anything in depth and they thought anyone who sought out silence to spend time reflecting was an idiot. It annoyed them that Jacob chose this son, whom they thought a fool, above them. It irked them that Joseph was popular with women and that women treated him as if he were one of them, while they could only sheepishly observe the world of women from a great distance, never to be admitted.

And so, in this story too, jealousy raised its poisonous head, but Joseph did not see it. He noticed neither the admiration nor the envy he aroused; he was like a foal that finds only joy in life and in all its playfulness does not notice that it has hit others with its hooves. It is not vanity that makes the foal jump and prance; it is a pure zest for life that has not yet been tamed by the bridle. It would have been wise of Jacob to rein Joseph in a little, but he took pleasure in watching his son's antics and he let him run free. Rachel lived on inside him, who had also been a frisky young filly, and the more Jacob saw his beloved wife in Joseph, the more he loved him.

As like attracts like, so Joseph attracted everything that was beautiful. He had an eye for the foal that would grow into a beautiful adult, and so he always rode the most beautiful donkey. He saw the starry sky and pointed out its beauty to me. He pointed out the flowers and showed me their splendor. When he was with me, my eyes opened and I saw beauty where I had not suspected it, but my brothers mocked us, because you cannot take ahold of stars and you cannot eat flowers. We lived in two different worlds: the world of Leah, who had to live without her husband's love and saw life as a bitter struggle, and the world of the high-spirited Rachel, who had known she was loved and saw goodness in everything.

Jacob could see that Joseph loved beautiful things, so he had a magnificent coat made for his son, which Joseph wore with great pleasure, not out of vanity but because it was beautiful and because his father had given it to him. That caused bad blood with my brothers, because they thought he was trying to elevate himself above them with his wonderful coat.

Joseph did have dreams as well as thoughts, though. So my brothers weren't entirely wrong to call him a dreamer, but they didn't understand that for him dreaming was a form of thinking: dreams came to him at night just as thoughts came to him in the daytime. "I do not make the dreams," he said. "The dreams come to me. I do not make the thoughts; the thoughts come to me."

And because he believed his dreams and thoughts were sent to him, he gave enthusiastic accounts of them. Not like some smart-ass who thinks himself wiser than everyone else, but as a humble messenger passing on what he has been told.

He would have been better to keep some of his thoughts and dreams to himself, because even if they come to you, you are still responsible for them. But he was young and could not keep his mouth shut. Usually it did no harm. His dreams and thoughts were typically so cryptic that no one could make any sense of them, but one day he told of a dream whose meaning was all too clear, even to me, though I cannot have been any older than ten.

"Listen," he said to his brothers. "I had a dream. We were binding sheaves in the field. We set our sheaves upright and when mine was standing straight, your sheaves surrounded it. My sheaf remained upright and yours all bowed down to mine."

Everyone who hears this dream will wring his hands and exclaim, "But, Joseph, how could you be so dumb, you who are so wise! Do you not understand how insulting this is for your brothers?"

They were, of course, furious. They said, "Do you wish to be our king? Do you want to rule over us?" And they hated him more than ever.

But Joseph took me aside and said, "I do not want to rule over them. The dream says I will rule over them whether I want to or not. I had to tell them—perhaps the gods wish to warn them about something."

I understood that his motives were noble, but I also knew he had put himself in danger, and I said, "You must learn to hold your tongue. Do you want to die?"

He laughed at me with Rachel's laugh.

There are those who speak, not because they are reckless, but because they cannot be silent. They think their words can make all hatred and jealousy evaporate like boiling water, because they are not hateful and jealous themselves, and so they do not understand the blind forces with which they are dealing. But I, who carried all of my forefathers' stories inside me, knew very well and my heart was in my mouth for Joseph. He was my big brother and my mother at the same time. I could not imagine a life without him as anything other than one long nightmare.

The brothers sometimes wandered far with their herds. When we had pitched our tents in the valley of Hebron, my father heard they had ventured near to Shechem, and so he was worried about them. It angered him that they had so shamelessly revisited the scene of their crime and at the same time he was concerned for their safety. So he said to Joseph, "I have heard those idiots are near Shechem. Go to them and see how they are. And tell them to get the hell out of there. We cannot return to Shechem for another one hundred years."

Joseph set off and he naturally took me with him, for we were inseparable. When we came near to Shechem, we heard that things had gotten too hot for the brothers there and they had left for Dothan. So we traveled northward. And there we found them. Ruben, Leah's most human son, later told me they saw us coming in the distance. Simeon said to his brothers, "Ha, look, here comes our dream king. Now we can finally deal with that asshole once and for all. Let's kill him and throw him in a pit. Then we'll tell Father a wild beast ate him." Almost all the brothers applauded his plan.

Their hatred was deep.

But Ruben thought it was going way too far, not because he cared so much for Joseph, but because he knew his death would destroy their father's life. He saw that the brothers were so furious that he could not calm them down completely. So he said, "Let's not kill him. Do not spill his blood, for he is our brother. Throw him into this pit here, in the middle of the desert, and then he'll die anyway and his blood will not be on our hands."

He planned to rescue Joseph and to pull him out of the pit at the first opportunity.

When we arrived at our brothers' camp, to my horror, they grabbed hold of Joseph, tore off his clothes and dragged him toward the pit. I screamed and kicked and cried, but they held me, gagged me, and I had to watch helplessly as Joseph was thrown into the pit. I heard the dull thud as he hit the bottom and I realized the pit was dry.

"What will come of your dreams now, dream king?" someone cried. I heard the forced laughter of people who are imitating happiness without being happy. I hate such laughter. It is meant only to mock and humiliate.

How they did it, I do not know, but after they had committed their scandalous deed, they began to eat, even though they knew Joseph would die of hunger and thirst! I was nauseated by the smell of the bread and vomited. Ruben apparently had no appetite either, since he walked over to me and said, "Come."

I followed him. When we were out of earshot, he said, "When they've finished eating, they will head out into the field, and then we'll return. We'll pull Joseph out of the pit and the two of you can race back to Father."

I cheered up because I had found an ally in Ruben, but when he drove the animals so far away that we could no longer see the brothers, I became uneasy.

"We mustn't lose sight of them," I said. I was afraid they might still do something to Joseph.

"They don't trust me," said Ruben. "They won't believe I'm leaving Joseph to his fate until I'm out of sight. And only then will they go out into the field. Then we'll go in a big loop and return to the pit to rescue him."

It sounded like a good plan but it wasn't. Real life is so improbable that you can't predict it. Our detour took up half the day and all that time we couldn't see what was going on at the pit. That was Ruben's mistake. As soon as you lose sight of someone, you abandon him to his fate—and fate does not need much time to strike.

When we returned to the pit, Joseph had disappeared. I looked at Ruben, completely at a loss, but I could see he had no other plan up his sleeve. I thought to myself: Do not say everything you think, keep your dreams to yourself, as if that could change anything about the situation. The pit was empty. My heart was empty. For the first time, I felt what emptiness means: the absence of love, the triumph of hatred. I looked around and saw that the world was dead.

Ruben could think of nothing better to do than wait for the brothers to return, and that made me furious.

"Go after them!" I cried. "I'll look after the herd." But there was no moving him. He tore his clothes. Then he fell to the ground beside the pit like a sack of flour. There was not a trace of emotion on his face.

We waited and waited. The sun dragged itself down to the horizon so slowly that I wondered if the day would ever end. It ended, but it was the longest day I've known.

The brothers returned. They sat down around the pit and said nothing. I felt like pulling their tongues out of their mouths and making them talk, but I did nothing. I just sat there as if I were dead.

Then Ruben mumbled, "The boy is gone, what now, what should I do?"

I knew Ruben was afraid to see our father again. What could he say to him if he did not want lose his birthright?

"Listen," said Judah. "He's not dead. We were still eating beside the pit when a caravan of Ishmaelites appeared on their way to Egypt. They were carrying gum, balm, and aromatic resin."

Such a long silence fell that I lost my patience. I cried out, "What do I care what those people were carrying? Where's Joseph?"

Judah started speaking again, with an unpleasant grin on his face.

"So I said to my brothers, 'What good is it to us to murder our brother when he could earn us some money? Then we won't have to get rid of his bones either, because this way we'll leave no traces. Let us sell him to the Ishmaelites instead of killing him.

After all, he's our brother, our own flesh and blood.' So we sold him for twenty shekels, which I thought was a good price, and the Ishmaelites took him to Egypt."

After a brief silence, he added these terrible words, "So, in fact, I saved his life."

How is it that a person can transform a misdeed into a good deed with such great ease? I think Judah was actually really proud of himself, all because of his weak and transparent argument. Joseph sold as a slave! God, my God, why did you forsake him?

"And that's what you're going to tell Father?" I screamed. "That you saved Joseph's life by selling him as a slave?"

Only then did it seem to dawn on the brothers that they'd have to face their father again at some point. They looked around in panic, first at me, then at each other.

"Yes, tell us, Judah, what are we going to say to Father?" asked Ruben.

Judah was tongue-tied. I'd happily have tied the rest of him into a knot if I were bigger and stronger.

"Here's my suggestion," said Ruben. "We'll say, 'Father, we wanted to kill Joseph at first, but out of compassion we decided to sell him as a slave, so you should be grateful to us. Here are the twenty shekels we earned for him.'"

Judah looked at Ruben as if he'd seen a ghost. The other brothers started to curse him, calling him a blockhead and a stupid camel, but that only revealed how desperate they were. They had not considered the consequences of their crime and now they were tearing their hair out.

"All right, then," said Ruben. "I can see we'll have to handle it differently. Father can't find out you've sold Joseph as a slave, because then he'll lose all his sons except for Ben-Oni. What else could he do but drive us all into the desert and take away all our rights? So Joseph is dead, but not by our doing. He was torn apart by a wild animal."

Everyone thought that was a great idea. Hands clapped and shoulders were slapped.

"Do you understand, Ben-Oni?" asked Ruben. "Joseph was torn apart by a wild animal."

I nodded. I understood, but I was determined to tell my father the truth.

"What kind of animal?" I asked.

"I don't know, just an animal," said Ruben.

"An ostrich?"

The brothers glared at me, because they could tell I was trying to provoke them.

"It was a lion, of course," growled Judah.

"But we don't know that," said Ruben, "because we weren't there."

"Oh, I see," I said. "You just happened to find him somewhere. And where was I?"

The brothers had to think hard about that, because of course I was a problem.

When I've heard others tell this tale, they have Joseph leaving for Shechem without me,

but, believe me, I was there.

"I know why your mother called you Ben-Oni," said Judah, "'son of my pain,' because you're a pain in the ass."

He reminded me of my mother's death and I was filled with melancholy.

"Why not sell me as a slave to the Ishmaelites?" I said grimly. "Then I can make some money for you too."

I will never forget the look on his face. I was overcome with foreboding. His descendants and mine could well come to blows one day.

Ruben had had enough.

"Think of something yourselves," he said. "And if you can't convince Father, I'll knock your heads off your shoulders."

I knew where I stood with my beloved family, but I did not fear death. I would avenge Joseph by telling my father the truth. Anyone who allows injustice is himself an accessory; I could not let my feelings fester in my heart.

I watched in disgust as my brothers slaughtered a kid goat and smeared Joseph's coat with blood. As I thought about my father, I felt his heartrending grief. It was as if an invisible hand were squeezing my throat shut.

I do not remember exchanging a single word with my brothers on the long way back to Hebron. They said very little to one another either, just the occasional bark or growl, since criminals cannot stand their own kind.

The reunion with my father was awful. The brothers showed him Joseph's bloodstained coat and said, "We found this. Take a good look, is it not your son's coat?"

Jacob recognized it immediately and exclaimed, "My son's coat! He must have been devoured by a wild beast! He has been torn apart, Joseph has been torn apart!"

He tore his clothes, put on sackcloth, and mourned his son for many days.

He cried, "I shall wear sackcloth for my son until I follow him into the realm of the dead!"

His sons and his daughter tried to comfort him, but he did not wish to be comforted. And what about me? I was silent. I am not like Joseph. I cannot handle the truth, and I keep silent when the truth is too hard for me.

I understand that about myself now that I am old, but at the time I thought the hand squeezing my throat shut was the hand of God. I have learned that people are only too happy to explain their weakness as the consequence of divine intervention.

After a few weeks, when my father briefly surfaced from the fog of his mourning, he suddenly said, "Where were you, Benjamin, when Joseph was torn apart?"

I felt my heart freeze in fear. I stammered, "I do not know, Father. I know only that I saw his bloodstained coat. I know no more than that."

To my surprise he was satisfied by my answer, but I was not, and I have never forgiven myself for that lie.

The story I am going to tell now I heard from Joseph's own mouth, but since he is too modest, I shall add my own thoughts to his account. It is, I believe, almost impossible to tell someone else's story without becoming involved. The stories we pass on to one another cannot be traced back to one single person, since they've been kneaded by many different hands. I think this makes them all the richer, because they speak to us not from one mouth but many. My children will add their own stories to "my" tale, and I will encourage them to do so, because how can a story stay alive if others do not make it their own?

The Ishmaelites took Joseph with them to Egypt and brought him to the market there. On that same day, Mene, Potiphar's wife, was looking for a new house slave, and so she visited the different dealers with her steward to see if there was anything suitable for her. When she spotted Joseph, she began whispering behind her hand to her steward, then, feigning indifference, she walked away and left the negotiations to him.

Potiphar, who worshiped Apis the divine bull, was a rich man, one of the pharaoh's courtiers and captain of the palace guard. So Mene had little else to do than wallow in luxury and amuse herself. When she saw Joseph, she set her sights on him. He was an exceptionally beautiful boy. Mene's life was all about beauty, primarily her own. She spent the first hours of the day bathing and perfuming her body, making up her eyes, coloring her lips, and selecting her wig. She was no longer very young, but she barely looked her age and men still turned their heads as she walked by. She deserved to have a beautiful young slave around, whom she could watch to her heart's content, and who would look up to her with humility and longing. She was planning to present the boy with a feast for his eyes and to bask in his desire.

When Joseph entered Potiphar's house for the first time, he couldn't believe what he saw. It felt like coming home for the first time. For a boy who had lived in tents, growing up among sheep and passionately longing for a kind of beauty whose existence he only suspected, Potiphar's house must have seemed like Paradise.

The sophisticated furnishings, the wall paintings, the fabrics, the gleaming ornaments, not to mention the mistress of the household herself—everything was dazzlingly beautiful. God has brought me here, he thought, because this is where I belong.

He soon forgot the dreadful events at the pit, where his brothers had left him to die, the awful journey through the desert, the slave market; he even forgot about Canaan, the land God had promised his forefathers, because he was so enchanted by Egypt.

Mene gave him light tasks and commanded him with kindness. She kept him close to her. He took care of her clothing, served her food, and poured her wine. If he ever had to clean a room, it was always wherever she was at that moment.

She watched him as she had her nails painted. She made him wear only a loincloth with his torso bare so she could delight in his beauty. She was pleased with her purchase, but as time went by it began to annoy her that she could not see a trace of desire in his eyes. He looked at her, but not as a man looks at a woman. He seemed to see her as one of the magnificent pieces of furniture in her house and not as a seductive and desirable woman of flesh and blood. It was unseemly for a slave to treat his mistress like a piece of furniture, particularly after she had purchased him to flatter herself with his undying longing for her beauty. She considered ordering him to show his desire but realized that would do no good: she wanted him to yearn for her, then to suffer because she was unavailable. It would relieve a few hours' tedium to have such a beautiful boy following all her movements with a look of longing and to bask in his burning desire.

But it simply did not happen. He obediently did as he was told and nothing more.

One day, her niece Asenath came to stay with her. Asenath was a daughter of Potipherah, a priest from On, in the north of Egypt. She was sixteen or so. She worshiped Neith, the goddess of wisdom, and this veneration had made her a contemplative young woman. Mene found her niece dull and so she decided to seek some entertainment with Joseph.

She called him to her and, as Joseph bowed to both women with his hands crossed on his chest, she asked, "Boy, do you know what my name means?"

"No, mistress."

"It means 'exquisitely beautiful.'"

"Oh."

"What do you think of that, boy?"

"The name suits you, mistress."

She sighed impatiently. "And why does that name suit me?"

"Because you are exquisitely beautiful, mistress," said Joseph. "I have never seen a woman more beautiful than you."

The answer was perfect, but there was not a trace of passion in it. Mene felt a powerless rage rising up within her like a storm and at that moment she realized she was in love. It was not Joseph but she herself who was hopelessly lovelorn, not he but she who was the slave of desire.

"There are thousands of exquisitely beautiful women walking around Egypt, sheep farmer," she snorted. "But not one of them looks like me. Can't you come up with anything better than repeating what my name already says?"

Joseph bowed his head and whispered, "If your husband did not know better, he would surely think you a goddess."

"My husband? Leave my husband out of this, you desert rat!" she hissed. "My husband whispers what he thinks into my ear at night when he is crazy with love. What would you know about that?"

"Nothing, mistress."

"So, tell me, what do you think of me?"

Joseph fell onto his knees in a desperate attempt to calm her anger. With his forehead on the ground, he cried, "If I didn't know better, I would think you're a goddess."

Mene gazed at his gleaming back and his ebony hair. This was not an answer that would allow Asenath to witness her triumph.

"Why don't you honestly admit that you're jealous of my husband? Is it not true that you look at me with covetous eyes?"

Joseph stayed on the ground and kept silent.

She had not achieved what she wanted and she tasted the bitterness of unrequited love. "Stand up," she said. "Prepare my bath. And get this into your head: you can forget about this 'knowing better' nonsense. I am indeed a goddess!"

She waved her hand and Joseph ran from the room. She watched him go and said to Asenath, "I shall have him yet."

Asenath remained silent, with pain in her heart, because Joseph had made an impression on her. As soon as Mene was in the bath, she went to find Joseph, and said, "Don't anger her. When she's angry, she can do harm. I know her."

"I shall do my best, mistress," said Joseph.

"I am not a mistress," said Asenath. "I am Asenath."

They looked at each other and both felt at the same moment that something was happening between them, but they did not yet know what.

"Obey her in everything," said Asenath. "She wants to be loved. So love her."

As she spoke those words, her eyes suddenly turned moist, but she did not understand why. She knew only that she wanted to protect Joseph from her aunt's whims.

"I am her slave," said Joseph. "A slave does not love; a slave serves."

Asenath helplessly looked him in the eyes. Did he not understand what she was trying to warn him about? Or was this boy incapable of faking love as other men do when required? She didn't know what else to say. She just looked at him and saw that she was dealing with an extraordinary man, the kind of man rarely encountered among the Egyptians. He appeared to take love so seriously that he would not make a sham of it, not even to save his own life. She would have liked to have such a man for herself, but he was a slave and a Hebrew to boot.

"When the time comes, remember my words," she said. She turned around and walked away, but it seemed as if she were dragging him behind her on a rope, so heavy was her step. I must let him go, she thought. I must. But she could not. She would be bound to him for the rest of her life.

It is doubtful whether Mene knew what love was. She knew it only as a trick to manipulate her husband or a way to relieve her boredom. But perhaps this was the most important thing for her: love was something that was her due, something that had to be given to her naturally and eagerly whenever she felt like it.

The master of the house was a man with an open mind. He worshiped the bull with the disk of the sun between its horns, a god of masculine strength and light. He had no prejudices against foreigners or people of lowly birth, because the sun rose for everyone and the strength of the bull resided in every man. He noticed that Joseph was a diligent boy who went about his work with care, and so he began to make use of his services. To Mene's fury, he even made Joseph his personal servant, leaving the household affairs to him and giving him control over everything he owned. Joseph acquitted himself so well that Potiphar's household flourished as never before, and his trust in him was so great that his master only concerned himself with what he was provided to eat.

When Mene saw that something resembling a friendship was developing between her slave and her husband, a fierce jealousy was kindled inside her. She wanted to have Joseph for herself and to share him with no one. Precisely because he seemed to be drifting away from her, she desired him more and more every day, until she could no longer control herself.

Asenath had returned to On, called back by her father. Saying farewell, she had cried, and Mene had seen her tears as a sign of Asenath's love for her, but in reality they were spilled for Joseph, since Asenath believed she would never see him after this. She didn't know that God had noticed her and held her in his thoughts.

When Asenath had left and Potiphar was away for a long time serving at the pharaoh's court, Mene was left at the mercy of her own unbridled lust. She lay down on her bed, scantily dressed, and sent for Joseph. The boy appeared in her bedchamber, as hand-some as a young god. He looked at her quizzically with his eyes of black velvet and waited for her command. She thought: He belongs to me, so why should I not have him? I will take him, as is my right.

She said as sweetly as she could, "Come here, my boy, and lie with me."

Joseph did not move, but stood and looked at her. Before, he would have lowered his eyes, but no longer. Before, he might have obeyed her, but no longer. His position in Potiphar's house had changed and Mene had misjudged the situation.

"Do as I say, boy," she said. "Come lie with me." The tone of her voice made it clear how much effort it was taking her to remain friendly.

"I have as much authority in this house as my master," said Joseph.

Mene was speechless. Never before had she heard a slave say such words. Joseph was claiming not that he was her equal, but that Potiphar had placed him above her!

"Don't talk nonsense, boy," she hissed. "I bought you, you belong to me, so do as I say."

Joseph bowed, turned around, and left the room.

Of course, he was concerned. He remembered Asenath's warn-ing and realized he was in danger, but he didn't know how he could protect himself from someone who was beyond reason. If he told Potiphar, he would bring misfortune upon his house, so he had to remain silent and put up with Mene.

How long would he be able to resist her charms? He'd never known a woman who so openly showed her desire for him; he was afraid that if he didn't hold fast to his loyalty to Potiphar, Mene's beauty would eventually prove irresistible. He prayed that she would come to her senses, but his prayer was in vain. Once again God needed Evil: Mene's desire was the tool God had used to get Joseph to the place he wanted him to be. Israel's God truly is a wondrous god, whose ways are unfathomable, and who does not shy away from Evil while striving for Good.

Mene tried again the following day. She sent for Joseph and he appeared at her bedside. There's no need to detail all she exposed to his eyes; it's sufficient to remark that few men would have felt obliged to reject so much beauty.

She said, "If you don't come lie with me now, I'll make your life so miserable you'll be sorry you were born."

The contrast between her offer and her threat tore Joseph's world into two irreconcilable pieces and made him feel as if the ground beneath his feet had been snatched away. His legs shook like an old man's, but he said, "I owe your husband everything. He has given me everything, except his wife. I cannot betray his trust, surely you understand that? You are the most beautiful woman in all of Egypt. You know that I admire you, that I love you, that I shall obey you in all things, but you also know that I may not lie with you, no matter how much I might wish to."

But Mene didn't want to understand what he was saying, or perhaps God had clouded her understanding so she had no say in the matter.

"I don't know anything!" she screamed. "All I know is that you are my slave and that you must obey me because I bought you."

She grabbed him by his loincloth, but Joseph pulled away and his garment was torn from his body. He ran from the room, desperate and almost naked. His loincloth remained behind in Mene's hands.

When Mene realized she could not have Joseph, her desire changed into blind fury and vengeance. She felt deeply hurt by the slave who had resisted the temptation of her body and who had refused to obey her. Such slaves were unmanageable; they had to be swept away as a threat to the reputation of Egyptian womanhood.

She started to scream and all her slaves came running. Lying on her bed, she held up Joseph's loincloth. "What do you think of this? My husband insisted on bringing a Hebrew into this household, so that he could have his fun with us!"

She forgot for a moment that she had bought Joseph at the market herself, thinking him such a beautiful boy. She "forgot" because it was better for her if all the blame was placed on Potiphar, so that he would react as she wanted him to.

"That man came bursting into my room," she told them between sobs. "He wanted to lie with me, but I screamed out loud. When he heard my screams, he fled and left his loincloth behind."

That was how she ensured she had witnesses. She left Joseph's loincloth lying beside her until Potiphar came home. Weeping, she repeated her story and concluded, "You brought that Hebrew slave into this house and if I had not screamed out loud, your slave would have dishonored me."

Potiphar flew into a rage and everyone thought his fury was aimed at Joseph, but he knew his wife and knew she was lying. He was aware that Mene had little more to offer than her beauty and that she was addicted to the effect she had on men. Potiphar cursed the situation she had placed him in, but she was his wife. He could not forsake her now that she had made his entire household her witness. All of Egypt would turn against him if he took a slave's word over his own wife's.

Mene saw the fury on his face, but she didn't realize that she had lost Potiphar's love for good. She cast down her eyes to hide her satisfaction, while inside she was purring like a cat.

Potiphar looked around the room and determined never to set foot in it again. For him, it would forever remain the loathsome scene of his disgust, the place where he was forced to commit the most heinous injustice of his life. Love dies a painful death when it causes unloving behavior toward others, and nothing can bring it back to life.

Potiphar sent for Joseph and held him tight. It was like the embrace of a father saying farewell to his son. They did not speak, both thinking themselves the victims of inexorable fate, for how can anyone suspect that a deity would employ such cruelty with the best of intentions?

Potiphar had Joseph arrested and the pharaoh's soldiers took him to the "House of Saru," a fortress where the pharaoh's prisoners were held. Once again, Joseph was in a pit, thrown there by a man he had regarded as his brother. But Joseph did not grow bitter and did not lose his faith in others. Potiphar, on the other hand, was a broken man who was disgusted with himself, with his wife, and with life. He resigned as captain of the palace guard because that position also meant he was in charge of the jail where Joseph was held. He took another job, he did his duty, but everyone could see that he had lost all joy in his existence.

Joseph did his best to help his fellow prisoners. He comforted and cared for them, cleaned, and listened. Since he was friendly and kindhearted, people trusted him with their sadness, their desires, and their dreams. His actions calmed the prisoners, and the new prison commander noticed the change. Joseph was put in charge of the prisoners and supervised their work.

The prison was a terrible place. Some of the prisoners had been thrown into that filthy hole by the previous pharaoh and forgotten by everyone. They stumbled around like hollow-eyed, soulless ghosts. There were misshapen men among them who were missing arms or legs; there were blind men and deaf men. One man was covered in scabies and had forgotten his name. He scratched all day long and tried to relieve his deadly boredom by provoking his fellow prisoners. When he thought one of his jokes was particularly good, he burst out into insane laughter and tears rolled down his cheeks. Anyone who'd been there longer than a year lost all hope of ever being set free, and their despair drove them to listless apathy or cackling madness.

Dealing with so many people who all had their own stories and who had nowhere to hide their peculiarities gave Joseph the opportunity to learn more about human nature. He learned to tell the difference between good intentions and bad intentions, he began to hear the difference between a lie and the truth, and he saw sadness and joy even when they were kept hidden beneath jokes and silliness. He realized that his own thoughtless behavior had made his brothers so angry that they'd sold him as a slave. He learned to

236 ⊙ The Bible for Unbelievers

be silent when it was wiser than speaking. He learned that words that sounded innocent to his own ears could have a deafening and disorienting effect on others.

One day, two courtiers were brought in: the pharaoh's head butler and head baker. Even before Joseph knew what they were accused of, he could see that one was guilty and the other innocent—there is, after all, a world of difference between feigned innocence and real innocence—but he remained silent because he had learned not to pour out his thoughts.

What happened? One day the pharaoh had become unwell after eating and he suspected that someone had poisoned his bread or his wine, so in his fury he had both his butler and his baker thrown into jail, assuming that some intelligent questioning would reveal which of the two was guilty. So the men were given a good torturing, but neither of them admitted his guilt.

"Well, let them see where that gets them," the prison commander said, and both the butler and the baker were ordered to stay in prison until one of them confessed.

Joseph knew which one was guilty, so he waited for an opportunity to have the innocent one freed, hoping that he would be able to put in a good word for him at court.

Joseph did not know that Asenath, Mene's niece, had been unable to put him out of her mind and was suffering because of his terrible fate. She requested an audience with the pharaoh and, being the daughter of a high priest, she was granted one.

No one knows exactly how her discussion with the pharaoh went, but a few snatches of the conversation have been passed down.

"Does the pharaoh know that in his prison there is a Hebrew who has likely committed no crime? May I ask the pharaoh why the commander of the prison resigned immediately after the Hebrew's arrest? Is the pharaoh aware that this commander is the same man who accused the Hebrew?"

The pharaoh's answers to these questions are unknown. All that was passed on to me was this one statement: "Every prisoner is guilty until proven innocent."

Since it was impossible to prove Joseph's innocence, it seemed unlikely that he would ever be released from the prison, but fortunately he didn't know that. He kept hoping, believing that eventually justice would prevail.

Asenath returned empty-handed to On, but she refused to accept any other potential suitors for all the years Joseph was in prison.

Since the butler and the baker were important gentlemen, the commander ordered Joseph to serve them and to help them bear their fate.

The two men had been in prison for some time when Joseph found them in a rather melancholy mood one day. That did not surprise him. Captivity doesn't exactly put anyone in a good mood, but their faces were gloomier than ever.

"Why are you looking so miserable today?" he asked. Until then, he had always been able to cheer up the gentlemen with a friendly chat.

Maybe the hardest thing to bear about being in prison is that a person is never alone. The baker and the butler would rather have presented their problem to Joseph in private, but in every corner loomed eager ears and curious eyes. Nothing could be said without unsolicited comments; no gesture could be made without some kind of joke or witticism in return. It was almost impossible to share something intimate without wicked scoffers making sport.

But their need must have been great, because the baker said, "We both had a dream."

"But there's no one here who can explain it," added the butler.

There were rowdy reactions all around.

"I have dreams every night!" someone yelled. "And can you guess what I dream about?" Snickering, he began to list all kinds of obscenities and soon had the whole uproarious audience on his side.

Joseph let him rattle on for a while, but then held up his hand as a sign that he had heard enough. Joseph had gained a little authority among the prisoners because he was always so helpful, and sometimes they did as he asked. They fell silent.

"Dreams come from the gods," said Joseph, "and they have a purpose. Tell me what message they wanted to pass on to you."

The butler went first. He said, "In my dream I saw a vine. On that vine were three branches. And as soon as the vine budded, it blossomed, and bunches of ripe grapes were hanging from it in an instant. I had the pharaoh's cup in my hand. I picked the grapes, squeezed them into the cup, and presented the cup to the pharaoh. That was the end of my dream."

The prisoner who was covered in scabies and had forgotten his own name crept closer and heard the words the butler spoke.

"This dream is not hard to explain, my lord!" he cried. "You are a dead man. Because you should have tasted that wine first. What grapes ripen so quickly without magic being involved? Those grapes must have been poisoned! In three days they will come for you and chop off your head."

The butler cringed in terror, but Joseph cried, "You're talking nonsense! You don't understand it at all." And he told the butler, "Listen to me, noble lord, and not to that fool who wants only to entertain his fellow prisoners." He knew only too well that the man's explanation could be defended, but he'd seen the butler's innocence and so he said, "This is how the dream should be interpreted. Those three vines are most likely three days. In three days' time, the pharaoh will restore you to your former position and you will once again pass the pharaoh his cup, as you did before, when you were his butler."

The man with scabies burst out laughing. People were rarely released from the pharaoh's prison, unless as a corpse.

"Keep dreaming, noble lord," he brayed. "And let that pretty boy explain your dreams, because then you can spend the rest of your life counting to three over and over again in hope." He started to cough because he'd laughed too loud.

Being innocent, the butler paid no attention to the man. He embraced Joseph and thanked him for his interpretation.

"I had already suspected the gods wanted to say something favorable to me," he said, "but now I know for sure."

The butler was an important man at court. He was allowed to come so close to the pharaoh that he could touch him. With this man's help, Joseph could appeal to the pharaoh directly and beg for his freedom.

He said, "I hope you will remember me when you are free and put in a good word for me with the pharaoh. I am innocent, too, just like you. First I was abducted from the land of the Hebrews and then I was thrown into jail, even though I'd done nothing wrong."

The butler solemnly promised to do his best to help him.

When the baker heard Joseph's favorable interpretation of the butler's dream, he hoped his dream would also bring him good fortune, which is strange, since he knew he was guilty. That is often the way with criminals: they feel guilty only when caught. He hoped against hope that the gods might have been looking the other way when he put poison in the pharaoh's bread. No one knows why he did it, but presumably he was part of some plot to murder the pharaoh. It was his misfortune that the pharaoh ate only a small piece of the bread and became unwell for just a short period of time.

He said, "I dreamed something very similar. I had three baskets of white bread on my head. In the top basket was bread of the finest quality, which was intended for the pharaoh, but birds kept pecking away at the tasty food inside the basket. And that was the end of the dream."

"Well, that's more good news!" cried the man with scabies. He rubbed his hands with glee because he thought it was amusing to give a prisoner false hope, just as Joseph had done. "Those birds are, of course, ordinary Egyptians, who would also appreciate something nice to eat once in a while. Your dream says that in three days' time you will be released and that you will bake for the entire nation."

The baker leapt up with joy and embraced the man, in spite of his scabies, but Joseph told him, "Pay no heed to that fool, but listen to me. I have seen the guilt in your eyes. Those three baskets are three days. In three days' time the pharaoh will place you in a high position: he will have you beheaded and impaled, and then the birds can peck the flesh from your bones."

That was not a pleasant interpretation for the baker to hear, so he very much preferred the explanation of the nameless man with scabies. He glared contemptuously at Joseph and said, "Who do you think you are, little slave, that you believe you can interpret dreams? Have you lost your mind?"

The man with scabies began to roar with laughter again. He had not been bored for quite some time now.

"Dream!" he cackled. "Just keep on dreaming!" Still giggling, he hobbled away from the men and disappeared into the darkness.

In the meantime, the pharaoh instructed his doctors to carry out an investigation into the facts of the case, which was as enlightening as it was simple. The doctors chose two healthy slaves and had one of them drink the full jug of wine from which the pharaoh had taken a sip; the other ate the whole loaf of bread from which the pharaoh had eaten a morsel. When the slave who had eaten the bread dropped to the floor writhing in pain, the pharaoh had his answer.

Three days after the baker and the butler had explained their dreams to Joseph, the pharaoh held a big party for all his servants on the occasion of his birthday. The whole palace was decorated with garlands and the air was filled with cries of "Hip hip hooray!" That same day, to the amazement of their fellow prisoners, the baker and the butler were fetched by an escort of the pharaoh's soldiers to attend the party. Everyone was dumbstruck, except for the nameless man with scabies who launched into a loud rendition of "Happy Birthday to You," almost choking on his own laughter.

Joseph watched them leave, one on his way back to life, the other to death. His hope was kindled, since he trusted the butler would not forget him.

Both men were warmly welcomed at the palace. They were bathed, shaved, and dressed. The pharaoh gave them places of honor at his table and everyone merrily feasted and drank. Everything seemed to have been forgiven and forgotten, and the pharaoh was the very image of amiability; it would not have surprised anyone if he had restored both men to their former positions. The birthday boy was clearly having a fine time and he gave many people, including the baker, hearty slaps on the back.

The cruelty of a cat playing with a mouse: ten, twenty, one hundred times, it gives the mouse hope of escape, enjoying its mortal terror, reveling in its own power. Are humans above cats? Apparently not. Is a king above a common man? Apparently not.

The pharaoh spoke flatteringly to the butler, "You have always poured me pure wine, you have been loyal to me, your slate is clean and I am ashamed at the wrongs that I've done to you. I restore you to your office."

Then the pharaoh had the butler bring a pitcher of wine and raised his glass so that the butler could fill it.

Next he turned to the baker. "You have always baked delicious bread for me," he said, "and one tasty treat after another, but the last batch you baked for me was a nasty trick that I barely survived. So I intend to mark my birthday with your celebratory beheading and impaling, after which the birds may feast upon your flesh."

The baker was led away screaming, with the pharaoh and his entire court following, since the partygoers did not want to miss any bit of the spectacle.

Kings rule with cruelty because otherwise they are not sufficiently feared. Perhaps the gods learned this art by watching them. Kings and gods who are not feared would, after all, be better off herding sheep. But then, they must also be merciful so that they are loved by their people, because a man who is unloved will one day be pushed aside or be poisoned by some baker. I learned this from the stories of my forefathers and from my beloved brother Joseph's trials and tribulations: this combination of cruelty and mercy is the foundation of power.

One type of cruelty involves the infliction of physical pain, but there are many forms of cruelty. Breaking a promise is one of them. It is possible the butler was waiting for an opportunity to draw the pharaoh's attention to the innocent slave in his prison, but it's also possible that Joseph overestimated his influence. Perhaps the butler was not in a position to offer the pharaoh unsolicited advice. He tasted wine, he poured wine, he asked the pharaoh's opinion of the wine he poured. The pharaoh would have been surprised if he had suddenly started talking about the innocence of one insignificant slave or another. That might be the reason for the butler's silence, though it's more likely that he had quite simply forgotten Joseph. A cruelty stemming from indifference.

However that may be, Joseph remained languishing in the pharaoh's jail. He tried to keep his hopes up and not to surrender to the apathy and lethargy he saw all around him, but it became more and more difficult as the years passed by. Time took its toll. He often thought back to the dream that had made his brothers jealous. Why in the name of God had their sheaves bowed down to his? And how heartless had it been to shout a dream like that from the rooftops? He was starting to believe that he deserved his punishment and that the butler had been right not to go to the trouble of pleading his case to the pharaoh. He was beginning to resemble those prisoners who, guilty or innocent, stumbled through life in numb resignation, like the living dead, for whom time had ceased to exist. Who had sent him the dream in which he elevated himself above his brothers? Which of the gods had whispered that foolish notion into his ear, thereby bringing disaster upon him? In one of his moments of clarity, he realized that man must carefully choose which gods he wishes to listen to and which to ignore, but usually Joseph spent his days without one single thought and was barely even aware he existed. When, two endless years later, soldiers came to the prison gates and said the pharaoh had sent for the Hebrew slave, he heard their words but he did not understand them. They took hold of him, pushed him out of the jail, and lifted him onto a camel. He could not move by himself.

The pharaoh had had a dream that troubled him greatly. So he sent for all the magicians and scholars of Egypt, but there was no one who could explain his dream to him. Only then did the butler remember Joseph and the promise he had made to the Hebrew slave. Although he was neither a magician nor a scholar, and his advice had not been sought, the butler dared to speak.

"When I was in the prison," he said, "together with the baker whom you so rightly beheaded and impaled, I met a Hebrew slave who, three days before you restored me to my position, interpreted a dream of mine and predicted my release. This young man is truly a seer and an interpreter of dreams. There is no other man like him in all of Egypt."

The pharaoh was grateful to his butler for his advice and gave the order that Joseph should be brought to him. This required some preparation, for Joseph had not been able to wash and change his clothes in all those years and so he stank to high heaven. He was thoroughly bathed. And thoroughly shaved, for Egyptians had no beards. The pharaoh removed his own beard at night, which was false. For an ordinary mortal like Joseph a beard was inappropriate, because it was a symbol of divinity. The Egyptians also had a loathing for all body hair because of the inevitable lice, so everything had to come off. Joseph was given a fine wig and new clothes that made him look like the very model of an Egyptian. When he stood before the pharaoh, he was still dazed. Time had suddenly started racing, and it was a rhythmic thud inside his head. But when the pharaoh told him that he'd had a disturbing dream, Joseph called time to order. Life returned to him.

"Listen carefully," said the pharaoh. "I am of course something of a god myself, but I do not always understand the messages of the other gods. I dreamed I was standing on the banks of the Nile. Then I saw seven cows come out of the water, beautiful and sleek. They came to graze on the riverbank. It was a wonderful sight to behold; the world was peaceful and prosperous. But then seven more cows came out of the water and they were terribly gaunt, just skin and bone. I have never seen such ugly cows in all of Egypt. They walked up to the beautiful cows on the riverbank. And those ugly gaunt cows ate up the seven beautiful sleek cows. But after they had gobbled them up, it made no difference, there was no sign: they looked just as ugly as before. And then I woke up."

The pharaoh looked at Joseph hopefully. "Can you explain my dream for me?"

"I cannot," said Joseph modestly, "but perhaps the gods will give an interpretation that is favorable for the pharaoh." He closed his eyes as if trying to concentrate on voices from the world of the gods, but in reality Joseph was frantically thinking. What was he to make of this ridiculous dream? His freedom depended on cows eating cows. He broke out in a cold sweat. He could not keep the pharaoh waiting for long. He opened his eyes and began desperately improvising; to his relief, when he spoke, his voice revealed none of his anxiety.

"Let me begin with the cows," he said. "In your dream they exhibit unnatural behavior. In reality one cow eating another would be an insane cow that was suffering from some kind of mad-cow disease. So the cows in your dream are not literal, but must have some different meaning."

Joseph fell silent. A different meaning, but what? What could cannibal cows possibly mean? He needed to say something else, and quickly.

"And now for the number seven, which appears twice in your dream," he said. "Numbers in dreams usually express a period of time. So it could be seven days, months or years, but I suspect it means a good length of time."

He was beginning to suspect where he should be going; he really felt inspired now. "A farmer would call those beautiful, sleek cows 'good,' and the gaunt cows 'bad.' If I attach the notions of 'good' and 'bad' to periods of time, that means a good time is coming, which will then be swallowed by a bad time. Seven bad days wouldn't trouble the farmer, nor would seven bad weeks, and seven bad months wouldn't be pleasant, but seven bad years would be a disaster. So the dream is warning you of a disaster. Egypt is now thriving. The Nile overflows its banks every year and fertilizes the ground, and that will remain so for a good period of time, maybe seven years. Good times are always followed by bad times. The Nile won't burst its banks for a long while, maybe seven years, and the ground will become dry and will fail to produce any harvest. There will be famine and all the prosperity that once was will be eaten up by those seven lean years. No one will remember anything about Egypt's abundance. Famine will bring the country to its knees."

The pharaoh gaped at Joseph, because never before had anyone dared to be the bringer of such bad tidings. An indignant hubbub broke out among the courtiers, because the pharaoh could not possibly allow such impudence to stand. Everyone expected the immediate arrest and execution of the Hebrew slave who had been so foolish as to speak his thoughts freely. Joseph felt their hostility piercing his skin like poison arrows and realized his honesty had once again put him in danger. He had to try to put a positive spin on his devastating message or another pit would await him, the final one, his grave.

"The gods have warned the pharaoh of this disaster because wise leadership can prevent it," he said. "What sense does a warning have otherwise? This is what the gods wish to say to you: Do not eat everything in times of plenty, but save some so that you might have food to eat in times of need. The pharaoh would be well advised to seek a wise and discerning man and to entrust him with the government of Egypt. I advise you to appoint supervisors throughout the whole land, and during the years of plenty to demand a fifth of what the land yields. Of course there will be those who do not wish to pay the tax and who will rebel. Those are the people who do not understand that the common good is also good for them. They need to be dealt with firmly. The wheat must be stored in the cities, where the stores can be guarded well. So there will not only be sufficient supplies to make it through the lean years, but you will also be able to set the price of every single deben of grain you sell. Imagine what good it will do the treasury when only the state is in a position to satisfy the nation's hunger!"

Joseph fell silent. The silence rang in his ears and he could hear his heart beating. What had he done? Had he really spoken up without being asked and given the pharaoh advice? He shook his head; he could hardly believe it himself. This was his death, his certain death.

What happened next is the most unlikely thing that has ever happened and will surely never occur again. I would not have believed it myself if I had not, years later, seen the consequences with my own eyes.

The courtiers closely watched the pharaoh's expression, because it was important to guess whether they should applaud or disapprove. The Hebrew had spoken wisely, as everyone knew, but that did not mean you could simply show your admiration, not without the pharaoh's consent.

"Could we ever find someone so filled with the divine spirit?" asked the pharaoh.

Then the courtiers knew they could cheer and so they did. The slave would most certainly be freed, and perhaps be given a nice position at the palace, or a house and a piece of land, which would make him a citizen of Egypt. A free Egyptian could be applauded with a clear conscience.

But what the pharaoh said next must have left the courtiers speechless.

He turned to Joseph. "If the gods have told you all this, there can be no one more wise and discerning. You are the one to whom I will entrust my palace, and all my people will do as you command. Only I will stand above you."

After his words, the only sound to be heard in the throne room was the sound of breathing. It was as if a breeze had arisen within those walls, a deep sigh that came from all sides at once. It surprised no one that the slave was rewarded, but that he was suddenly higher in rank than any courtier whatsoever was almost impossible to believe. Only when the pharaoh slid his signet ring onto Joseph's finger and put a gold chain around his neck did everyone understand that the incredible is sometimes true: the Hebrew slave had become the vizier of Egypt.

Joseph must have been overwhelmed, even dizzy. Maybe he

questioned his sanity and thought he was losing his mind, like a man who sees things that aren't there. But he too realized that sometimes the unbelievable must be believed. He soon regained his wits and said, "I thank the divine pharaoh for the honor he has shown me and I would like nothing more than to serve him and protect Egypt from a disaster. But I have one request. I would ask you to send for Potipherah, the high priest of Neith who lives in On, so that I may ask him for the hand of his daughter, Asenath. And if he agrees and she wants me, then I would like to celebrate my wedding before I embark upon my task."

With a wave of his hand, the pharaoh indicated that he granted Joseph's request and a messenger was immediately sent to On.

"And one more thing," said Joseph. "I would appreciate it if Potiphar, the former captain of your palace guard, and his wife, Mene, could be present at my wedding."

Perhaps at that moment the pharaoh remembered the slave whom Potiphar had thrown in jail, but that is not certain. He simply smiled.

"So?" I asked Joseph years later. "What did you say to Potiphar?"

"That he should make sure his wife does not become bored." He burst out laughing when he told me that.

Joseph set to work and traveled throughout Egypt in the chariot the pharaoh had given him. It was the second most beautiful chariot the pharaoh owned. Slaves ran ahead of it shouting, "Respect! Respect!" at every turn, and people threw themselves to the ground. The pharaoh had given him white linen robes, because the Egyptians found the multicolored finery of the "sand dwellers" ridiculous, and when Joseph thought back to the brightly colored coat he had worn as a young man, he was a little ashamed. He felt like an Egyptian, particularly after the pharaoh gave him an Egyptian name, Zaphenath-Paneah: "The gods say, long may he live."

He had storage houses built in every city and collected a fifth of the grain that was harvested from the surrounding fields. The grain from distant fields was transported by ship down the Nile. Joseph made sure the farmers understood the purpose of this heavy tax, so that they did not revolt. After a few years Joseph could confidently say:

> The stores are full,
> the sheaves are overflowing,
> the broad ships are piled so high
> that the grain is spilling over.

So much grain was gathered that the scribes stopped keeping records: they could no longer keep up, since it was like the sand of the sea.

Joseph was happy with Asenath because she loved him and he loved her. She sat beside him on his throne; he did not want her to be his inferior. He never allowed the Egyptian sculptors to depict him without her, and they sat beside each other, both the same size and with happy smiles on their faces. Even though he had lost his father and his brothers, he felt secure in an extended family of Egyptians who loved him. Finally, after years of misery, he had come home.

Asenath gave birth to two sons: Manasseh and Ephraim, which are Hebrew names; Joseph did not deny his origins. "Manasseh" has to do with "forgetting," because this boy made him forget his sadness and he no longer missed his brothers and father. The name "Ephraim" carries the meaning "fertile" within it. He gave the boy that name because he'd borne fruit in the land where he'd endured so much misery.

He did not forget the god of his forefathers, but of course he respected the gods of his wife and met the religious obligations that were the norm in Egypt. Only a fool neglects the gods of the land where he dwells.

Now that he was so happily in love and was valued for his quick mind, he lost the vanity that had made him so unpopular with his brothers. When a person is finally in the right place, boastfulness and ostentation can be dismissed as the folly of youth. So it could be said that the real Joseph first appeared when he stood before the pharaoh at thirty years old. People bowed down before him, but unlike in his dream of the bowing sheaves, he felt ashamed because it reminded him of his time as a slave. He knew how humiliating it was to have to bow to your masters. He quickly tried to set people at ease, particularly poor farmers, and helped them back to their feet after they had thrown themselves to the ground before him.

But he could also be stern. That stood him in good stead when one day he received some visitors who caused the ground beneath his existence to shake and brought to the surface feelings he did not know he had.

After seven years or so famine broke out after a long drought, not just in Egypt but all over the world. Jacob was a rich man, but if your money cannot buy food, then you're as poor as a beggar. He was close to despair and furious with God.

"Do you remember our fight by the Jabbok?" he screamed at the heavens. "Is this the blessing you promised me? I challenge you to fight another round! I intend to beat you to a pulp and to force you to give me your blessing once more."

But no matter how he yelled, God did not appear.

His sons saw their father's desperation and they laughed at it, because they considered it the madness of old age. They did nothing, and if it had been up to them, Jacob's entire camp would have died of starvation.

"Why don't you do something?" asked Jacob. "Are you waiting for God to come rescue you? As you can see, God won't lift a finger to help us. I've heard there's still grain for sale in Egypt. Go there and buy some, otherwise we'll all die."

Grumbling, my ten brothers set off for Egypt. My father did not allow me to go, for, he said, "A wild animal could tear Benjamin apart. That often seems to happen when a man depends on his half-brothers' protection."

I heard from the mocking tone of his voice that he had never believed the story my brothers had told about Joseph's disappearance, and I was deeply ashamed that I'd never told him the truth.

So I was not there when my brothers arrived in Egypt. Everything I know about what happened to them was later told to me by Joseph. I will tell his stories to my children. They will pass on the same stories in their own way, leaving out an event or a remark they don't like and adding others, because a story is like a living organism, which matures and changes shape until maybe one day it is fully grown. I tell Joseph's story as accurately as possible, but I know that I am adding and omitting without noticing, because no mouth speaks like any other, and no two people have the same tongue.

Throughout Egypt the storehouses were opened and the grain was sold to the people, and also to foreigners, who flocked to the stores. Joseph did not have to sell the grain himself, of course—he had people to do that—but when he heard that ten brothers had arrived from Canaan and called themselves "sons of Israel," he sent out the order that no one should sell even a single grain of wheat to these men until they had appeared before him. He thought he was acting purely out of curiosity; he could not imagine that these "sons of Israel" were truly his brothers; he even hoped they were not, because he felt absolutely no desire for a reunion. He was mistaken about his feelings, though, because when the men entered the throne room his soul was squeezed so hard by an invisible hand that tears came to his eyes. All the pain his brothers had inflicted on him, and which he had endured for all those years by hiding it deep in his soul, was forced out at once. It was like having nails driven through his heart and, for a moment, before he had come to his senses, he thought he was overwhelmed by hatred. What would be more natural than revenge? Who could resist the temptation to crush without mercy the men who had been the torturers of his youth, as soon as he had the chance?

They threw themselves to the ground before him and in that humble gesture he recognized his dream about the bowing sheaves of grain, but he experienced no joy in it, as he had once imagined he would. Still he let them lie there for a long time, because he was not sure he could bear to look at them. Then the image of his father came to him, and of me, Ben-Oni, and he suffered the pain of the loss he had long suppressed.

Was Father still alive? And Ben-Oni, how was he doing? Longing can take the form of an agonizing thirst that must be quenched. The men on the ground were his tormentors, but at the same time they were the guardians of events that he had missed. They knew what he did not, and Joseph was burning with longing for that knowledge.

"Stand up," he had his interpreter say, and the men stood up.

They failed to recognize him, because their jealousy had distorted their memory of him. They saw a mighty Egyptian who could decide their fate at will.

"Where do you come from?" asked Joseph in a brusque tone, which his interpreter echoed.

"We come from Canaan and we wish to buy food."

Joseph looked at the man who had spoken. It was Ruben, the least bad brother. Beside Ruben stood Simeon, the worst brother of all.

"You are spies," he said. "You have come to see where the land's defenses are at their weakest." He gestured at his guards as if he wished to have them arrested.

"Oh no, my lord," the brothers cried in unison. They threw themselves to the ground again because they feared for their lives. "Your slaves have come only to purchase grain," cried Simeon.

Joseph looked down at him and remembered how scared he'd been, particularly of this brother, who had wanted to murder him.

"We are brothers," said Ruben. "We are all sons of the same man, we are honest men, we have never been spies."

Joseph looked down at Ruben, the man who had saved his life but had been unable to prevent his slavery. He reflected on the words "honest men" and decided to put their honesty to the test.

"You are lying," said Joseph. "You have come to see where the land is vulnerable. I know the Canaanites."

The brothers began to wail at the top of their voices and begged for their lives to be spared.

Ruben said, "Your slaves are actually twelve in number. We are brothers, sons of the same man from Canaan. Have you ever heard of a whole family coming to spy in Egypt? Surely no sensible father would take such a risk. Only the youngest is still with him at this time, and one has died. Our father is elderly and cannot bear to lose another son."

Joseph turned around. He knew he could not conceal his emotions now that he had heard his father was alive! He had long ago resigned himself to never seeing his father again, but now there was suddenly a glimmer of hope. He quickly pulled himself together.

"I maintain that you are spies," he had his interpreter say to them. "We shall put this to the test: you may not leave until your youngest brother comes to me. I swear this by the divine pharaoh. Send one of your number back to fetch him. The rest will remain as prisoners until proof is provided that you speak the truth. Otherwise I shall have you sentenced as spies. This, too, I swear by the divine pharaoh."

He made another gesture to the captain of his guard, who saw that the vizier meant it this time. His men threw the brothers in jail, where they remained for three days.

During those three days, Joseph had time to recover from the reunion. He talked to Asenath.

"If your old father sees only one son returning, it will be the death of him," she said.

"So what should I do?" asked Joseph.

"Do it the other way around: keep one brother in prison and send back the rest."

On the third day, Joseph had his brothers fetched from jail and said to them, "If you wish to stay alive, then do as I say, for I am a pious man and I fear the gods, including yours, and I do not want to sin by committing an injustice. If you are truly honest men, one of you must remain here in prison. The rest can go home with grain to satisfy your family's hunger. If you then return to me with your youngest brother, not one of you will be put to death."

The brothers bowed their heads. The three days in prison had made them realize how serious their situation was. They agreed to do as Joseph commanded.

Then they began to talk among themselves, in Hebrew, of course. They did not know Joseph could understand them, because he had only ever spoken to them with the help of an interpreter.

"This is our punishment," said Ruben, "for ignoring Joseph's pleas, even though we could see that he was terrified. Didn't I tell you not to hurt the boy? You wouldn't listen. Now we are being made to pay for his death."

Joseph walked away from them because he couldn't hold back his tears. But you agreed they could throw me in the pit, he thought. And then: They think I'm dead. They know they committed a terrible crime.

When he had his emotions back under control, he returned to his brothers. He knew which of them he wanted to punish most— the most murderous one—but he kept them guessing.

"I shall now choose one of you to remain a prisoner in Egypt."

He walked past them and studied their faces, one by one. He felt that he loved them in spite of everything and that, in fact, he wanted to embrace them. The venomous snake of jealousy had crippled the conscience of these men, but they had become older and wiser, and it seemed they regretted their crime. But they did not appear to have been punished for their actions. He wanted them to have to tell their father once more that a son was missing; they needed to face his grief and fury again so that they would really understand what they had done.

He stopped beside Judah and saw the fear on his face. He thought: You, too, Judah, deserve for me to throw you into a dungeon and load time upon your shoulders like a lead weight. But he walked on. These were the men who had carried out a massacre of innocent people in Shechem. Did they now have their violent nature under control? Apparently so, for they seemed more like sheep in search of a shepherd. Joseph would not be that shepherd himself, but the predecessor of the shepherd who would come from Egypt. He did not understand how he knew that, but still he did. Egypt would be the spring from which the people promised to Abraham would drink. It was from Egypt that the man would come who would lay down the law to the sons of Israel, so that they could no longer do whatever came into their crazy heads.

Joseph thought the grain must not go to Israel. Israel must come to the grain.

He understood his mission: The descendants of Jacob must be raised in Egypt. That was the will of the gods. He had to make Israel come to him.

He stopped when he reached Simeon.

With the help of his interpreter he asked, "What is the name of your youngest brother?"

"His mother named him Ben-Oni, but my father calls him Benjamin."

"Is he healthy?"

"Oh yes, my lord," said Simeon. "He is young and strong."

"Good," said Joseph. "You will remain my prisoner until I have seen Ben-Oni." He had Simeon thrown into shackles before his brothers' eyes. The man did not protest, because he knew only too well that it was he who had incited his brothers to murder. Quietly and with his head bowed, he allowed himself to be led away.

Then Joseph ordered his slaves to fill the brothers' sacks. He sold the grain at the same price he asked of the Egyptians, but secretly had the money hidden inside with the grain, not wanting to accept any money from his family.

The brothers loaded the grain onto their donkeys and left.

Jacob saw immediately that Simeon had not returned from Egypt and began to lament, fearing his son was dead. Then the brothers told him what had happened to them in Egypt.

"The vizier will release Simeon when he has seen Benjamin," they said, concluding their story. They hoped this message would bring some consolation, but that hope was in vain.

"You are robbing me of my children!" cried Jacob. "Joseph is no longer here, Simeon is no longer here, and now you want to take Benjamin away from me as well!"

Then Ruben said, "You may kill both of my sons if I do not bring Benjamin back to you."

At that point Jacob fell silent for a long time. Now he knew for certain that Leah had given birth only to madmen. How could Ruben ever imagine he would find any comfort in the murder of his own grandchildren? Why did he have to listen to such insane cruelty in his old age? How was it that he had fathered only idiots with Leah? Was it because he had spilled his seed inside her without loving her? Was this his punishment?

He tried to shake these futile thoughts from his mind, for what was done was done. He had loved Rachel but not Leah. There was nothing he could do about that now.

"Oh no!" Jacob violently shook his head. "Oh no, Benjamin is not going with you, because his brother Joseph is dead. He is the only son of Rachel I have left. If anything were to happen to him on the way— should an animal tear him apart or something like that—it would send me tumbling straight into the grave. It is out of the question."

But the wind from Cyprus did not blow, and the land cracked open with thirst, and the famine continued. Animals died in the fields and infants wailed heartrendingly at their mothers' dry breasts. People desperately studied the horizon, looking for just one little cloud, but the sky seemed carved from blue marble and the sun was a glowing ball of copper.

When the slaves' children died and hunger hollowed the eyes of Jacob's grandchildren, the brothers tried again to convince him to let them take Benjamin so that they might buy grain in Egypt.

This time it was Judah who spoke up: "Give the boy to me," he said, "and then we can leave and none of us will have to die, not us, not you, and not our children. I will vouch for his safety."

Jacob reflected on these words and not without bitterness. He was, after all, sure that one of the murderers of his beloved Joseph was speaking to him. What good is the promise of a man who is capable of murdering his own brother?

But the need was great and the thought of his whole family, including Benjamin, dying of hunger was unbearable. What would become of God's promise to Abraham then? The tribe of Israel would be smothered in its cradle. All he could do was nod and, if necessary, offer up Rachel's last son on the altar of God's mysterious ways.

He attempted to fathom why such a powerful man as the vizier of Egypt wanted to see Benjamin. He tried to understand why this divine Egyptian had asked, "Is your father still alive?" He pondered the question of how the money had come back. He found no answer to any of these questions, but a vague suspicion grew within him that he could not put into words. It was all so strange that perhaps a miracle was involved, some divine intervention with consequences that surpassed all understanding.

Jacob was old and more than tired of life. It was time for him to pass his authority to the next generation, even if that generation consisted of a select company of madmen.

He called his sons to him and said, "If this is the only way, then it must be so. Take Benjamin with you, but also take gifts for the Egyptian: balm, honey, gum, myrrh, as well as pistachios and almonds. And take twice the money, since you must return the money you found in your sacks. That may have been a mistake. Before you know it, you'll be accused of theft and we'll be in a bind that's even worse. Take Benjamin with you. I hope that God, the Almighty One with whom I wrestled, will ensure that the Egyptian is merciful to you and that he frees Simeon and also lets Benjamin go."

He bowed his head and whispered, "And if I have to lose my children, fine, then so be it."

I heard these words and shivered, not because I was afraid something might happen to me, but for my father's sake. I hoped

I would not have to suffer what he had been through: losing children, to death or to life, seemed to me the worst that could happen to someone.

But joy at the prospect of a journey to world-famous Egypt soon won out over my sadness at my father's fate. I had heard exciting stories about that country: about colossal buildings, finely carved statues of humans and animals, beautiful women who walked around less modestly attired than our women, and the Nile, which they said was as wide as the sea.

After my father had seen Joseph's bloodstained coat, he guarded me like his prisoner, rarely letting me out of his sight, so afraid that something might happen to me. I loved him, and yet his protective hand had clutched me so tightly that I sometimes thought I would suffocate. Now he was forced to set me free and I could go out and explore the world. We set off on our journey.

When Joseph looked out from his palatial offices and saw us coming, he recognized me, even though he had last seen me as a child. He told me later that my appearance and behavior had not changed much, and I think he was right: I had remained a child under my father's overprotective regime.

Joseph's steward came outside and said, "I will take you to my lord's private palace and you will eat with him there at noon." And he led us to the palace where Joseph lived with Asenath and their children.

I thought it a great honor to be permitted to eat with the vizier of Egypt, but my brothers' hearts were seized with terror. They believed they were being lured into a trap and that they would be enslaved. They felt guilty about the money they had found in their sacks and were afraid of being accused of theft. Just as they were about to enter the palace, they took the steward into their confidence and told him everything.

I did not understand their concern and was not afraid, and so I noticed something my brothers missed: the steward understood

Hebrew! And yet the man looked like a real Egyptian and, when he spoke, you could hear that Hebrew was not his mother tongue.

He reassured my brothers. He said, "You have nothing to fear. Your gods, the gods of your father, must have placed a treasure in your sacks, for I received your money. You have no debt with us."

Where had the man learned Hebrew? Who was his teacher? If the people in this palace had an interest in our language, who had awakened it?

"Wait here a moment," said the steward. "I have a surprise for you."

He walked away from us and disappeared around the corner of the building.

I felt that nothing but goodness could await us in Egypt. We'd been so kindly welcomed, and so I saw my brothers' suspicion as the foolishness of desert dwellers. They didn't say a word, but looked around with searching eyes as if they expected at any moment to be arrested.

When the steward returned, someone was walking beside him. We did not recognize him at first, but as they came closer we saw it was Simeon! He had been released before the vizier had even seen me! At least, that's what I thought at the time, but now I know better. Again it made me feel as if something miraculous was about to happen. My spirit prepared itself for a great secret to be revealed.

Finally the brothers shook off their suspicion. We took turns embracing Simeon and the air filled with cries of joy.

We were taken inside and given water to wash our feet, and our donkeys were fed. We had, of course, unloaded the gifts for the vizier and laid them out in the palace.

When the vizier came home that afternoon we were taken to his dining room, where he awaited us in his full regalia. And then it happened: he smiled. That was the miracle I'd been waiting for, but still it shocked me, as if lightning had struck the ground beneath my feet. The miracle was a smile.

My father always comforted me by saying, "If you want to see your mother, look at Joseph's smile."

The vizier smiled and I saw my mother's smile! This mighty Egyptian, the second most powerful man in the world, was my brother Joseph. My head felt light and I could barely hold back a cry of shock and joy, but Joseph stared at me and I could tell from the look in his eyes that I should remain silent, that I should hide my shock and my joy from the others. I bit my tongue, I clamped my jaw shut and told him with my eyes that he had no need for concern. My face showed no sign of emotion, but a storm raged inside my head. Joseph was alive! I had found my brother and my mother again in a royal palace in Egypt. It felt like a dream.

"Is all well with your elderly father?" asked Joseph. "Is he still alive?"

"Oh yes," said the brothers, "he is still alive."

"And is this your youngest brother, the one you told me about?"

But before the brothers could reply, he turned to me and said, "May the gods have mercy on you, my son."

Then he immediately fled from the room, because he could not hold back his tears. After washing his face, he returned with a silver cup in his hand.

"Listen," said Joseph, "the pharaoh gave me this cup when he elevated me to the position of vizier. It is no ordinary cup, but a cup of divination, which means I can consult it when I want to find out the truth."

He filled the cup with water and then dripped a few drops of olive oil onto the water's surface. After studying the shapes the oil formed on the water, he said, "I am going to seat you at the table in the order of your birth."

He pointed first at Ruben, followed by all the brothers, from the eldest to the youngest. When I saw my brothers' amazement, I had to bite my tongue again so as not to burst out laughing.

Then everyone sat down at the table. The Egyptians sat at another table because they did not want to eat together with Hebrews, to them that would be loathsome, but the vizier joined us. I was afraid for a moment that the brothers would notice Joseph was not acting like an Egyptian, but fortunately in their confusion they noticed hardly anything. What was served to Joseph was served to each of us; the only difference was that I was given five times as much. Joseph said I was "still growing." We ate like wolves and drank until we were legless.

When we awoke the next morning from our intoxicated haze, our sacks had been filled to the brim and the money we had paid was on top of the grain.

We went on our way, but we had only just left the city when we saw a group of riders pursuing us. We stopped. When the group had reached us, we recognized among the armed men the steward who spoke Hebrew. He looked far from happy. He strode toward us, fists clenched, and said, "Why have you repaid good with evil? Of all things, you have taken the cup from which my master always drinks, the gift from the pharaoh, in which he can see what is still hidden!"

I was scared out of my wits, because I interpreted his words to mean that one of my brothers, in his drunken state, may have helped himself to the silver cup. Was it possible that one of them had shown his very worst side yet again? Were they beyond hope? I thought it quite likely.

"How can you say that?" asked Ruben. "We would never do such a thing. If you can find anything stolen on one of us, then that man must be put to death, and the rest of us will serve you as slaves."

High stakes, for how could Ruben be so sure that his brothers had behaved decently on this occasion, when they had stopped at nothing in the past?

The sacks were searched, one by one, and when they had searched all of them except mine I sighed with relief: no one had been guilty of theft. But, in a flash, my relief turned to terror as my sack was opened and the cup was found inside. I froze as if I were standing on a high mountain and afraid to fall.

The steward held the cup high above his head so that everyone could see it. My brothers started to wail and rend their clothes with grief, but I could not speak and I was incapable of moving. My mind began to churn, repeating the same words over and over: It wasn't me, it wasn't me. Unlike my grandfather Isaac, I had absolutely no desire to be sacrificed when I had done nothing wrong.

Everything was loaded onto the donkeys and we rode back to the city. I could feel the accusatory looks like daggers in my back. It hurt me that my brothers held no doubt about my wrongdoing, but at the same time it made me feel wide awake. I thought: It was Joseph who did this. I didn't understand why, but I grew full of hope that all would end well, because I knew he loved me.

When we were standing before Joseph, though, I began to have my doubts. There was nothing but haughty contempt on his face. He stared at us in silence for a long time and all we could do was fall to our knees once again. Then he said, "Did you not realize that a man such as I can see what is hidden to others?"

Judah lifted himself up and said, "My lord, we are prepared to become your slaves, not just the man in whose sack the cup was found, but all of us."

"Out of the question," said the vizier. "Only the boy in whose sack the cup was found will be my slave. The rest of you can go."

Slave! That was better than death. I was quite prepared to become Joseph's slave, but Judah said, "Lord, you are as lofty and divine as the pharaoh, and I hope you will not be angry. If we return without Ben-Oni, it will be my father's death. Ben-Oni is the only remaining son of Rachel, the wife my father loved, and their elder son is dead, so my father is very attached to Ben-Oni."

"Touching," said Joseph. "Very touching. Tell me what Rachel's elder son was called."

"His name was Joseph," said Judah.

"You say that he's dead. Did you protect him as well as you now appear to protect Ben-Oni?"

"No, my lord," said Judah. "We failed him. For that very reason I beg you to take me as a slave instead of Ben-Oni."

Then my mother's smile unfurled on Joseph's face, like a flower with petals opening wide. He took off the *nemes*, the headdress that showed his authority, spread his arms wide, and said, "It's me, Joseph!"

I stood up and fell into his arms, but my brothers were rooted to the spot with shock.

"Don't be afraid," said Joseph, as he kissed my hair, "and don't reproach yourselves. I know now that you've changed. The gods sent me on ahead to Egypt to save your lives."

As he hugged me, I thought: Or the gods could, of course, have sent us better weather. Then there would have been no need for this whole complicated story.

"Come closer," said Joseph to my brothers, who were still looking up like fearful rabbits at their hunter. "Go on, stand up."

Hesitantly, the brothers came closer. Joseph let go of me and embraced and kissed them, one by one. Only then did they realize that it really was their brother Joseph standing before them and that he had forgiven them.

We stayed in the palace that day. Many tears were shed and we told each other the stories of our lives until deep into the night.

The news that Joseph's brothers had arrived in Egypt soon reached the royal palace. The pharaoh was pleased for Joseph. He said, "Tell your brothers to load up their animals and return to Canaan. Have them fetch their father and their families and return here."

The sons of Israel did as they were told. The pharaoh gave them chariots to transport their father and their families.

And so they left Egypt. When they reached Jacob, they said, "Joseph is still alive and he rules over all of Egypt." But Jacob was unmoved, because he did not believe them. Then, shamefully, they told their father about their crime, and about everything that had happened to Joseph since then. But it all sounded so implausible that Jacob did not believe them, not until he saw the expensive chariots sent by the pharaoh. Joyfully, he said, "I have seen enough. My son Joseph is still alive. I want to go to him. I want to see him before I die."

Then the whole tribe of Israel left for Egypt to settle there and to fill themselves with the ideas and the thoughts that reigned in that land.

Epilogue from Jochebed

These are the stories of my ancestors. I have given them each a voice of their own: Adam, Ham, Shelah, Sarai, Isaac, and Ben-Oni, to bring them to life, because these are the ancestors of the people who struggle with God.

I am Jochebed, mother of Moses, Miriam, and Aaron, and daughter of Levi, who was a son of Jacob and Leah. I have passed on these stories to my children so that they would know how we came from Mesopotamia to Egypt.

I am Jochebed, whose eldest son grew up as an Egyptian prince, but who never forgot he was a Hebrew.

I am Jochebed, but beware: stories are usually told after darkness falls, so you can't always tell exactly who's speaking. Someone may be using my name to lend his story more authority than it deserves. Always decide for yourself what you believe and what you don't.

Afterword

The stories you have just read are all in the Bible. If, like me, you were raised with the Bible, you know that already, but it may perhaps surprise some readers. Does it really say in the Bible that Jacob wrestled with God and that God could not defeat him? Yes, that's really in there. All the stories in this volume can be found in Genesis, but of course I've retold them in my own way.

I was raised with the Bible close at hand, but from the age of ten I began to realize I was not a believer. I remember lying in bed and trying so hard to pray that I cried, but still feeling like I was pretending. I was performing the part of a boy who was praying; in short, I was playacting. The Bible stories continued to fascinate me, though, not because of their religious content, but because of their astounding narrative force.

Sometimes the stories, as presented by the Bible, seem too brief to make any real impact, but my teachers at school knew how to tell them. Some of them conjured up a desert for us to behold, something they and we had never seen for real; they painted pictures of massacres that made our hearts race, and knew just how to fire up our fury about wicked folk who sold their own brother as a slave.

It became clear to me that these stories were meant to be told. My schoolteachers did so with passion and brought the stories to life. But of course each narrator's own interpretation crept unnoticed into the tale, as is inevitable and only right. A story does not come to life unless the storyteller makes it his or her own.

With *The Bible for Unbelievers*, I am following the tradition of the storytelling schoolmaster, with the difference that he was probably a believer and I am not. Unlike that schoolteacher, I searched for traces of doubt, contradiction, disobedience, and even disbelief, which I believe can be found in the Bible. Genesis is, in my opinion, not first and foremost a religious treatise, but more an account of a journey whose destination and purpose are uncertain. It is furthermore an account of human nature, an *Ecce Homo*, an invitation to "behold the man" in all his greatness, but also in his pettiness.

Life is a quest and humankind, in spite of its unique intelligence, does not know where it might possibly end. I believe this is what the stories in the Book of Genesis want to tell us. The struggle with God is the struggle with the mystery called life.

About the Author and Translator

GUUS KUIJER was born in Amsterdam in 1942, and is one of the most popular writers for both children and adults in the Netherlands, where he is perhaps best known for his Madelief and Polleke series of books. Polleke was made into a successful movie. He has won numerous major awards and his works have been translated into several languages, with several of his books being made in successful plays, The Book of Everything being staged in Australia for several years now, and was also staged in New York. In 2012 Kuijer won the prestigious Astrid Lindgren Memorial Award for his writing for children, and in 2014 he was shortlisted for the prestigious AKO Literature Prize for adult fiction. Kuijer currently resides in Zuidschermer, a small, rural town in the Netherlands.

LAURA WATKINSON has translated books by authors including Cees Nooteboom and Tonke Dragt. Her translations have won the ALA's Mildred L. Batchelder award for children's books in translation three times. She lives in a tall, thin house on a canal in Amsterdam.

About Seven Stories Press

SEVEN STORIES PRESS is an independent book publisher based in New York City. We publish works of the imagination by such writers as Nelson Algren, Russell Banks, Octavia E. Butler, Ani DiFranco, Assia Djebar, Ariel Dorfman, Coco Fusco, Barry Gifford, Martha Long, Luis Negrón, Hwang Sok-yong, Lee Stringer, and Kurt Vonnegut, to name a few, together with political titles by voices of conscience, including Subhankar Banerjee, the Boston Women's Health Collective, Noam Chomsky, Angela Y. Davis, Human Rights Watch, Derrick Jensen, Ralph Nader, Loretta Napoleoni, Gary Null, Greg Palast, Project Censored, Barbara Seaman, Alice Walker, Gary Webb, and Howard Zinn, among many others. Seven Stories Press believes publishers have a special responsibility to defend free speech and human rights, and to celebrate the gifts of the human imagination, wherever we can. In 2012 we launched Triangle Square books for young readers with strong social justice and narrative components, telling personal stories of courage and commitment. For additional information, visit www.sevenstories.com.